Emergent Technologies and Design

Michael Hensel, Achim Menges and Michael Weinstock

Routledge
Taylor & Francis Group

LONDON AND NEW YORK

To Defne, Diane and Eva

First published 2010 by Routledge

2 Park Square, Milton Park, Abingdon, Oxfordshire OX14 4RN
605 Third Avenue, New York, NY 10017

Routledge is an imprint of the Taylor & Francis Group, an informa business

First issued in hardback 2020

Designed and typeset by Gavin Ambrose
Printed and bound by CPI Group (UK) Ltd, Croydon, CR0 4YY

British Library Cataloguing in Publication Data

A catalogue record for this book is available from
the British Library

Library of Congress Cataloging-in-Publication Data

Hensel, Michael.
Emergent technologies and design : towards a
biological paradigm for architecture / Michael
Hensel, Achim Menges & Michael Weinstock.

p. cm.

Includes bibliographical references.

1. Architecture and technology. 2. Architecture-
-Technological innovations. 3. Design and
technology. 4. Design--Technological innovations.
5. Architectural design. I. Menges, Achim. II.
Weinstock, Michael. III. Title. IV. Title: Towards a
biological paradigm for architecture.

NA2543.T43H46 2010
721--dc22
2009035639

ISBN13 978-0-415-49343-7 (hbk)
ISBN13 978-0-415-49344-4 (pbk)

Contents

Preface

There was no singular point in time that marked the beginning of the Emergent Technologies and Design programme, but rather an episodic convergence of individual interests that occurred during a series of collaborations. In November 1998 an exhibition entitled Advanced Technologies and Intelligent Materials was co-curated by Michael Hensel and Michael Weinstock at the Architectural Association (AA) in London. This exhibition displayed images, texts and models of a number of physical and digital experiments that set out key areas of interest that later became characteristic of the interdisciplinary Emergent Technologies and Design agenda. Among these interests were algorithmic computational methods, tools and techniques that originated from mathematical approaches in evolution and biological systems modelling, new technologies in computer-aided manufacturing, advanced construction techniques, and material science research in adaptive and responsive material systems and high-performance products in advanced prostheses for athletes. The initial collaboration between Michael Hensel and Michael Weinstock in co-curating the exhibition was key to what followed.

Michael Weinstock brought his particular interests in the mathematics of biological evolution and in the cultural evolution of material constructions in maritime artefacts and systems, ancient and vernacular buildings, and contemporary architecture.

Michael Hensel contributed his interest in investigating the relation between building operations and the human environment, challenging the discreteness of buildings and exploring alternative models, through a series of speculative projects, originating in the research of OCEAN NORTH and from Diploma Unit 4, which he co-taught with Ludo Grooteman. Advanced computer-aided design, material logics and computer-aided manufacturing were key areas of investigation in OCEAN NORTH (today OCEAN Research and Design Network registered association), while Johann Bettum and Michael Hensel, both members of OCEAN NORTH, pursued a re-articulation of the material threshold in architecture along a biological model in an unpublished paper from 1999 entitled 'Issues of Materiality'.

The opportunity to extend this influential exhibition into a more directed agenda in the form of a curriculum presented itself in 2000, when Mohsen Mostafavi, at that time chairman of the Architectural Association, appointed Michael Hensel and Michael Weinstock to be the programme directors of a new Masters programme at the AA, focused on emergent technologies. Over a period of a year, and with many consultations with eminent experts and practitioners in architecture, engineering, industrial design, computational sciences and biomimetics, the Emergent Technologies and Design curriculum was written and developed. The first intake of students followed in 2001. In the same year the programme was validated by the Open University. In 2002 Achim Menges joined the Emergent Technologies and Design programme as Studio Master and began to introduce and explore a wide array of computational approaches, including associative modelling and parametric design, with advanced computer-aided manufacturing and material logics. The programme continued to develop, and focused on the exploration of higher-level functionality in the built environment, driven by algorithmic procedures, computer-aided analysis and an integration of material and computational form-finding. Professor George Jeronimidis, Director of the Centre of Biomimetics at the University of Reading, also joined the programme in 2002, bringing his long experience of the analysis of biological systems and the application of abstracted principles to the design and development of engineering structures and material systems across a range of scales and industries. The extended collection of our joint and several interests was consolidated in the exhibition at the Architectural Association in February and March 2003 entitled Contours: Evolutionary Strategies in Design. The Emergent Technologies and Design programme continued to develop and evolve its research, published in two guest-edited issues of *AD* entitled *Emergence: Morphogenetic Design Strategies* (*AD* Wiley, 2004) and *Techniques and Technologies in Morphogenetic Design* (*AD* Wiley, 2006). In addition to these collaboratively edited issues, the members of the Emergent Technologies and Design team also published a series of other books and magazines that explored new areas and developed those already under investigation. These publications include *Morpho-Ecologies* (M. Hensel and A. Menges (eds.) London: AA Publications, 2006, with a contribution by Michael Weinstock), *Versatility and Vicissitude* (M. Hensel and A. Menges (eds.) London: AD Wiley. 2008, with a contribution by Michael Weinstock), and *Space Reader: Heterogeneous Space in Architecture* (M. Hensel,

C. Hight and A. Menges (eds.) London: John Wiley & Sons, 2009). Michael Weinstock's book entitled *The Architecture of Emergence: The Evolution of Form in Nature and Civilisation*, to be published by Wiley in February 2010, addresses the origins of the theories and 'Emergence' through to the analysis of the dynamics of natural and cultural complex systems, and sets out the likely outcomes of the accelerating cascade of transitions through their critical thresholds.

This book presents an overview of the research of the Emergent Technologies and Design programme and the way it has contributed to practice over the last eight years. It is our ambition to make the work accessible to a broad readership of scholars, researchers, students and practitioners with the sincere hope that future research and design collaborations may contribute to a built environment that is less concerned with idiosyncrasy and more with performative capacity.

Michael Hensel, Achim Menges and Michael Weinstock
London, June 2009

Acknowledgements

We would like to offer our heartfelt gratitude to Mohsen Mostafavi, previous Chairman of the Architectural Association School of Architecture in London, for making it possible for us to initiate the Emergent Technologies and Design Master Programme in 2001. Many thanks also to Brett Steele, current director of the Architectural Association, for his support.

We are immensely grateful to our distinguished collaborators, first and foremost Professor Dr George Jeronimidis – Director of the Centre of Biomimetics at Reading University, Professor Dr Toni Atkins, Professor Max Fordham, Dr Emma Johnson, Professor Dr Remo Pedreschi, Dr Christina Shea, Dr Chris Williams, Professor Chris Wise, the Smart Geometry Group and Bentley Systems – in particular Robert Aish, Buro Happold – especially Mike Cook and Wolf Mangelsdorf, Expedition Engineering, and our current and past teaching staff including Daniel Coll I Capdevila, Christina Doumpioti, Evan Greenberg, Stelianos Dritsas, Martin Hemberg, Nikolaos Stathopoulos, our visiting staff Professor Dr Birger Sevaldson and Defne Sunguroğlu Hensel, as well as our Chile project coordinator Juan E. Subercaseux and the Chile project client representative Martin Westcott.

Frei Otto's and his team's work at the Institute for Lightweight Structures at Stuttgart University has been a constant source of inspiration to us, and to our students over the last eight years.

We offer our deep gratitude to Caroline Mallinder for her unwavering encouragement and support in making this book possible and to our project editor Katherine Morton.

Finally, we would like to thank our families for bearing with us during the many occasions when our collective obsessions blurred the boundaries between family life and work.

Introduction
Emergent technologies and design: towards a biological paradigm for architecture

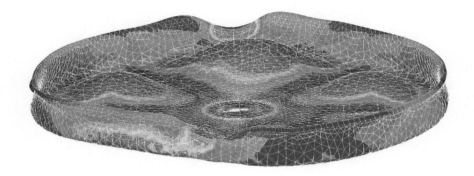

DISPLACEMENT
STEP=2
SUB =1
TIME=2
DMX =1.83

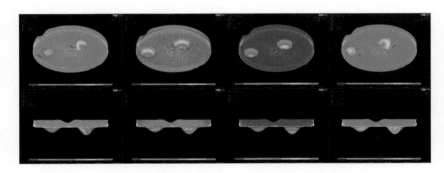

DISPLACEMENT
STEP=3
SUB =1
TIME=3
DMX =1.802

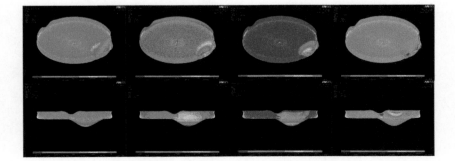

'Emergent Technologies and Design' is more than the name of our academic programme at the Architectural Association. It nominates a very specific interdisciplinary approach to design that is embedded in technological development and design innovation. The programme might also have been titled 'Emergence, Technology and Design' or perhaps 'Biology, Technology and Design'. While the programme title does acknowledge the importance of new technologies, it also emphasises the key concepts of *emergence* in relation to design. Emergence is a new science, a new field that has initiated a significant change in the culture of architecture. To engage with emergence requires more than the development of a catalogue of new materials that are coupled to innovative production technologies; it requires an understanding of the behaviour of complex systems and the mathematics of their processes, and of the systematic transference of that knowledge to design and production. Emergence is a consolidation of a profound change in knowledge and materialisation that has made significant changes to science and technology, and to the way in which we think of architecture and the way we produce it. Emergence provides an explanation of how natural systems have evolved and maintained themselves, and a set of models and processes for the design and fabrication of architectural forms that exhibit complex behaviour, and perhaps even real intelligence. Emergence has radically transformed the frontiers of science, mathematics and industry in recent decades, and it is central to a way of design across many fields that is rapidly making

obsolete what was once a strict distinction between design and production. The set of available analytical instruments that are commonly used in architectural and engineering design have undergone substantial recent development, and are increasingly incorporating temporal parameters such as lifespans and generations. New design software enables the writing of scripts and codes, that when coupled to simulations of dynamic structural and environmental loads have the potential to extend design processes from the development and fabrication of a singular static artefact or building to families of variant forms that can respond to varying conditions. Computationally driven design and production processes are enabling the fabrication of the complex forms and materials of almost all of the products of the contemporary world that we use in our daily lives, the complex geometries of many contemporary buildings, and the complex topologies of infrastructural and information networks. Emergence demands new strategies for design, strategies that are derived from the evolutionary development of living systems, from their material properties and metabolisms, and from their adaptive response to changes in their environment.

0.1

Natural systems analysis: water lily *Victoria amazonica*. The leaf of the giant water lily, which supposedly inspired the structure of Paxton's Crystal Palace, was investigated in regard to its structural performance and buoyancy resulting from the network of air-filled ribs on the leaf's underside. The digital model includes the leaf's morphology and material information such as the stiffness of the plant fibres and fibre orientation. Using finite element analysis (FEA), different loading scenarios were investigated, applying a distributed pressure over the surface of the structure as well as applying forces directly to discrete positions on the structure. EmTech Natural Systems Module, Pablo Cabrera, Efrat Cohen and Thomas von Girsewald, 2005.

THE DYNAMICAL ARCHITECTURE OF BIOLOGICAL SYSTEMS

> The relationship between biology and building is now in need of clarification due to real and practical exigencies. The problem of environment has never before been such a threat to existence. In effect it is a biological problem … Not only has biology become indispensable for building but building for biology. (Otto 1971: 7–8)

It has often been stated that biology was the leading scientific discipline of the twentieth century, and is set to continue at the centre of scientific discourse in the twenty-first century. All disciplines are in the process of a major revision, within which concepts that originated in biological studies gain new impetus and offer insights and new paradigms for all the creative practices across many fields of creative endeavour. New research topics, new modes of analysis and development, and new ways of working have emerged from the cross-fertilisation of what were once separate and discrete professions and academic disciplines. Living systems, their relation to one another and to the physical environments within which they come into being and coexist are complex, but there is a large body of work over the last century that has had a profound impact on our understanding of the natural world.

The study of ecological systems provides concepts and models for the complex energy relations of organisms to their environment, that extends from the analysis of the metabolic behaviour of a single plant or animal to the dynamics of the patterns of species within an ecological system, and the flow of energy and material between them that regulates their behaviour down through the generations.

> Ecological systems have at least five features that make them interesting. First, they are comprised of many parts; most contain hundreds of billions of individual organisms and tens of millions of species. Second, ecological systems are open systems that maintain themselves far from thermodynamic equilibrium by the uptake and transformation of energy and by the exchange of organisms and matter across their arbitrary boundaries. Third, ecological systems are adaptive, responding to changing environments both by behavioural adjustments of individuals and by Darwinian genetic changes in the attributes of populations. Fourth, ecological systems have irreversible histories, in part because all organisms are related to each other genetically in a hierarchic pattern of descent from a common ancestor. Fifth, ecological systems exhibit a rich variety of complex, non-linear dynamics. (Brown 1994: 419)

The dynamical systems of nature, the systems of living beings and the systems of the physical world including climate and geological forms, display a variety of organisational and behavioural characteristics that are central to the study of emergence. There are many definitions of evolutionary and developmental processes that unfold over time. One that is widely quoted is that put forward by Tom de Wolf and Tom Holvoet, who proposed the following working definition of emergence:

> A system exhibits emergence when there are coherent emergents (property, behaviour, structure …) at the macro-level that dynamically arise from the interaction between parts at the micro-level. Such emergents are novel with regards to the individual parts of the system. (De Wolf and Holvoet 2005)

They also suggested that 'Self-organisation is a dynamical and adaptive process where systems acquire and maintain structure themselves without external control' (De Wolf and Holvoet 2005). Emergence and self-organisation may occur separately or in combination, driving the development of systems towards new properties, behaviour, organisation and structure. Dynamical processes that unfold over time develop complexity of form and behaviour through the interaction of simple constituents, proceeding without central directions.

Living organisms can be regarded as systems, and these systems acquire their complex forms and patterns of behaviour through the interactions, in space and over time, of their components. The dynamics of the development of biological forms, both the growth of individual being from a single cell to fully developed adult, and the evolutionary development of new species over time, are strongly coupled. Biological forms and their behaviour emerge from pro-cess. It is process that produces, elaborates and maintains the form or structure of biological organisms (and non-biological things), and that process consists of a complex series of exchanges between the organism and its environment. Furthermore, the organism has a capacity for maintaining its continuity and integrity by changing aspects of its behaviour. Form and behaviour are intricately linked. The form of an organism affects its behaviour in the environment, and a particular behaviour will produce different results in different environments, or if performed by different forms in the same environment. Behaviour is non-linear and context specific. Norbert Weiner, who developed the first mathematical descriptions of responsive behaviour in machines and animals, founded his study, cybernetics, on anticipation, feedback and response.

Cybernetics, system theory and complexity have a common conceptual basis. They are sometimes referred to collectively as the 'sciences of complexity' or 'complex adaptive systems' in the extensive literature of thermodynamics, artificial intelligence, neural networks and dynamical systems. Mathematically too, there are commonalities in the approach to models and simulations. It is axiomatic in contemporary cybernetics that systems increase in complexity, and that in natural evolution systems emerge in increasing complexity, from cells to multicellular organisms, from humans to society and culture. System theory argues that the concepts and principles of organisation in natural systems are independent of the domain of any one particular system, and contemporary research tends to concentrate on 'complex adaptive systems' that are self-organising.

The principles of 'General Systems Theory' (Bertalanffy 1969) were set out by the biologist Karl Ludwig von Bertalanffy (1901–72) et al. Ervin Laszlo stated in the foreword to Perspectives on General Systems Theory that 'Von Bertalanffy opened up something much broader and of much greater significance than a single theory ... he created a new paradigm for the development of theories' (Bertalanffy 1976).

Complexity theory formalises the mathematical structure of the process of systems from which complexity emerges. It focuses on the collective behaviour that emerges from the interaction with each other of millions of simple components, such as atoms, molecules or cells. The complex is heterogeneous, with many varied parts that have multiple connections between them, and the different parts behave differently, although they are not independent. Complexity increases when the variety (distinction) and dependency (connection) of parts increases. The process of increasing variety is called differentiation, and the process of increasing the number or the strength of connections is called integration. Evolution produces differentiation and integration in many 'scales' that interact with each other, from the formation and structure of an individual organism to species and ecological systems.

The pattern of distributed variation within systems and the effects of natural selection on those patterns are common to many models of self-organisation. The complexity of individual organisms, species and ecological systems are all evolved and developed from the interactions of elements that combine into a variety of 'assemblies'. Some 'assemblies' survive, and go on to form 'naturally selected' wholes, while others collapse to undergo further evolution. The process repeats at higher levels, so that what is a 'whole' at one level may become a component within a yet more complex system that has emerged from the collapse and reorganisation. An emergent whole form can be a

0.2

Natural systems analysis: bamboo. In order to investigate the relation of bamboo's overall morphology and its anatomy, digital models of different scales were constructed. The relative densities and strengths of the fibres and surrounding matrix were established, so that FEA simulations of the response to different stresses and loadings could be conducted. For example, the deflection behaviour of the stem (top) was investigated in relation to the local stem morphology around the diaphragm and the intermodal transition of the stem cross section (centre) as well as the interaction between stiff fibres and the much softer surrounding material matrix on the microscopic scale (bottom). EmTech Natural Systems Module, Atul Singla, Juan Subercaseaux, Li Zou and Taek Yong Yoon, 2005.

component of a system emerging at a higher level – and what is 'system' for one process can be 'environment' for another process.

Evolution is not a single system but is rather is distributed over many scales of time and space, so that multiple systems co-evolve with partial autonomy and some interaction.

BIOLOGICAL MATERIAL SYSTEMS

The evolution of all the multiple variations of biological form should not be thought of as separate from their structure and materials. It is the complex hierarchies of materials within natural structures from which their performance emerges. Form, structure and material act upon one another, and the behaviour of all three acting on each other cannot be predicted by analysis of any one of them separately.

The self-organisation of biological material systems is a process that occurs over time, a dynamic that produces the capacity for changes to the order and structure of a system, and for those changes to modify the behaviour of that system. The characteristics of self-organisation include a three-dimensional spatial structure, redundancy and differentiation, hierarchy and modularity. The critical factor is the sponta-neous emergence of several distinct organisational scales, produced by the interactions between lower or local levels of organisation, the molecular and cellular level, and higher or global levels of the structure or organism as a whole. The evolution and development of biological self-organisation of systems proceeds from small simple components that are assembled together to form larger structures that have emergent properties and behaviour, which in turn self-assemble into more complex structures.

All living forms are hierarchical structures, made of materials with subtle properties that are capable of change in response to changes in local stresses. Biological material systems are self-assembled, using mainly quite weak materials to make strong structures, and their dynamic response and properties are very different from the classical engineering of traditional man-made structures. Biology uses very few materials to construct its structures, and

they are mostly organised as fibrous composites. There are only four polymer fibres: cellulose in plants, collagen in animals, chitin in insects and crustaceans, and silks in spider's webs. These are the basic materials of biology, and they have much lower densities than most engineering materials. The geometrical and hierarchical organisation of the fibre architecture is critical to their structural capacity, and that capacity emerges from the way in which they are put together. The same colagen fibres are used in low-modulus, highly extensible structures such as blood vessels, intermediate-modulus tissues such as tendons, and high-modulus, rigid materials such as bone.

Fibre composites are stiff and strong in the direction and magnitude of the loads applied. The anisotropic properties provide structural performance superior to that possible with isotropic, homogeneous materials. It is the growth under stress that produces this material organisation, as the forces that the living form experiences while it is growing encourage the selective deposition of new material where it is needed and in the direction in which it is needed. This process continues during the adult life of the living being when changes in stress and load occur. The formation of reaction wood in trees, needed to straighten a trunk towards the vertical where it has experienced inclined growth or to offset loads from prevailing winds, and the mechanism of bone remodelling are perhaps the most widely studied examples. In bone, for example, material is removed from any parts that are not stressed and re-deposited in more highly stressed ones, and in trees a special type of wood, with a fibre orientation and cellular structure different from that of normal wood, is produced in successive annual rings that vary in width and density as specific circumstances require. Biology produces a large number of patterns of load-bearing fibre architectures, each a specific response to a specific set of load conditions.

All biological forms assemble themselves, and they do so under the load of gravity, and have to gather their materials and energy from their environment. Biological self-organisation takes place under stress. Most biological materials have marked stiffness non-linearities. The range of their elastic behaviour, their ability to accept large stresses and deformations and return to their previous state, is far greater than that of engineered structures. Animals and plants regulate their structural behaviour in a way that provides new models for engineered structures. Plants, for example, can accept very high temporary loadings, and even in high gusting winds and severe storms it is more common for palms and bamboo to be uprooted than for their stems to buckle and snap. They resist gravity and wind loads through variation of the stem sections and the organisation of their material in successive hierarchies, using small quantities of 'soft' materials in each organisational level to achieve a high level of structural performance without rigid materials. Variable sections produce anisotropic properties, and a gradation of values between stiffness and elasticity along the length of the stem that is particularly useful for resisting dynamic and unpredictable loadings. Unlike mechanical structures, in natural biological systems there isn't a single boundary or contour where one component ends and another begins, as fibrous material is continuous right through the joint – in fact there do not seem to be joints at all in the conventional engineering sense.

These engineering principles can be abstracted from biological forms and applied to the design of engineered materials, artefacts and buildings. Variations in the section and material properties of biological 'structural members' offer very considerable advantages over the constant section usually adopted in conventional engineered structures. The differentiated distribution of cells, fibres and bundles, according to height and slenderness, offers a very interesting model for the production of fibre composite materials systems. Differentiation also offers the potential for variable stiffness and elasticity within the same material, so that the variations in the section produce anisotropic properties, and a gradation of values between stiffness and elasticity along the length of the stem that is particularly useful for resisting dynamic and unpredictable loadings. Fibres are most efficient when they carry purely tensile loads, either as

reinforcement in composite materials that are used as membrane structures in biaxial tension, or as independent structures such as cables and nets. Fibres do not perform well in compression, as they tend to buckle, even when partially supported laterally by the matrix in composites. In biological material systems there are four known solutions: [i] pre-stress the fibres in tension so that they hardly ever experience compressive loads; [ii] introduce high-modulus mineral phases intimately connected to the fibres to help carry compression; [iii] heavily cross-link the fibre network to increase lateral stability; [iv] and change the fibre orientation so that compressive loads do not act along the fibres.

Biomimetic strategies that integrate form, material and structure into a single process are being adopted from the nano scale right up to the design and construction of very large buildings. Artificial materials and material systems can be manufactured with specific performance characteristics. Such new materials have already transformed everyday consumer products, motor vehicles and aeroplanes. Manufactured cellular materials, especially new metals and ceramics, offer an entirely new set of performance and material values, and have the potential to re-inform and revitalise the material strategies of architectural engineering and construction.

On the long timescale of evolution, the complexity and diversity of living systems developed in response to environmental pressures and instabilities. The most important principle of adaptation, unregarded by classical engineering, is small random variation in the 'design', repeated transitions over time. It is these stochastic processes that produce robust systems that persist through time. In mathematical terms 'stochastic' is often used in opposition to the word 'deterministic'; deterministic processes always produce the same output from a given starting condition – stochastic processes will never exactly repeat the output. It follows that developing processes that include small random mutations over many iterations is a significant 'evolutionary' strategy for design, architecture and engineering, and

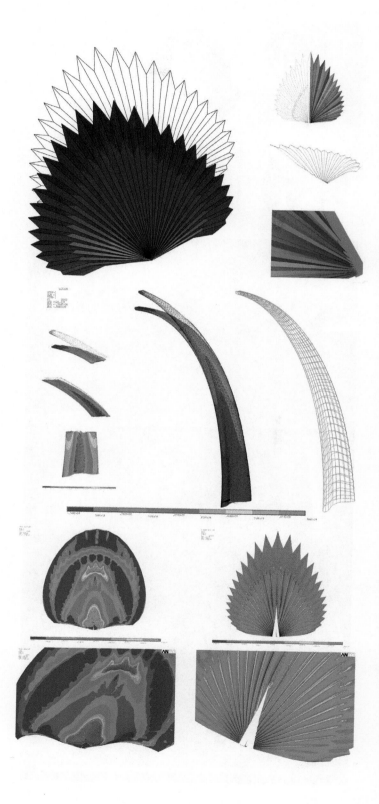

0.3

Natural systems analysis: palm
tree. For the investigation of the
palm tree's exceptional capacity
to respond to very high dynamic
loading, the morphology of
both the leaf (top) and the stem
were accurately modelled. The
analysis of the bending stresses
occurring at different section of
the palm stem (centre) shows
different local bending stresses,
indicating the global relationship
of bending and torsional stiffness
resulting from the locally
differentiated cross section. The
structural performance of the
leaf was investigated by means
of comparing the stress patterns
developing over the leaf (bottom
right) due to wind pressure with
the stresses that would occur in
a leaf with no folds (bottom left)
under the same loading conditions.
EmTech Natural Systems Module,
Zoe Saric, Biraj Ruvala, Michel
da Costa Goncalves and Jennifer
Boheim, 2005.

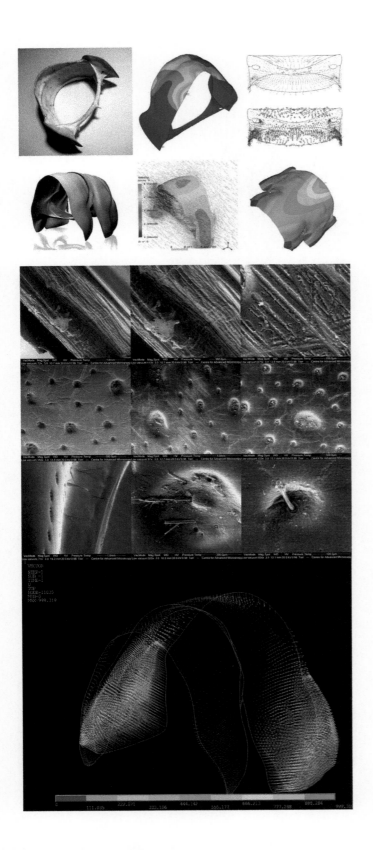

0.4

Natural systems analysis: lobster shell. An abdominal shell of a lobster was digitally modelled in order to analyse its capacity to bear different directional loads. Finite element analysis served to deduce loads and loading directions to be subsequently compared with the intrinsic directional material make-up of the shell segment (top). The electron microscopic imaging undertaken at the Centre for Biomimetic Engineering at the University of Reading shows that there are two different types of fibre organisations. Fibres and pore channels are oriented to best cope with the constant mechanical stresses and strains acting on them (centre). The findings of the research enabled the building of a precise analytical model of the upper part of the shell (bottom). EmTech Natural Systems Module, Maria Bessa, Christina Doumpioti, Karola Dierichs and Defne Sunguroğlu, 2006.

one that bypasses the limits of standardised material components.

MODELS AND SIMULATIONS

In the sciences of complexity, the term 'model' means more than the geometrical description of an object that is conventional in architecture and engineering. A model is a mathematical description of a process, and can begin as a simple set of rules that are progressively refined as the understanding of the process develops. Such models run as processes, with inputs and outputs, and when the parameters are changed related changes in the output form and behaviour are produced. Many physical processes are modelled in this way in the computer, producing interactive simulations of the physics of the world. Optics and light, springs and masses, pendulums and waves, harmonics, mechanics and momentum, and even nuclear physics are commonly available simulations.

Simulations are essential for designing complex material systems, and for analysing their behaviour over extended periods of time. Simulations of the acoustics of spatial designs and material systems, or of the flow of air and heat through spaces and in materials, or the stress response of structures under imposed loads, are now standard modules in most engineering software, and increasingly used in design studios. Once strictly within the domain of engineering practice, they now can and should

be used as part of the generative design processes. The advanced physics of non-linear behaviour, the dynamic changes that structures and materials undergo in response to changing conditions, are all readily and inexpensively available to be incorporated into the design processes of architecture.

The simulation of prototyping, sometimes known as 'virtual prototyping', usually requires multiple iterative dynamic simulations prior to the production of a physical rapid prototype. In aerospace, maritime and automotive engineering, the wear and fatigue throughout the life of a vehicle is simulated during the design phase. In many industries, manufacturing processes are also simulated digitally in the design studio. Simulation of the machine processes and tool paths of Computer Numerically Controlled (CNC), rapid prototyping and laser cutting is a standard procedure of preparing designs for fabrication, and extends to the casting, milling, extrusion and bending machines by which many architectural components are now produced. Simulations allow the development and refinement of designs prior to the construction of physical models and prototypes.

The simulation of non-linear fluid dynamics of air movements is, for example, essential for the computational generation of responsive architectural 'skins' and for adaptive intelligent environmental systems for buildings. The design development of 'responsive' artefacts or buildings that have the capacity to make controlled changes to themselves, capable of adapting to dynamic loading conditions and environmental changes, requires the incorporation of several inter-related simulations. Computational form-generating processes that are based on 'genetic engines', derived from the mathematical equivalent of the Darwinian model of evolution and from the biological science of evolutionary development, combine the processes of embryological growth and evolutionary development of the species. Experiments that couple such generative processes to advanced structural and material simulations are still in their infancy, but have the potential to bring many advantages to the design of buildings. These processes are currently focused on the form, structure and behaviour of single buildings, but there is a further area of investigtion, the design of cities. This is a rapidly expanding area of focus for new experimental computational processes, and has the potential to explore new urban forms and systems that are adapted to the changing climate, ecology and economies that are emerging. This new research proceeds from the ecognition of architectural constructions not as singular and fixed bodies, but as complex metabolic and intelligent material systems that have a finite lifespan, that are interlinked as part of the environment of other active systems, and that can be symbiotically related to the flow of energy and material in the systems and processes of the natural world.

To further the discussion in a few words introduced above and to contribute to innovation relative to this discourse by way of extensive research has been the mission of the Emergent Technologies and Design programme. The aim of this book then is to share the research undertaken thus far – or, owing to limited page numbers, at least a number of key aspects – with the interdisciplinary creative field that may have an interest in the matter at hand.

0.5

Natural systems analysis: nest of Swedish magpie. Owing to its complex structure, the Swedish magpie's nest (top right) required the use of computer tomography scans of rotational slices (top left) for digitising the morphology: 450 slices were generated to describe the nest configuration through a high-resolution spatial database, with precise documentation of the varying material density levels using feature enhancement techniques (centre). The computer tomography scans are described as a voxel dataset (bottom, upper image), which was subsequently converted to vector based information employing a 'marching cube' algorithm that generated a polygonal surface model (bottom, lower image). MA Dissertation of Lina Martinsson, 2003.

Part 1
Theoretical framework

Chapter 1
Evolution and computation
Michael Weinstock

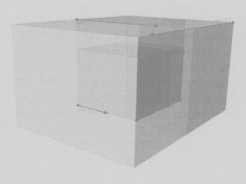

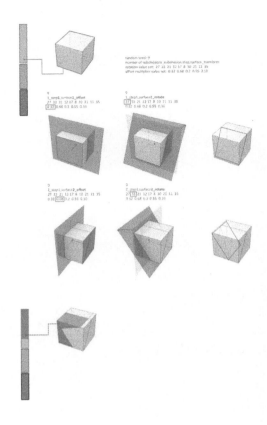

Architecture is undergoing a systemic change, driven by the changes in culture, science, industry and commerce that are rapidly eroding the former boundaries between the natural and the artificial. The conceptual apparatus of architecture has always given a central role to the relations of mankind and nature. The human body has been a source of harmonious proportions and the shapes of many living organisms have been adapted for architectural use. The current widespread fascination with nature is a reflection of the availability of new modes of imaging the interior structures of plants and animals, of electron-microscopy of the intricate and very small, together with the mathematics of biological processes. New working methods of architectural design and production are rapidly spreading through architectural and engineering practices, as they have already revised the world of manufacturing and construction. The material practices of contemporary architecture cannot be separated from this paradigm shift in the context within which architecture is conceived and made. The study of natural systems suggests the means of conceiving and producing architecture that is more strongly correlated to material organisations and systems in the natural world.

Computational form-generating processes are based on 'genetic engines' that are derived from the mathematical equivalent of the Darwinian model of evolution, and from the biological science of evolutionary development that combines processes of embryological growth and evolutionary development of the species. Evolutionary computation offers the potential for relating pattern and process, form and behaviour, with spatial and cultural parameters. Evolutionary computational strategies for morphogenesis have the potential to be combined with advanced structural and material simulations of behaviour under stresses of gravity and load. This approach is part of the contemporary reconfiguration of the

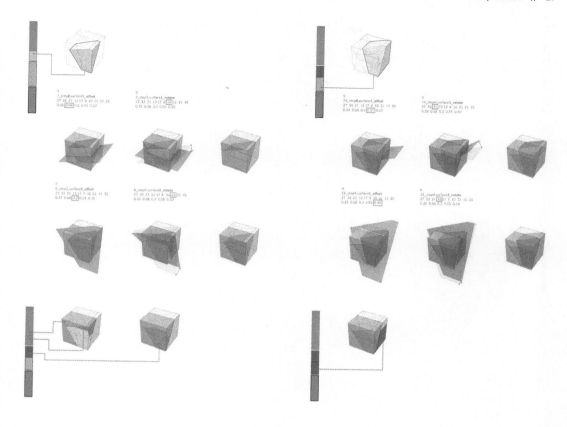

understanding of 'nature', a change from metaphor to model, from 'nature' as a source of shapes to be copied to 'nature' as a series of interrelated dynamic processes that can be simulated and adapted for the design and production of architecture.

The development and use of computational systems for architectural design is central to the theoretical and experimental explorations of the Emergent Technologies and Design programme. The seminar courses 'Emergence' and 'Biomimetics and Natural Systems' introduce the origins and instruments of the sciences and technologies associated with emergence, commencing with Darwin and D'Arcy Thompson, through analysis of the mathematical logics of evolution and biological development, to the experimental development of evolutionary algorithms within the limited computational environment of architectural design software.

1.1

Spatial subdivision algorithm (SSD): An offset operation is performed using multiple faces (red quad) of a three-dimensional polygon (white) to accommodate a pre-defined program hierarchy (2D-program bar). After each offset a rotation of the resulting cutting plane (grey 2D plane) is performed and the polygon solid is subdivided into smaller volumes. The program is inserted (yellow) based on optimal size and proximity to similar program classification. The algorithm repeats to distribute the various classifications of program utilising local geometric definitions of the polygonal solids. Offset and rotation values are determined by cycling systematically through a limited set of numbers. Each assembly of uniquely subdivided volumes is generated through using only nine rotation values and five offset values. Emergence seminar research by Sean Ahlquist and Moritz Fleischmann, 2008.

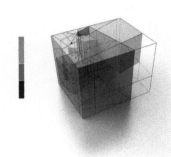

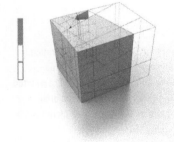

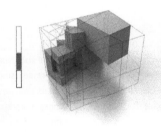

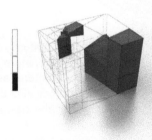

1.2

The program hierarchy, based on position and size in the 2D-program bar (input 1), applied to a cubic three-dimensional polygon (input 2, white) results in a highly differentiated accumulation of sub-volumes (yellow, green, grey). As the grey program was defined as a 'void space', it is deleted in the final result. Emergence seminar research by Sean Ahlquist and Moritz Fleischmann, 2008.

EVOLUTION AND DEVELOPMENT

The development of 'evolutionary' algorithms commences with an understanding of the two distinct but coupled processes that bring about the morphogenesis, variation and distribution of all living forms. Every living form emerges from two strongly coupled processes, operating over maximally differentiated time spans: the rapid process of embryological development from a single cell to an adult form, and the long slow process of the evolution of diverse species of forms over multiple generations. Fossil evidence suggests that the history of biological evolution is a sequence, from simple cell organisms to the higher complexity of plants and animals. Charles Darwin argued that all living and extinct beings were the offspring of common parents, 'descended from an ancient progenitor', and that 'all past and present organic beings constitute one grand natural system'. The diversification and proliferation of all living forms, the historical development of all the species of life, was driven by variation and selection. 'I have called this principle, by which each slight variation, if useful, is preserved, by the term Natural Selection' (Darwin 1859: 61). In Darwin's view variations are random, small modifications or changes in the organism that occur naturally in reproduction through the generations. Random variation produces the raw material of variant forms, and natural selection acts as the force that chooses the forms that survive. Just as humans breed livestock and vegetables by 'unnatural' selection, methodically organising systematic changes in them, so wild organisms themselves are changed by natural selection, in a slow, steady, gradual and continuous process of change. Darwin did not, as is sometimes said, assume that selection was the only mechanism of evolutionary change. In the last sentence of the introduction to *The Origin of the Species* he wrote: 'I am convinced that Natural Selection has been the most important, but not the exclusive, means of modification' (Darwin 1859: 6).

The development of a single being from an embryo to an adult form was at that time regarded as related to but distinct from the evolutionary 'descent from ancestors'. Darwin stated that 'the early cells or units possess the inherent power, independently of any external agent, of producing new structures wholly different in form, position, and function' (Darwin 1859: 389). His account of the properties of cells included their ability to proliferate by division, and to differentiate themselves to form the various tissues of a body. Almost a hundred years later Gould published *Ontogeny and Phylogeny* (Gould 1977), in which he argued that all changes in form are the result of changes to the timing of the developmental processes relative to each other, and to the rate at which they are carried out. His synthesis of embryological development and evolution was focused on changes in the timing and rate of development.

At the end of the nineteenth century William Bateson published a substantive account of the mutations in living forms, *Material for the Study of Variation* (Bateson 1894). Bateson's interest lay in how living forms come into being, how they are adapted to 'fit the places they have to live in', and in the differences between forms, and particularly in the causes of variation. Although an admirer of Darwin, he believed that the process of evolution was not one of continuous and gradual modification, but was rather discontinuous. New forms and species could not come into being through a gradual accumulation of small changes, and distinct parts arose or disappeared rapidly. He argued that distinctive variations, entire new forms, could spring up, already perfectly adapted. His argument rests on his analysis of the morphology of living beings, observing that 'the bodies of living things are mostly made up of repeated parts', organised bilaterally or radially in series, and many body parts themselves are also made up of repeated units. The parts are already functional, pre-adapted so to speak, so that morphological changes or variations can occur by changes to the number or order of parts. Another common variation he named 'homeotic', in which one body part is replaced by or transformed into a likeness of another part, for example appendages such as legs and antennae that have similar morphological characteristics. He regarded most variations between species as differences in the spatial arrangement, number and kind of repeated parts or modules. Furthermore, he thought that these changes were initiated during the development of the embryo by fluctuations in 'force'. He described this force, to much derision at the time, as rhythmic or 'vibratory', harmonic resonances or similar wave-like phenomena capable of dynamic response to environmental changes. Discontinuity in evolution is suggested by the fossil evidence, which implies long periods of relative stasis punctuated by sudden short periods in which many new species appear (Eldredge 1995). Gould's 'punctuated equilibrium' is perhaps the best known, if not most widely accepted, version of the theory that forms tend to persist unchanged for great lengths of time, and undergo brief but rapid change to produce new species in response to severe changes in their environment.

D'Arcy Thompson agreed with Darwin's argument that natural selection is efficient at removing the 'unfit', but in his view all forms are influenced by the physical properties of the natural world, and the form of living things is a diagram of the forces that have acted on them (Thompson 1917). The physical forces act on living forms and determine the scales, bounding limits and informing geometries of the development of all adult forms. Evolution and differential growth during the process of development produce the material forms of living things. The combination of the internal forces such as chemical activities and the pressure in their cells, and the external forces of the environment such as gravity, climate and the available energy supply determine the characteristics of the field in which they act; the effect of these natural forces is expressed in different ways depending on the size of the organism. 'Cell and tissue, shell and bone, leaf and flower, are so many portions of matter, and it is in obedience to the laws of physics that their particles have been moved, moulded and conformed' (Thompson 1917). His recognition of growth as the principal means of achieving variation in inherited forms predates Gould's synthesis, but most significantly, D'Arcy Thompson proposed that 'a new system of forces, introduced by altered environment and habits' would, over time, produce adaptive modifications of forms. Living forms, like non-living forms, exist in a field of forces, and alterations in those forces will inevitably produce the response of evolutionary changes to forms. Furthermore, these changes will be systemic, to the whole being rather than to a specific part, 'more or less uniform or graded modifications' over the whole of the body (Thompson 1917).

Animals and plants that have quite different evolutionary lineages may have striking similarities in the general organisation of their body parts, their anatomical structures, and the processes of their organs. Common organisations and anatomical architectures emerge from the coupling of processes that are strongly differentiated in time and by scale: slow processes acting over multiple generations, and very fast processes acting only in the short period of embryological development (Berril and Godwin 1996). In the first process, some biological forms, structures and metabolic processes are better able than others to withstand the physical stresses of the world, the rigours of the environment and the competitions of life. Natural selection will gradually tend to produce a generalised response of adaptation to specific environmental stresses, and this will occur across many species. Over sufficient time, forms will tend to converge. In the second process, the genome acts on the construction of individual forms. The accumulated complexity of the genome manifests in a general tendency to initiate cellular differentiation along common sequences and pathways. Common sequences of development, in a stress field that all developing organisms share, tend to lead to rather generic outcomes.

Furthermore, a large portion of the genome is similar across groups of species, and the sequence of development is also similar, as is the molecular chemistry of the biological materials of which living forms are constructed. All materials experience the same physical forces, are subject to the same stresses and react in similar patterns. Small variations in the sequence of inhibition and acceleration or in the duration of either inhibition or acceleration may produce changes in the development of the embryo at many scales, through the reorganisation and recombination of biological components.

INFORMATION AND MUTATION

Genetic information passing down through the generations modifies the forms of living beings and their interaction with their environment and the materials and energy that they extract from it. As each generation succeeds its ancestors, information is propagated down through time. Changes or modifications to living forms occur both by mutation or 'copy errors', and by the recombination of existing information into new sequences and patterns. This may be seen in evolution in general, in the emergence of new species, and in the emergence of social or collective behaviour and material constructions of insects, animals and humans. Energy and information produce effects that act upon the architecture of material in space and over time, and the interaction between them is neither exclusively 'bottom' up nor 'top down'. It is clear that both the living forms of nature and the constructed forms of human artefacts emerge from complex processes that are coupled to the transmission of information.

Cultural information is also transmitted down through time, and material practices manifest that information in the social activities of humans and in the forms of artefacts and buildings they construct, from the simple pit dwellings of the first anatomically modern humans to the cities of the ancient world, and on to the built forms and 'megacities' of the contemporary world. It is clear that material culture is also inherited by descendants, that there is 'descent with modification' in artefacts, and that the forms of buildings and even cities can be grouped into morphological taxonomies in a similar manner to the grouping of species. As mutations to the known forms of organisms occur naturally, so too have the small innovations, theoretical 'errors' and design mutations of ancient architectures produced the 'populations' or cities of buildings, and driven the historical evolution of architecture, with its limited morphologies and convergent set of available forms. There are, however, significant differences between the mode of operation of material cultural evolution and biological evolution. Perhaps the most significant difference between biological and cultural evolution lies in the 'selection' of forms that survive to pass on their genes or information to their descendants. Other differences include the mode of inheritance, which in culture may be horizontal or oblique, as cultural practices concerned with material construction diffuse between distinct social groups. Information transmission has been an essential characteristic of human culture since anatomically modern humans evolved from the great apes, although the means of transmission were slower, with less immediate effects. The transmission of the information of material practices and architectural forms has been accelerated exponentially several times, with the sequential emergence of large trading networks, mathematical notation, writing and drawings systems, printing, and most recently by computation. The built forms of material culture may also be said to have evolved, commonly producing variation more rapidly than biological evolution but still at multi-decadal and millennial time scales. Computation offers a new design environment, one that has the potential to develop algorithms that mimic biological evolution, and compress the evolution of architectural designs into extremely rapid processes.

In biological evolution it is the sequential activation of the genes that 'express' the proteins and hormones needed for the construction of biological materials. The sequence of activation is regulated by a small subset of the genome, the 'homeobox'. It is thought that this regulatory set of genes emerged long before the evolution of physical complex forms, and many of the regulatory genes are similar across species. The differential growth of cells occurs in a field of stresses induced by the physics of the earth and the tendencies of biological materials to self-organise into differentiated patterns. The regulatory set of genes produce the initial spatial organisation of the embryo, by accelerating or inhibiting growth in varying sequences and patterns, and so act as differentiated feedbacks on the process of growth. Small variations in the strength of inhibition or acceleration induce a periodicity in the self-organising patterns, and that in turn produces yet more complex spatial and anatomical organisations across the range of scales.

1.3

The SSD algorithm can be performed on more articulated shapes. In this example, the shape is a zoning envelope in lower Manhattan, NYC (white polygonal solid). The algorithm functions through the two inputs (program bar and polygonal solid), but is easily expandable to consider more specific contextual inputs. Emergence seminar research by Sean Ahlquist and Moritz Fleischmann, 2008.

Mutations to the forms of animal and human bodies occur naturally. Cyclops mutations, for example, are a frequent occurrence in many species. Fish may become cyclopic if their embryos are thermally or chemically traumatised, pregnant ewes grazing on corn lilies can produce cyclopic lambs, and in humans diabetes or the consumption of excessive amounts of alcohol during pregnancy dramatically increases the chances of the embryo mutating to the cyclopic form. It is a very common mutation, a deviation at the very beginning of the normal development of the embryo. The morphological characteristics of Cyclopia are similar in all species, including humans. The mutation produces an undivided brain, lacking the normal two hemispheres, and a single eye, usually with the nostrils located above the eye. Biological mutations reveal the space of morphological variation or differentiation of any given species. In evolutionary terms, they are subject to strong negative selection, but are produced in every generation by the processes of embryonic development. Morphological differentiation of the full adult form is produced by small variations that occur very early in development, and may be initiated by genetic errors or environmental changes or may be induced by experimental manipulation. The process of embryonic development determines the morphological variation or differentiation in the population of any species, the total set of available forms.

Changes arise in the genome by mutation, often as 'copy errors' during transcription, when the sequence may be shuffled or some modules repeated by mutation. The changed genome in turn produces changes to physical form or phenome. Most mutations are either neutral or harmful to the living form, and beneficial mutations are rare. Differentiation during the development of an individual is controlled by the homeobox genes (originally discovered in the fruit fly *Drosophila*) that turn other genes on or off during development, controlling the order of morphogenesis and the position of different parts in relation to the body plan. In the case of the fruit fly, the mutation of a single gene, known as antennapedia, produces changes to the morphology and function of the fly's antenna, so that it develops as a leg rather than an antenna. This is possible because all cells in the fly have all of the information necessary to become leg cells or antennae. Every cell in an organism carries a complete genome, all of the information necessary for the development of the complete organism. Antennapaedia and its homologues control limb development in all vertebrates, so that the forelimbs of birds develop as wings, or the extremities of the forelimbs develop as hands in humans or flippers in seals. Homeobox sequences have been conserved throughout evolution and are controlling factors to the development of even distantly related organisms. Changes to the homeobox genes have substantial effects on the morphology

1.4

The SSD algorithm executed on a building envelope, depicting a distribution of space, both continuous and dispersed. The high degree of articulation is driven by the more detailed 2D-program bar, as compared to the example in figure 1.2. The more strategic program bar assigns the grey-value as a 'void space'. These elements are therefore removed. Emergence seminar research by Sean Ahlquist and Moritz Fleischmann, 2008.

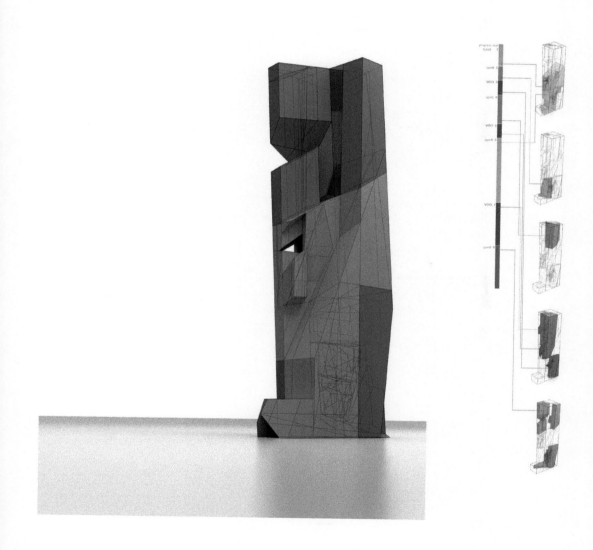

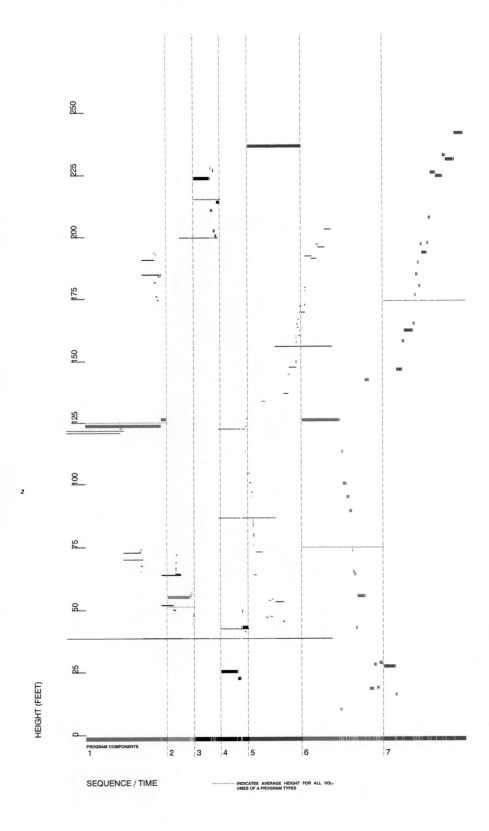

2

HEIGHT (FEET)

250
225
200
175
150
125
100
75
50
25
0

PROGRAM COMPONENTS

1   2   3   4   5   6   7

SEQUENCE / TIME

.... INDICATES AVERAGE HEIGHT FOR ALL VOL-
UMES OF A PROGRAM TYPES

of individuals, and when these changed individuals survive the rigours of natural selection, new descendant species are formed. If individual mutations offer the advantage of superior functionality in some capacity, then the mutant organism will have an enhanced reproductive fitness. If its progeny inherit the changed genome, then evolutionary change will occur. Differentiation by speciation, new species arising from a common ancestor, is normally described in phylograms, or tree-like charts. The underlying logic is to plot the sequence of morphological differentiations that lead from the 'form' of a common ancestor to the multiple differentiated forms of the whole group or taxa. For example, the common ancestor of all arthropoda, including crustaceans, centipedes, spiders, scorpions and insects, was a simple tube-like worm. The arthropoda group has over one million species alive today, with a fossil record that starts in the early Cambrian era, and it accounts for over 80 per cent of all known organisms. The sequence of morphological differentiation produced segmented bodies, exoskeletons and jointed legs.

The co-option or recruitment of existing genes into new organisations means that no new molecules are needed, so that repetition and reconfiguration produce a higher complexity within the genome. Living forms have an anatomical and spatial organisation that consists of repeated modules that vary in size, shape and number. The genome too is modular in organisation, consisting of many repeating sequences arrayed in distinct groups, each of which may contain common or multiple sequences that also occur in other groups. If small changes occur in the regulatory genes, they have the potential to produce changes to the size, shape and number of repeating modules in the living form. Over evolutionary time the genome has grown in size and complexity, but there is no apparent correlation between the size of the genome and the complexity of a living form. It has been observed that large living forms with very large genomes, such as trees in temperate climatic regions, tend to produce variant descendant species less often than other species. In the history of biological evolution, the emergence of small complex anatomical organisations made possible the emergence of ever larger and even more complex organisations. Complexity builds over time by a sequence of modifications to existing forms. There is both fossil and genetic evidence that the emergence of the general vertebrate organisation, and its subsequent modification into amphibians, reptiles, birds and mammals, occurred in this sequence.

1.5

As the SSD performs offsets and rotations within a randomised region to produce varying results each time it is executed on a given input shape, it is necessary to keep track of these transformations if a desired solution needs to be reproduced or passed on. This is done in a two-dimensional map (fate map). The map records the vertical position (top of y-axis = top of polygonal shape), distribution and sizes (length of strips) of a certain program (colour), within the 3D-envelope (same as figure 1.3). As the program bar is rotated by 90 degrees (bottom of fate map), the programs on the right are lower in the hierarchical level. It can nicely be seen that a low hierarchical level (red, on the right of x-axis) results in a high distribution of very small sub-volumes. This depicts the overall distribution of volumes, by size and vertical position. It purposefully avoids specifying a volume's interior and/or exterior position. Emergence seminar research by Sean Ahlquist and Moritz Fleischmann, 2008.

EXPERIMENTS IN EVOLUTIONARY COMPUTATION

Evolutionary algorithms are iterative processes that are structured on simplified logics abstracted from evolution, and are commonly used in many fields for solving non-linear and intractable problems. There are several different techniques, but they have in common several operations on the information or genome of each candidate form that are derived from biological evolution, including selection, reproduction and mutation. The process usually commences with the initiation of a random population of candidate forms, from which those that best match the desired criteria, the 'fittest' individuals, are selected. The use of evolutionary algorithms has been quite limited in architectural design, and algorithms that combine both growth (embryological developments) and evolution (operating on the genome) over multiple generations have not yet been successfully produced. The ambition of the experiments within the Emergent Technologies and Design seminar course is to explore the means of evolving context-sensitive and functionally specific architectural forms within typical architectural design software, such as Rhino, and with limited computational resources, typically a laptop computer.

The experiments begin with a series of geometric transformations (scale, rotate, move) that are applied to simple primitive geometries such as the cube, sphere, cone or torus. The first generations are run without scripts or code, using simple rules with parameters that allow for variation. These early generations are used to refine the relationships between 'breeding', the amount of random variation permitted in the genome, and the resultant complexity of form within the computational environment. The subsequent iterations of the process include both evolution over successive generations and the rules of embryological development of each individual within each population.

The numbers of successive generations and the number of individuals within each population of a single generation have an impact on the computational resources available and so have to be carefully calculated. The distribution of variation within each population, the percentage of deviation from the norm, has an impact on the calculation of fitness of the whole population. This is a significant point of bifurcation in the design of the algorithm, as 'fit' populations may have many very similar individuals and thus a good 'gene pool' but less fit populations may have one or two outstanding individuals within them. There are many ways of inducing environmental pressure on the populations, for example constraints on the total amount of surface 'material' available for the whole generation. The interaction of environmental constraints and population strategies are also amplified or inhibited by the kill strategy, how many if any of the parent individuals survive into the next generation, and how many individuals are bred from.

The 'growth' of each individual form within each population is manipulated by a set of actions that are designed to be the equivalent of the regulatory or homeobox genes acting on the axes and subdivisions of the 'bodyplan'. The earlier that 'mutation' or changes to the regulatory set are applied in the growth sequence, the greater the effect is on the completed or adult form. Random mutation applied to the homeobox produce changes in the number, size and shape of each of the subdivisions of the 'bodyplan'. Very significant differences in populations and individuals are produced by small changes in how much mutation is permitted in each generation, by varying the percentage of mutation in different segments of individual forms, and by constraining the differentiation of axial growth across the population. A simple example is that constraints on the ratio of lateral growth to vertical growth will tend to generate tall slender tower-like forms, whereas constraints on the range of permitted ratio of surface area to interior volume will tend to generate more rounded forms. Ratios may also be used for ranking the fitness of individual forms, such as the ratio of a linear dimension to a cross section, or the ratio of cross section to surface area.

Adding further constraints on the interactions between various modules or subdivisions of the 'bodyplan' may produce quite unexpected results. This is well known in living forms, for

1.6

The SSD algorithm outputs highly articulated three-dimensional volumes every time it is run. These individuals can be reproduced or re-combined. Emergence seminar research by Sean Ahlquist and Moritz Fleischmann, 2008.

example in the growth of molars in mammals. Accelerating the growth of some molars will also tend to inhibit the growth of adjacent teeth, so that a great variety of different patterns and sizes of molars, canines and incisors can be achieved without having to have genes that act separately on each tooth.

The production of new and varied 'genomes' require the parameters for form-generation and the analysis of how well each form matches the desired performance criteria to be made readable and calculable, to be ranked and to be recombined to create successive generations. In embryological development, the 'homeobox' is able to generate and evolve structures without itself having to continually evolve higher complexity. In computational terms, it may be

regarded as a collection of switches that turn other processes on or off, at various times and in various regions during the digital growth of the specific structures. The combinations of switching, in differing sequences and at differing times and locations, is extremely powerful, capable of generating enormous variation and differentiation from a very small and computationally lean set of instructions.

SPATIAL SUBDIVISION ALGORITHM

This architectural algorithm derived from the study of evolutionary development was developed within the 'Emergence' seminar course by Sean Ahlquist and Moritz Fleischmann. The computational experiment explores digital mechanisms for the integration of multiple tasks and conditions. Based on the logic of evolutionary development, the algorithm is modular, non-hierarchical and uses the simplest tools, local interaction and feedback to develop higher-order structure, architectural form and behaviour. The strategy for evolving configurations of space and program is based on a spatial subdivision algorithm that was developed in McNeel's scripting language 'RhinoScript'. In this experiment, the algorithm begins with an overall building envelope and performs recursive steps of subdivision to distribute a series of spaces. The hierarchy of architectural programs is determined, from which information is derived regarding the subdivision of program functions and quantities, and their particular requirements of space and organisation. The hierarchy ranks, among other parameters, the necessity of a program type to be consolidated with similar or related types or to be more widely distributed. The algorithm works only on the local level. Subdivision is triggered by the relative balance or imbalance of two conditions. The priority is to find connected volumes and insert the same or related program type. If a connected volume is too big for a program type then it is subdivided and the 'connected volume' is searched out again. Subdivision, when triggered, works with the geometry of the individual volume. The surfaces of the volume become the armatures for the subdivision of itself. This provides for varied amount of articulation, shifts in topology, and a high degree of extensibility.

1.7

The SSD algorithm's strength is its quick production of comparable designs given a very limited and open framework of inputs. Combined with the strategy of genetic information mapping (fate maps), this algorithm works within the framework of a genetic evolutionary strategy. Fit individuals with their related fate maps are highlighted in black frames. Emergence seminar research by Sean Ahlquist and Moritz Fleischmann, 2008.

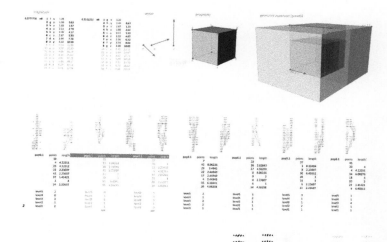

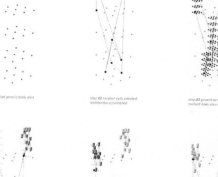

1.8

This is an example of some initial experiments in program evolutionary-based algorithms. The method of subdivision was easily derived from a method of 1D-scaling of a simple 3D polygonal shape. In this case a growth through simple iterative transform operations was desired, leading to highly articulated results of interconnected continuous geometries. Emergence seminar research by Sean Ahlquist and Moritz Fleischmann, 2008.

Chapter 2
Material systems, computational morphogenesis and performative capacity
Achim Menges

Architecture as a material practice is predominately based on an approach to design that is characterised by prioritising the elaboration of form over its subsequent materialisation. Since the Renaissance the increasing division between processes of design and making, as proclaimed by Leon Battista Alberti (Grafton 2002), has led to the age-long development of and increasing dependence on representational tools intended for explicit, scalar geometric descriptions that at the same time serve as instructions for the translation from drawing to building. Inevitably, and with few exceptions such as Antoni Gaudí, Frei Otto, Heinz Isler and some others, architects have embraced design methods that epitomise the hierarchical separation of form definition from materialisation. In today's practice digital tools are still mainly employed to create design schemes through a range of design criteria that leave the inherent morphological and performative capacities of the employed material systems largely unconsidered. Ways of materialisation, production and construction are strategised only after a form has been elaborated, leading to top-down engineered, material solutions that often juxtapose unfitting logics. The research presented in this book explores an alternative, morphogenetic approach to design that unfolds morphological complexity and performative capacity from material constituents without differentiating between formation and

materialisation processes. This requires an understanding of form, material and structure not as separate elements, but rather as complex interrelations that are embedded in and explored through integral processes of computational morphogenesis. It is important to note, however, that there is a crucial difference between established processes of material simulation and this design-oriented research: while material simulations require all variables of the system to be defined at the onset, the computational approach developed in this research enables the exploration of the design space established by the constraints of a material system, which leads to results that are not a priori fully determined.

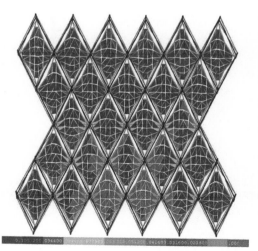

2.1 (above)

Full-scale mock-up of the AA Membrane Canopy examined by Michael Weinstock and Mike Cook at Buro Happold in London.

2.2 (left)

Example of a structural analysis of the AA Membrane Canopy's generic component setup showing the stress distribution in the tensile and compressive elements. Emergent Technologies and Design group 2006–07 in collaboration with Buro Happold.

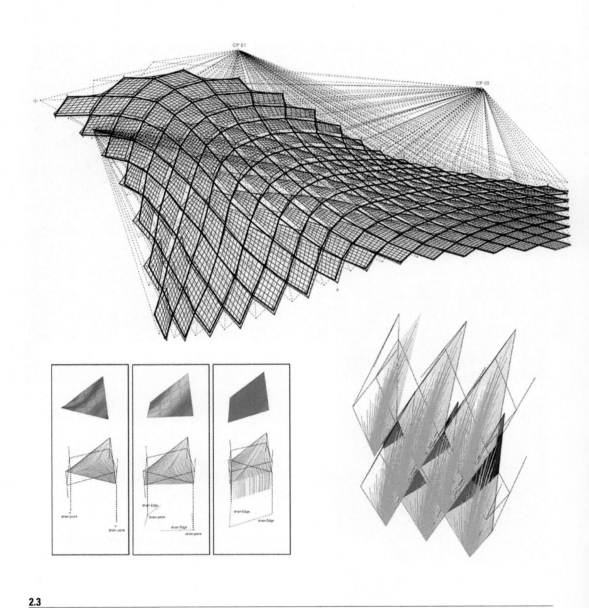

2.3

Computational model (top) and rainwater run-off analysis of the AA Membrane Canopy (bottom). Emergent Technologies and Design group 2006–07 in collaboration with Buro Happold.

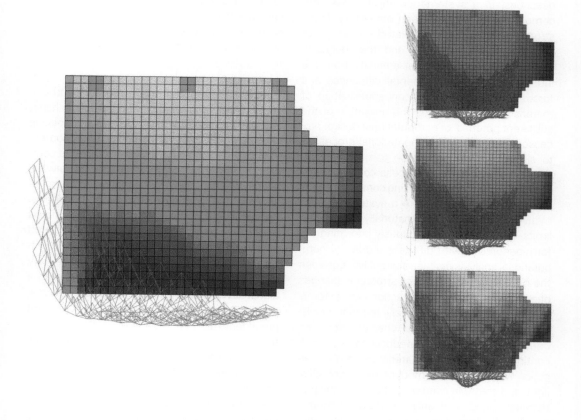

2.4

Examples of the shading analysis of different membrane canopy geometries over different times of the day and different seasons. Emergent Technologies and Design group 2006–07 in collaboration with Buro Happold.

MATERIAL SYSTEMS

The notion of the *material system* constitutes one central aspect of the research presented in this book. While it may initially seem obvious to consider material systems more or less as the equivalent of construction systems and tectonics, we conceive of material systems as a more profound and integral concept. In this way, *material system* does not refer to the material constituents of a building alone, but rather describes, in a system-theoretical sense, the complex reciprocity between materiality, form, structure and space, the related processes of production and assembly, and the multitude of performative effects that emanate from the interaction with environmental influences and forces. Interestingly, this conceptualisation of material systems enables the utilisation of the still latent potential of computational design processes. The ability of computational processes to simultaneously do both – to stochastically derive and systemically process complex datasets within a defined or evolving constraint space – can be utilised to explore a system's performative capacity within its materially determined limits. Furthermore, continuously informing the form-generation with different modes of computational analysis enables a direct link between the ontogeny, the history of structural changes of an individual, and its interaction with external forces and energy respectively. In other words, material and morphological characteristics are derived through iterative feedback loops, which continually process the material system's interaction with statics, thermodynamics, acoustics, light, and so on. In contrast to the currently predominant modes of utilising design computation first for formal explorations liberated from all constraints of construction, and then for the economically driven rationalisation of the resultant, tectonically complicated buildings, this approach utilises computation to recognise and exploit the material system's *behaviour* rather than merely focusing on its *shape*. This enables the designer to conceive of material systems as the synergetic outcome of calibrating and balancing multiple influencing variables and divergent design criteria, which always already include the interaction with the system-external environment. The resultant environmental modulations can now be understood as highly specific patterns in direct relation to the material interventions from which they originate. Hence they no longer rely on universal textbook principles of generalised behaviour. The design of space, structure and climate can be synthesised in one integral process rather than subdivided in a hierarchical workflow of separate actions or disciplines. Such an integral approach to architectural design based on the concept of material systems leads to considerable methodological changes and necessitates questioning some concepts deeply entrenched in current architectural practice.

In his seminal writings on morphology Goethe ([1796] 1987) draws the profound distinction between *gestalt*, the specific shape, and *bildung*, the process from which a specific shape unfolds. In this sense gestalt is a momentous snapshot in space and time. Thus the complex morphology of material gestalt always needs to be perceived in relation to morphogenesis, the continual process of becoming. Recognising that the gestalt of natural systems is always inherently and inseparably related to their processes of materialisation is of critical importance. Hence the works of the very few architects and engineers that pioneered a higher level integration of processes of formation and materialisation are far more relevant precedents for the work presented here than the superficially similar, yet design-methodologically fundamentally different avant-garde of contemporary digital design. Frei Otto's work is of particular interest for us, especially the synthesis of many of his investigations in his special research group *Natürliche Konstruktionen* at Stuttgart University. His realisation that 'the knowledge of the conditions under which forms develop opens up the possibility to qualify step by step the differentiation between design – the anticipation of reality in mind – and the construction of buildings – the production of objects' (Gaß 1990: 2–4), serves as a reference point in architectural research history. Frei Otto coined the term 'Selbstbildung', the process of *self-forming* that underlies most of his experiments on membranes, shells and other systems. This refers to the generation of a system's particular shape as the self-found equilibrium state of the forces acting upon it and its internal resistances determined by its material properties. In other words the designer defines a number of critical parameters and material characteristics, upon which the material system settles into the equilibrium state by itself taking on its specific shape in the process. This design method of *form finding,* as Frei Otto called it, is profoundly different from the still prevalent *form definition.*

As Frei Otto was mainly concerned with developing long-span lightweight structures with the primary objective of improving the ratio of a system's mass to its load-bearing capacity, he usually employed this method to form-find the overall shape of the structure. The work presented in this book aims at extending this research in regard to two points: [i] we have been investigating various possibilities of how form-finding can also be employed on additional levels of a material system, as for example each local element; [ii] we aim for integrating a much higher number of critical design criteria, which inevitably leads to systems that no longer have one equilibrium state, but a multifaceted and complex capacity of negotiating and balancing multiple functional and performative requirements. The related design process of *computational morphogenesis* of material systems will be explained in the next paragraphs.

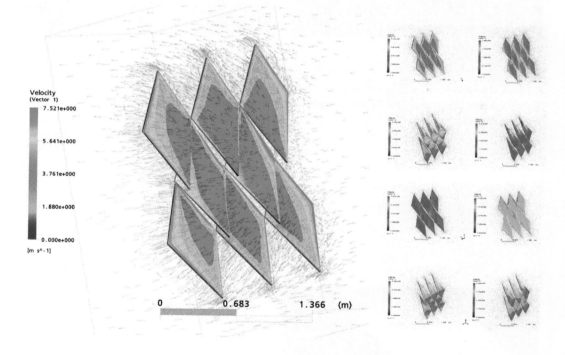

2.5

Examples of Computational Fluid Dynamics (CFD) analysis investigating pressure differentials and airflow acceleration of different areas of the membrane canopy. Emergent Technologies and Design group 2006–07 in collaboration with Buro Happold.

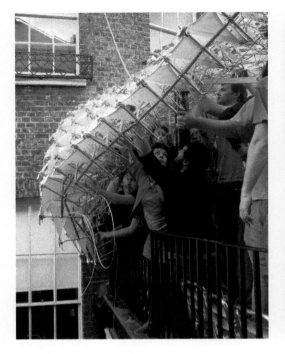

2.6

Assembly of the AA Membrane Canopy. Emergent
Technologies and Design group 2006–07 in collaboration
with Buro Happold.

2.7

Various views of the AA Membrane Canopy. The photo
in the centre shows an unexpected effect of the canopy
reflecting the low-angle sunlight during early morning
hours. Emergent Technologies and Design group 2006–07
in collaboration with Buro Happold. Photo: Sue Barr, 2007.

2.8 (opposite)

Close-up view of the steel and membrane elements.
Emergent Technologies and Design group 2006–07 in
collaboration with Buro Happold.

2.9 (left)

AA Membrane Canopy exposed to severe snow loads in
winter 2008–09. Photo: Tobias Klein, 2008.

COMPUTATIONAL MORPHOGENESIS

Computational design lends itself to an integral design approach as it enables employing complex behaviour rather than just modelling a particular shape or form. The transition from currently predominant modes of computer-aided design (CAD) to computational design allows for a significant change in employing the computer's capacity. CAD is very much based on computerised processes of drawing and modelling stemming from established representational techniques in architectural design (Terzidis 2006). In this regard one of the key differences lies in the fact that CAD internalises the coexistence of form and information, whereas computational design externalises this relation and thus enables the conceptualisation of material behaviour and related formative processes (Hensel and Menges 2006). In computational design form is not defined through a sequence of drawing or modelling procedures but generated through algorithmic, rule-based processes. The ensuing externalistion of the interrelation between algorithmic processing of information and resultant form-generation permits the systematic distinction between process, information and form. Hence any specific shape can be understood as resulting from the interaction of system-intrinsic information andexternal influences within a morphogenetic process (Menges 2008).

During the short history of so-called digital architecture, the notion of morphogenesis has almost become a cliché owing to excessive referencing to all kinds of design processes that operate most often merely on a metaphorical level. This has not deterred us from thoroughly investigating the powerful principles underlying natural morphogenesis and step by step transferring them into an integral computational process. As it is not possible to disentangle a material system's specificity from its morphogenetic development, we will present the most important characteristics of this design approach not in a generic manner, but along the specific example of the AA Component Membrane. This project aimed at accomplishing both, being an experiment that allows exploring and synthesising a number of research topics on a relatively large scale, while at the same time resulting in the completion of a commissioned project.

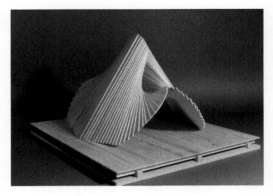

2.10

¹/₁₀ model of the viewing platform and shelter at Hazienda Quitralco in Patagonia, Chile. Emergent Technologies and Design group 2006–07 in collaboration with Buro Happold.

In the summer of 2007 the AA Component Membrane was developed, designed and constructed with our EmTech master students in collaboration with structural engineers from the London branch of the renowned engineering practice Buro Happold. The starting point for this project was a thorough analysis of the brief to construct a canopy for the AA terrace and the careful examination of its context in terms of the actual tectonic situation of the site, its specific environmental influences and the considerable limitations for the construction process. This led to the definition of a performance profile and related fitness criteria, which significantly constrained the design space in the following way.

The contact points between the canopy to be constructed and the surrounding building were limited to three existing columns. Upon closer examination, it transpired that the columns' base points could only withstand minimal bending moments, which seemed to be at odds with the requirement that the completed canopy needed to protect the terrace from crosswinds and horizontally driven rain. On the one hand, the canopy needed to provide a sufficient rain and wind shelter, while on the other, a high degree of porosity was necessary in order to minimise horizontal wind impact

pressure and to avoid blocking the view towards Ron Herron's landmark membrane roof of the Imagination building. Furthermore, the generally weak, existing substructure and the fact that the entire canopy was to be assembled without cranes or scaffolds greatly limited the overall weight and size of the individual components. Last but not least, owing to significant budget constraints, the material system to be developed needed to consist of common, inexpensive stock material and only to rely on fabrication processes operable in the school's workshop by unskilled labour. Only the membranes needed to be cut and the steel elements needed to be nickel-plated by specialised manufacturers.

For the subsequent steps of initiating the development and differentiation of the system, the first critical task was to capture and embed its parameters, their hierarchies, dependencies and variable ranges in a system-defining, genotypic dataset. The Danish genetics pioneer Wilhelm Ludvig Johannsen introduced the profound difference between *genotype* and *phenotype* in developmental biology in 1909 (Mayr 2002: 624). The *genotype* constitutes the unchanging genetic information, whereas the individual actual gestalt emerging from its interaction with the specific environment in which the development takes place is referred to as

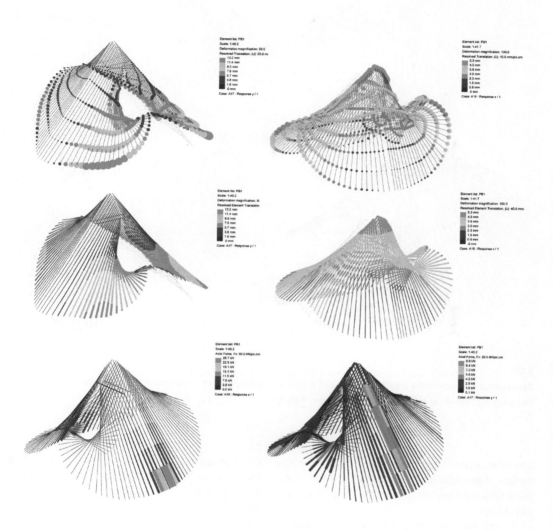

2.11

Structural analysis of the viewing platform and shelter exposed to seismic forces. Emergent Technologies and Design group 2006–07 in collaboration with Arup and Partners.

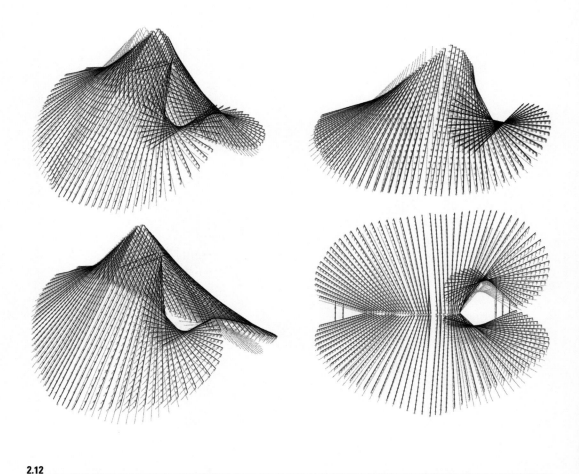

2.12

Displacement analysis of the viewing platform and shelter affected by seismic movement. Emergent Technologies and Design group 2006–07 in collaboration with Arup and Partners.

the *phenotype*. The possible degree of differentiation of an individual's gestalt in relation to its genetic determination is defined as its *phenotypic plasticity*.

First the definition of the basic system constituent, the variable system component, needed to be established. Because of the aforementioned constraints, the basic component of the material system developed for this project comprises [i] a framework of compression elements, simple galvanised steel tubes; [ii] steel wires as tension elements on the perimeter; and [iii] the membrane assembly. In the overall structure the membrane patches contribute

considerably to the structure's load-bearing capacity as the main tension elements and at the same time provide the system's skin. At this point it is important to reiterate that the material system is considered not so much as a derivative of standardised building systems and elements, but rather as the product of a whole range of generative drivers in the design process. This initially requires disentangling a number of aspects that later on form part of an integral computational setup in which the system evolves.

First of all the geometric description of the material system, or rather the notation of particular features of the system's morphology, needs to be established. The designer needs to facilitate the setup of a computational model not as a particular gestalt specified through cartesian coordinates, but rather as a framework of possible formations affording further differentiations that remain coherent with the system's characteristics. Hence, for the following development steps of the membrane component system the aim was to define the material system's inherent parameters and in particular their variable bandwidth determined by the affordances and constraints of the individual elements. This generic definition allowed for each individual component to be differentiated in response to the specific requirements of the overall system's sub location in which it is placed.

The parameterisation of the component was based on a large number of physical tests exploring the system's inherent constraints. First the self-forming behaviour of the membrane element was investigated in relation to the location of the points where it attaches to the compression framework. Depending on the relative position of the anchor points, the pre-tensioned membrane settles into different individual shapes. However, within a specific parameter range, all the individual shapes share certain characteristics: for example, they all adhere to hyperbolic-paraboloid (*hypar*) geometry with negative Gaussian curvature. In other words, the variation of the defining parameters, in this case the relative coordinates of the hypar's high and low points given by the steel framework, leads to variant equilibrium states of the acting forces and related membrane shapes. The parametric description of the tubular steel frame is hierarchically dependent on the membranes, in that its geometric variance is limited by the constraints of their self-forming processes to prevent wrinkles or more generally to ensure proper tensioning so that the membranes can become structurally active. In addition, the compression elements have their own inherent limits, for example the maximum deviation of the joint angles on both ends. Furthermore, in order to prevent local buckling, the relative maximum length of each tube is limited in

relation to the compressive force acting on it as the tubes' diameter range was restricted to 16 to 22 millimetres owing to manufacturing and weight constraints.

The notion of 'component' does not only integrate the possibilities and limits of making, and the self-forming tendencies and constraints of materials, but also needs to anticipate the processes of assembly of a component collective, opening up the possibility for building up a larger system. Similar to the definition of the elements, the definition of the relation between elements prioritises topological exactitude (Winfree 1987: 253) over the metric precision usually pursued when detailing the assembly of parts. In other words, the material system's component assembly is primarily defined through the topological relations of proximity and contiguity of its elements rather than the metric characteristics of length, angle or area as in Euclidean geometry. In Euclidean geometry the relation between elements or points is expressed as fixed length and distances that stipulate how far apart points are in relation to one another. However, in topological space distances expressed in length cannot characterise proximity as the length does not remain fixed. Such topologies can be stretched or scaled without changing the underlying characteristics of its defining points or elements. The summation of all these defining factors derived through and verified by a multitude of digital and physical test models leads to a first genotypic definition of the system's basic constituent. The relevant material properties, self-forming capacities, geometric characteristics, manufacturing constraints and assembly logics of the system elements are described as reciprocal interdependences operating within specific variable margins. Within these margins, associative computational geometry enables the differentiation of the elements' transformative behaviour, whereby more complex and adaptable interrelations across different systemic hierarchical levels can also be programmed.

INTEGRATIVE DIFFERENTIATION

In computational morphogenesis the genotypic definition unfolds a performative phenotypic material system. This takes place through integrative differentiation of its elements driven by multiple performative requirements. This comprises both the ontogenetic growth process of individual systems and the comparative, evolutionary development of system populations across many generations. The technical implementation of algorithmic growth processes can vary significantly according to system type and design strategy. In any case, the common and most relevant aspect is the proliferation of the elements across several growth steps, in which each element is regenerated rather than one added to another. In this iterative *bildungs*-process each element and component adapts its morphology by calibrating its functional requirements with its particular sub-location in the overall system. This computational generation of the performative, phenotypic components is driven by a feedback with different simulation and analysis tools. These tools are not only employed for cross-checking the self-forming limits of the systems. This setup enables iterative analyses and evaluation cycles, so that the specific gestalt of the system unfolds from the reciprocal influences and interactions of form, material and structure within a simulated environment.

Both evaluative and generative modes (Sasaki 2007) of structural analysis play an important role in this process. Depending on the system's intended environmental modulation capacity, the morphogenetic development process also needs to recurrently interface with appropriate analysis applications, for example multi-physics computer fluid dynamics for the investigation of thermodynamic relations, light and acoustic analysis. It is important to mention, though, that CFD does always only provide a partial insight as the thermodynamic complexity of the actual environment is far greater than any computational model can presently handle. Nonetheless, as the main objective lies not solely in the prediction of precise data, but primarily in the recognition of behavioural tendencies and patterns, the instrumental contributions of such tools are significant.

The full exploration of the design space as defined by the variables and evolving margins of the phenotypic plasticity, as well as the related development of a system's specific performative capacity, is possible in an evolutionary process. Similar to the algorithmic growth process, evolutionary computation offers different ways of implementing such generative processes and fitness evaluation techniques. What all such procedures generally have in common is using the evolutionary dynamics of combination, reproduction and mutation of the underlying genotypic datasets through a genetic algorithm as well as selection procedures. The continuous differentiation of the system and all its elements is driven by the open-ended, stochastic search of the morphogenetic process, in combination with the selective nature of fitness rankings at the interval of each generation. This fitness evaluation always happens on the phenotypic level.

In regard to the design approach presented in this book, it may be important to note that the fitness evaluation, as well as other aspects of the evolutionary design process, are not strictly limited to computational means. Similar to the definition of the material system through physical models and prototypes, the analysis and evaluation of the system's performative capacity may equally be cross-checked through empirical tests. The findings of analytical modes oscillating between the analogue and computational realm can lead to alterations in the weighing of evaluation criteria or even the system's underlying definition itself.

PERFORMATIVE CAPACITIES

Computational morphogenesis can be described as a process of perpetual differentiation. The increasing morphological and functional difference of elements enabling the system's performative capacity unfolds from their divergent development directions triggered by a heterogeneous environment and multiple functional criteria. For the example of the AA canopy project, this entailed the specific formation of each membrane component depending on its location within the overall system. In this case, the computational differentiation operates on three different levels: [i] the component level and its dependent elements and [ii] the level of multi-component subsystems, as well as [iii] the

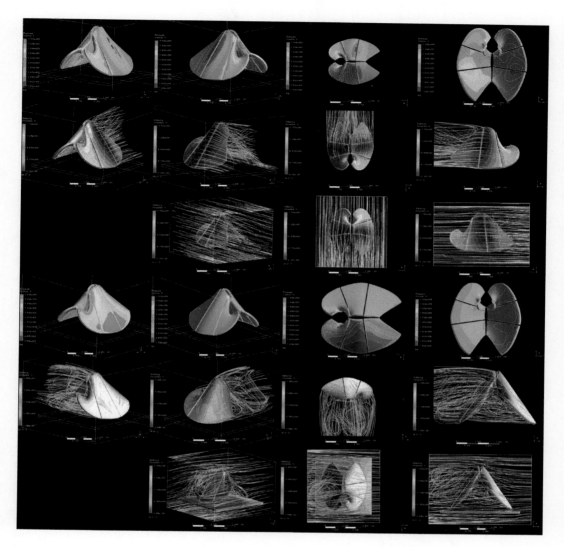

2.13

Computer fluid dynamics analysis of the viewing platform and shelter project. The top three rows are based on wind from the south, while the bottom three rows are based on wind from the west. In both cases the top row shows an analysis of the pressure zones on the envelope, the middle row shows the airflow velocity with selected streamlines, and the third row shows airflow velocity with full streamlines. The analysis served to determine horizontal loads and airflow conditions within the shelter as a design input. Emergent Technologies and Design group 2006–07 in collaboration with Buro Happold.

2.14

Construction process of the viewing platform and shelter at Hacienda Quitralco in Patagonia, Chile, 2007. Emergent Technologies and Design group 2006–07 in collaboration with Buro Happold.

overall system configuration. Each level is generated in direct feedback with different analytical tools and continual cross-checks with the given constraint space. Thus the morphogenetic process enables the balancing and calibration of multiple, or even conflicting, design criteria and the unfolding of the material system's inherent performative capacity. For example, a sequence of finite element analyses conducted by the engineers from Buro Happold during the design phase evolved the structure in such a way that the pre-tensioned membrane elements became an integral load-bearing part of the system, not just a cladding on a space frame. Concurrently iterative CFD tests of the system's aerodynamic behaviour were conducted on both the level of the overall system and local components assemblies. In feedback with analytical tools simulating the system's interaction with precipitation and its related drainage behaviour, this multi-criteria evaluation derived a finely calibrated level of permeability of the porous membrane skin that minimises wind impact pressure and simultaneously prevents local accelerations of airflow due to channelling gaps between the membrane elements. A further important factor that influenced the system's development was the shading behaviour of the canopy in different seasons and at different times of day, aiming for a mix of shaded and exposed terrace zones that changes from winter to summer.

Overall it is important to note that true morphological as well as performative differentiation requires the design and evaluation criteria, as well as their hierarchies and weighing, to develop alongside the evolution of the material system. Considering multiple influencing variables, which are negotiated and balanced during the process of differentiation, and the flexible hierarchy and evolving weighing of fitness criteria, shifts the potential of computational tools significantly. Rather than aiming for rationalisation or single-objective optimisation, computation becomes the means of integration: integration of the system-inherent constraints of materials, manufacturing and assembly, together with the system's interaction with a wide range of external influences and forces.

In the case of the AA membrane project, this integrative approach led to a highly differentiated, overlapping membrane structure cantilevering from three bearing points only. The information required for manufacturing forms an integral part of the derived computational dataset. The 600 geometrically different steel elements were manufactured in the school's workshop, and the 150 different membranes were automatically cut and labelled by a specialised manufacturer and subsequently finished at the London College of Fashion. The resulting overlapping membrane articulation shelters the terrace while at the same time remaining porous enough to avoid excessive wind pressure or blocking the view across London's roofscape. In addition, the integrative nature of the morphogenetic process derived a high level of robustness as compared to design processes aiming for single-criteria optimisation. Since its construction, the canopy has withstood gale-force winds and excessive snow loads, both conditions that the system was originally not designed for. Considering also that the entire structure was developed, designed, manufactured and erected within the short period of seven weeks, it demonstrates the potential inherent to the integral design approach of computational morphogenesis.

COMPLEXITY

Despite the fact that the presented design approach requires a serious engagement with technology, as may have become clear from the above description of computational morphogenesis, its use is certainly not limited to exotic materials, expensive manufacturing processes and vast budgets. The opposite is demonstrated through the following project, which is also based on the above explained computational approach, yet utilises more mundane building materials and the extremely limited manufacturing technology available in one of the world's most remote areas, Patagonia. In effect, as the main expenditure consists of the intellectual investment in an alternative conceptualisation of material systems and related computational processes, this design approach can remain operative in contexts of sparse resources. Here complexity, and related performative capacity, unfolds from the continuous evolution and differentiation of initially simple material elements and construction procedures.

The project entailed the design of a viewing platform and shelter, which was to be constructed within one week by a team of EmTech students on the land of Hacienda Quitralco in the Quitralco Fjord in Chilean Patagonia. The remote location imposed stringent constraints on the development of the material system: on site only one kind of locally cut timber plank was available, with the only tool for further fabrication being a chainsaw. The project comprised a generic platform on a raft foundation and a shelter that consisted of two ruled surfaces made from straight equal-width timber planks. The decision of constraining the basic computational definition of the system to so-called ruled surfaces was made in response to the pre-manufacturing constraints of timber on site, the available construction means and the local knowledge in timber construction. A ruled surface is a surface that can be swept out by moving a line in space. This implies that such a surface can be principally constructed from straight elements, such as, in this case, straight timber planks. However, the width and thickness of the planks require them to bend slightly along their longitudinal axis, which is possible as wood has the interesting characteristic of variable stiffness in relation to grain orientation. The considerable difference in modulus of elasticity in relation to fibre direction is particularly useful here, with the modulus of elasticity parallel to the main fibre direction generally being approximately fifteen times higher than that perpendicular to the fibres. This enables the ruled surface to be constructed from planks that are not all situated within parallel construction planes. Depending on the overlap and joint points with the adjacent elements, each plank can bend slightly along its longitudinal axis. This degree of deviation from coplanar plank assembly enables a specific curvature in the overall structure that is given as a function of each local plank joint.

The design space for the subsequent exploration of the system's capacity was defined by the possibility of varying both the guide curves in space, the length of each plank and the maximum angle between planks. Key design criteria for the evolutionary design process were basic functional requirements such as the enclosed volume in relation to envelope surface, the minimum ceiling height for inhabitation and the view axis towards the fjord and the Southern Cross. Considering the exposed location of the site and the harsh climate, additional essential criteria were the wind and rain protection of the inhabitable space. Furthermore, the structural capacity, particularly in regard to frequent earthquakes, was of critical importance. The considerable constraints determined by the availability of just one material element and the performative criteria outlined above provided the key constituents of the computational design process. Various generations of ruled surface configurations were derived and each generated instance individually evaluated, so that the results could inform the subsequent generation cycles.

In the final form the rotation points of the ruled surfaces shift along a curve in space, resulting in a surface that seems to turn upon itself. This creates a raised opening where the two surfaces meet and the timber planks cantilever. The entire structure is supported by an A-shaped frame constructed from eight planks, which form an integral part of the shelter's surface. This allows minimising the contact points between platform and surface in order to avoid moisture damaging the roof planks. The two surfaces that make up the shelter are symmetrical and lean against each other. The combination of the weight of the surfaces, their flexible connection and the slightly bendable planks enabled the resistance of the completed structure to the impact of the strong earthquakes of the region. This was put to the test the night after completion, which witnessed a number of earthquakes, with the strongest at the measuring 5 on the Richter scale. The shelter survived this first test without damage and has withstood a number of severe earthquakes and storms since construction was finished in spring 2007. In many ways this project demonstrates how an integral computational approach to design enables a high level of complexity and performance even in a situation where only the simplest means of construction are available. This indicates the importance of further developing the approach, as it may prove to be particularly relevant in contexts with very limited resources.

With regard to the concept of integral form-generation and materialisation processes and the related methodological framework of computational morphogenesis, one concluding remark needs to be offered in view of the research presented in the following chapters of this book. It is important to note that computational morphogenesis is not a universal procedure or design recipe, which, once established, derives any system from basic code to fully fledged material structure given the right input. On the contrary, beyond the common technological and methodological framework explained above, each material system requires the development of specific techniques corresponding with the system's particular composition, characteristics and performative criteria. Thus the work presented in the following chapters aims at providing an overview

of different material systems and related computational methods. Yet, one additional aspect they all share is the inherent questioning of the nature and hierarchies of currently established design processes and the promotion of an alternative approach, one that enables architects to exploit the resources of computational design and manufacturing beyond the creation of exotic shapes that are subsequently rationalised for constructability and superimposed functions. Rather, it promotes the unfolding of performative capacities and spatial qualities inherent in the material systems we construct. And this highlights the importance of the designer in an alternative role, one that is central to enabling, moderating and influencing an integral design process, which also requires novel skills and sensibilities. Exploring this challenge with the students has been one of the overarching educational aims for the research presented in this book.

2.15

Exterior and interior views of the viewing platform and shelter at Hacienda Quitralco in Patagonia, Chile, 2007. Emergent Technologies and Design group 2006–07 in collaboration with Buro Happold. Photos: Defne Sunguroğlu, 2007.

Chapter 3
Material systems and environmental dynamics feedback

Michael Hensel

It is a broadly acknowledged fact that today the majority of people on our planet live in cities, that the anthropobiosphere rapidly expands, and that two thirds to three quarters of Earth's eco-systems are interfered with by humans. These interferences effect a great deal of change of planet Earth's biosphere, including the local and global climate. It seems obvious that the vast amount of local interlinked material and ener-getic modifications of any context amount to significant regional and global changes. These local modifications are to a large extent affected by the built environment, and it is this realm that deserves greater attention and a broader scope of approaches than currently pursued. *Emergent Technologies and Design* offers an approach towards this thematic that does not compete with the current paradigm of the preservation of the natural environment or prevailing takes on sustainability, but that examines instead the capacity of material interventions in mod-ulating environments within specific contexts and empirically established ranges, while con-sidering a continuum between the inside and outside across the material threshold. Initially it is the immediate context of a built interven-tion that is in the focus of this line of research, although a new line of research introduced by Michael Weinstock is now also beginning to investigate processes of urbanisation in a fast-changing environment that is analysed and strat-egised on a metabolic level.

Michael Weinstock outlines this as a 'new line of research that proceeds from the recog-nition of architectural constructions not as sin-gular and fixed bodies, but as complex energy and material systems that have a finite lifespan, exist as part of the environment of other active systems, and as one instance of a series that pro-ceeds by evolutionary development' (Weinstock 2009). He continues to elaborate:

A metabolic model abstracted from natural systems can be developed to enhance the performance of indi-vidual buildings so that their 'meta-bolic' systems are responsive to their internal and external environment. Groups or clusters of environmentally

intelligent buildings can be interlinked with systems for material and energy flows, organised to generate oxygen, sequester carbon, fix nitrogen, collect and purify water, acquire solar, ground source and wind energy, and respond intelligently to the dynamical changes in local weather systems. The emer-gence of new metabolic forms will pro-liferate across the world as constructed material artefacts only if they are more closely and symbiotically related to the systems and processes of the natural world. As energy plays a critical role in all biological scales, from the cell to the ecosystem, so energy flows and metabolic systems for build-ings and cities will be central to the adaption of contemporary urban cul-ture to climate change.

(Weinstock 2009)

The following will focus, however, on a local level of environmental modulation, and dis-tribution of effects upwards in scale will be further discussed. This will require elaborating some scale-specific key features of climate and climatic processes. It is important to sys-tematically treat the distinct scales and differ-ences in altitude from the surface on which the climatic processes take place, starting with the notion of *microclimate*. Rosenberg *et al.* posit that:

Microclimate is the climate near the ground, that is, the climate in which plants and animals live. It differs from the macroclimate, which pre-vails above the first few meters over the ground, primarily in the rate at which changes occur with elevation and with time. Whether the surface is bare or vegetated, the greatest diurnal range in temperature experienced at any level occurs there. Temperature changes drastically in the first few tens of millimetres from the surface into the soil or into the air. Changes in humidity with elevation are greatest

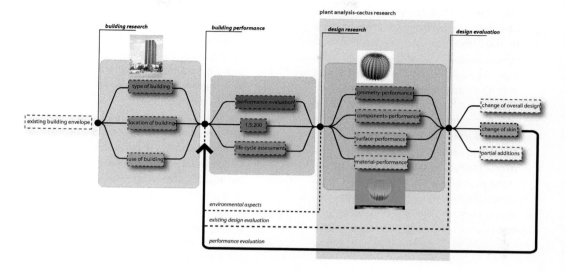

3.1

Flow chart of the iterative development process of a new envelope for the Piraeus Tower in Athens based on analysing the existing building, establishing relevant building performance criteria, implementing the findings of related design research and conducting iterative design evaluations. MSc Dissertation of Ioannis Douridas, October 2005.

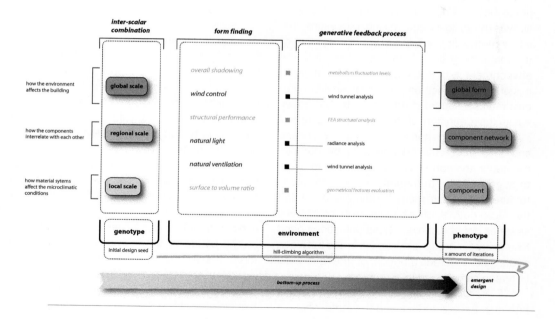

3.2

Diagram showing the relation between the computational design processes based on a 'hill-climbing' algorithm and the critical parameters of the new envelope's components, component networks and global form. MSc Dissertation of Ioannis Douridas, October 2005.

near the surface. Very large quantities of energy are exchanged at the surface in the processes of evaporation and condensation. Wind speed decreases markedly as the surface is approached and its momentum is transferred to it. Thus it is the great range in environmental conditions near the surface and the rate of these changes with time and elevation that makes the microclimate so different from the climate just a few metres above, where atmospheric mixing processes are much more active and the climate is both more moderate and more stable.

(Rosenberg et al. 1983: 1)

How far the microclimate, as determined by material surfaces and their properties, is significant also for the built environment is evident in the phenomenon of urban heat islands. Owing to the sealing of very large surface areas with high thermal mass, the local temperature of urban areas can rise by 3–4 degrees centigrade locally. While this is moderated, as stated above, by atmospheric mixing processes just a few metres above the surface, the amount of thermal energy stored and given back into the environment is of such magnitude that it yields a significant effect on the local environment past the usual strata of microclimate. Moreover, while the definition of microclimate is useful in understanding horizontal strata of climate and their interaction, it needs to be complemented with another set of definitions to begin to suggest an instrumental approach for architecture, given that many buildings are tall and therefore outside of the range of microclimatic strata as defined above. These definitions need to account for both the dynamics in and between strata and the redistribution of the threshold between climatic strata over time.

T. R. Oke explained that 'the interaction between Earth's surface and the atmosphere is limited to the *troposphere* that is a total height of circa 10,000 metres, and that this interaction is limited at certain time periods to the shallower zone of the *atmospheric boundary layer*' (Oke 1987: 3–4), positing that:

This layer is particularly characterised by well developed mixing (turbulence) generated by frictional drag as the Atmosphere moves across the rough and rigid surface of the Earth, and the 'bubbling-up' of air parcels from the heated surface ... The height of the boundary layer (i.e. the depth of surface related influence) is not constant with time, it depends upon the strength of the surface-generated mixing. By day, when the Earth's surface is heated by the Sun, there is an upward transfer of heat into the cooler Atmosphere. This vigorous thermal mixing (convection) enables the boundary layer depth to extend to about 1 to 2 km. Conversely by night, when the Earth's surface cools more rapidly than the Atmosphere, there is a downward transfer of heat. This tends to suppress mixing and the boundary layer depth may shrink to less than 100 m ... Naturally this ideal picture can be considerably modified by large-scale weather systems whose wind and cloud patterns are not tied to surface features, or the daily heat cycle.

(Oke 1987: 4–5)

Oke continued to elaborate the various climatic strata downwards in scale and height, distinguishing between [i] the *turbulent surface layer*, up to 50 metres high, that features 'intense small-scale turbulence generated by the surface roughness and convection'; [ii] the *roughness layer* that extends above the surface and objects one to three times their height or spacing and that is 'highly irregular being strongly affected by the nature of the individual roughness features'; and [iii] the laminar boundary layer 'which is in direct contact with the surface(s) ... the non-turbulent layer, at most a few millimetres thick, that adheres to all surfaces and establishes a buffer between the surface and the more freely diffusive environment above' (Oke 1987).

The matter becomes increasingly complex with buildings, which are affected by different climatic strata with increasing height and,

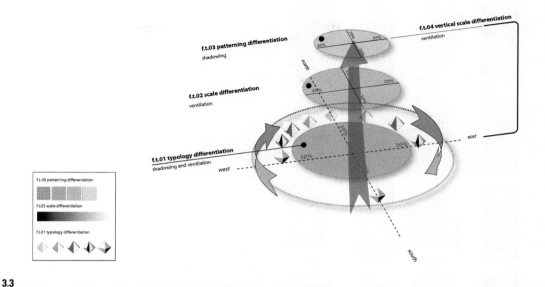

3.3

Diagram of the envelope's levels of differentiation in relation to its orientation and the performative capacity of self-shading and natural ventilation. MSc Dissertation of Ioannis Douridas, October 2005.

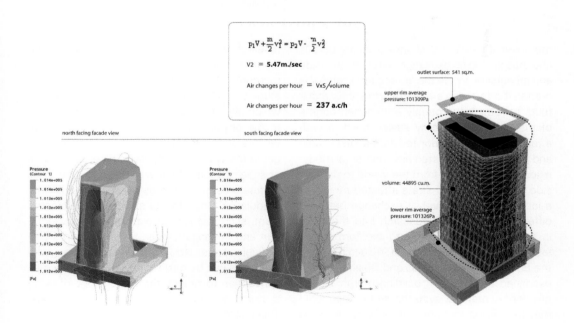

3.4

The envelope of the Piraeus Tower in Athens is derived through an iterative algorithmic procedure based on solar exposure and natural ventilation. The illustration shows the analysis of one envelope instance. MSc Dissertation of Ioannis Douridas, October 2005.

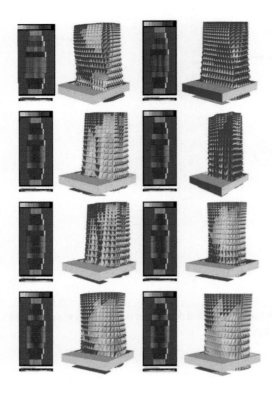

3.5

Multiple generations of the Piraeus Tower's envelope are computationally evolved and analysed in relation to a number of environmental fitness criteria in order to explore the self-shading capacity of both the global envelope shape and the local articulation of the skin components. MSc Dissertation of Ioannis Douridas, October 2005.

moreover, if their material envelopes are porous and thus enable an exchange between an inside and an outside. While the latter complicates the matter, it offers also a first opportunity for architects to rethink the deeply entrenched dogma of the quasi hermetically sealed building with a fully climatised interior towards a sustainable and carefully orchestrated environmental modulation over a gradient from the inside to the outside, and the climatic strata affected by this at a local level and a level of exchange between different strata. While research into the latter is still pending, research into the former has taken place. Various lines of research within the Emergent Technologies and Design context examined the way that building morphologies, envelopes, material systems and components may be utilised to contribute in effective ways to environmental modulation. In some cases this research incorporated also two-way interaction and feedback between material systems and environmental conditions.

Insights into how to approach this line of research were derived from studies in natural systems and their interaction with the environment. This entailed, for instance, detailed studies of plant morphologies and the way in which any particular morphology contributes to the physiology of a plant and its exchange with its environment. One line of inquiry investigated the way in which morphological features of specific cacti, all the way down to very small features, contribute to self-shading and airflow modulation close to the surface of a selected plant, such that loss of water through evaporation and transpiration can remain within a permissible range. However, listing such singular examples can be misleading. It would be a misconception to reduce the morphology of living systems to subsets with singular functions. This would just re-assert the prevailing prejudice based on which architecture and engineering strategises material assemblies as mono-functional building subsystems or elements that are optimised towards single objectives. Instead, a succinct attempt was made to conduct the

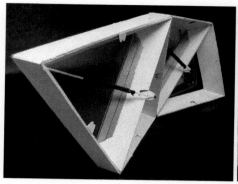

3.6

Photograph of a full-scale mock-up of three components of a responsive building envelope. Each component is equipped with a moisture-sensitive actuator that locally regulates the envelope's porosity without any additional electronic or mechanical control. MArch Dissertation of Juan Subercaseaux, February 2006.

inquiry into the morphology and material characteristics of living systems as performative systems that cannot be reduced to mono-functional elements. From this approach evolved a rather different understanding of the material envelope as an element of exchange. Thoughts in this direction have been stated for a while now:

> Contrary to heralding architecture's complete liberation from its material substrate ... an architecture of composite conditions can best be understood as based on material limitations and resistances. As with the highly ordered and complex cytoplasmic organisation of plasma cells in a cellular envelope, an architectural surface is a graded, permeable structure that can act as a selective barrier. If it is differentiated, the surface performs special functions in relationship to motile forces and informational flows that were exerted upon it. Furthermore, the complex organisation of simple cellular organisms provides an example of how the performative in architecture could be seen in conjunction with its formal components, first of all geometry and structure ... by closely engaging with the material variables.
> (Bettum and Hensel 1999)

However, it was not until the combined efforts of Emergent Technologies and Design and the Morpho-Ecologies research undertaken in Diploma Unit 4 (1996-2003) at the Architectural Association that the actual research began to take shape and to offer an alternative to prevailing modes of understanding and defining the relation between the built environment and climate. In the following paragraphs, three selected projects that characterise specific aspects of the research are discussed.

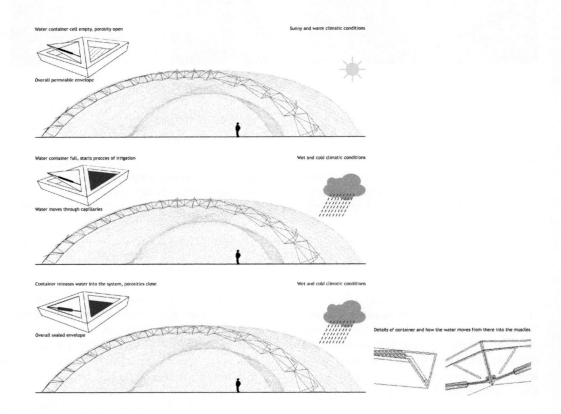

3.7

Illustration showing the three different states of the responsive building envelope. During sunny and warm times the water container is empty and the envelope remains open (top). In wet and cold climate conditions the water container begins to fill up and starts the irrigation process (centre) that causes the envelope to close (bottom). MArch Dissertation of Juan Subercaseaux, February 2006.

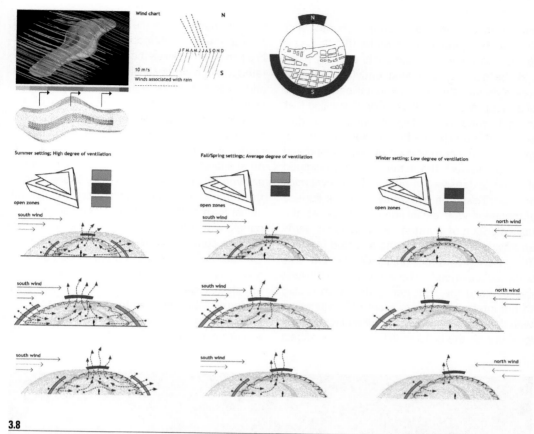

3.8

Illustration showing the envelope's capacity of naturally ventilating the interior in relation to seasonal climatic changes and changes of wind direction. MArch Dissertation of Juan Subercaseaux, February 2006.

Ioannis Douridas' MSc dissertation (2006) focused on how a new envelope for a climatically deficient 1970s mid-rise office building with a glass curtain wall, located in Athens (Greece), can make this building inhabitable without introducing a plethora of electrical and mechanical devices for climatisation. The research project utilised a bottom-up process facilitated by a hill-climbing algorithm based on multi-objective optimisation. Hill-climbing procedures are mathematical optimisation techniques that are used to solve multiple-solution problems, starting with a simple solution and making small changes to it until a more complex state is evolved. The process terminates when no further improvement is evident, thus not inevitably leading to an optimal solution. However, hill-climbing algorithms are comparatively easy to apply and

present a valid alternative to more complex algorithmic procedures.

The following phases characterise the research undertaken: [i] architectural analysis of the selected building – type, location, use, etc.; [ii] analysis of the environmental building performance; [iii] analysis of a plant morphology to extract relevant performance capacities vis-à-vis the criteria established in [ii]; [iv] setup of bottom-up algorithmic design procedure; [v] evolving of various designs and analysis and evaluation of their environmental performance; [vi] feedback of the findings into the next run of the algorithmic procedure; [vii] selection of the evolved envelope with desired environmental performance.

Owing to a lack of insulation, the selected building suffers from intense overheating of the interior space during the summer months and the inverse during the cold winter months. As a result, cooling and heating costs are very high, and the building is consequently uninhabited. Research into the environmental performance of a cactus (*Echinocactus grusonii*) revealed that the combined morphological features – hydrostatic and ribbed body – help in reducing thermal gain through a combination of self-shading and utilising airflow. The latter was investigated through extensive computer fluid dynamics analysis. Based on this study, an initial surface component was established to serve as the base element of a bottom-up approach towards an articulated surface for the selected building. The geometry of this initial component was analysed and modified based on its self-shading capacity and the light penetration with regard to the interior, leading to a set of components with different articulation to respond to different locations on the building envelope with respect

to their orientation to the sun path. In a second step apertures are introduced to the component in a similar process as the one before and elaborated through airflow analyses of homogeneous and heterogeneous regions of components, including acceleration and deceleration of airflow velocity and pressure zone distribution. On the north side the differentiated components serve only ventilation purposes, while on all other sides the combined effect of self-shading and ventilation must be operative. Subsequently the different logics driving the articulation of the global form of the envelope, the meso-scale of component regions and the local scale of the singular component needed to be established. On each scale criteria of aerodynamic performance, self-shading and light penetration are affected. Together the entire system fulfils its performative capacity with regard to these three criteria. Following this, a process for evolving the system needs to be established. A hill-climbing

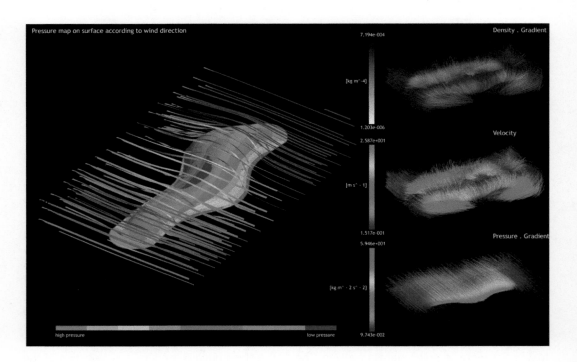

3.9

Computational fluid dynamics model: study of velocity streamlines and pressure gradients on the exterior of the building envelope. MArch Dissertation of Juan Subercaseaux with Nikolaos Stathopoulos as simulation and visualisation consultant, February 2006.

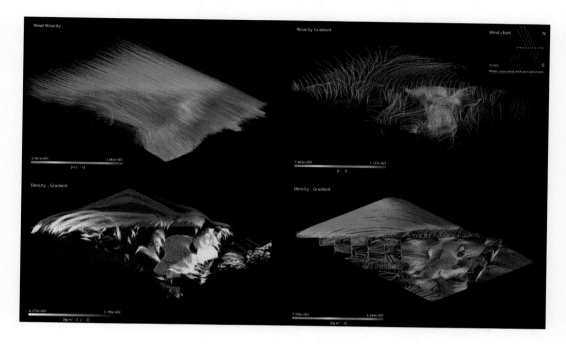

3.10

Computational fluid dynamics model: visualisation of the main airflow parameters around the proposed building envelope on a site in Valparaiso, Chile. The focus of the visualisation is on wind patterns at the scale of the extended context and the effect of the natural and built topography on the airflow. Velocity streamlines in different directions and pressure gradients are shown with colour coding that represents the value or intensity of the relevant parameters. MArch Dissertation of Juan Subercaseaux with Nikolaos Stathopoulos as simulation and visualisation consultant, February 2006.

routine was selected that is typically used in artificial intelligence applications that evolve from a starting condition towards an articulated global state in a non-linear algorithmic process. A large number of system configurations were evolved, analysed and evaluated with regard to local and global performance, gradually approaching a set of valid solutions to the multi-objective optimisation. However, the algorithmic procedure was based on a manual implementation and not on an integral method and toolset. This indicates one key area of further research. Likewise, the actual material characteristics of the component require elaboration and its performative impact would need to be embedded into the process.

Juan Subercaseaux's MArch dissertation (2006) focused on the development of a tessellated gridshell consisting of parametrically defined three-sided and four-sided frames selectively equipped with apertures that can open and close in response to the controlled presence of rainwater. The frames that have openable panels utilise pneumatic muscles made from a cylindrical bidirectional non-elastic mesh (Techflex) that is flexible and filled with CMC gel. The latter responds to the presence of rainwater directed to the muscle, by absorbing it and swelling until the water evaporates again and the gel shrinks. Upon absorbing water the gel, which is contained within an encasement, gains in diameter and shortens in length, and reverses its shape upon evaporation of the contained water. In this way a pneumatic muscle is established that does not require an external energy source. Since each muscle is stimulated and responds individually, no central control unit is required. The pneumatic muscles are utilised so as to individually affect the opening of the glass panels. Rainwater that is directed to the muscles affects the opening of the glass panels, which enables increased ventilation of the interior of the gridshell and in turn accelerates the evaporation of the water and the closing of the panel. Extensive physical modelling led to the development of a full-scale assembly of a set of frames equipped with modified functioning pneumatic muscles.

The overall geometry of the gridshell was subsequently elaborated through a series of environmental performance criteria within context-specific defined ranges of environmental conditions, including the utilisation of rainwater, ventilation and thermal modulation, as well as controlled sunlight exposure of the interior.

Form-finding experiments with form-active pneumatic systems served to extract the underlying geometric logic of the gridshell. This logic was used to set up an overall associative model. In a second step a process was developed that served to tessellate the overall geometry and to populate it with the three- and four-sided frames. Uniform and non-uniform tessellations were generated and subsequently tested for their environmental performance. Based on each modification of the overall geometry, neighbourhoods of frames were established that can receive rainwater from specified collection points. Once the associative interrelation between the overall geometry, tessellation logics and frame articulations was established, the setup was ready for iterative analysis and modification. Computer fluid dynamics analysis served as one of the main drivers for the iterative development of the design. At this stage the specific topographic context and the adjacent built environment were included in the digital model in order to account for the impact of the surroundings on the airflow velocity, direction and pressure zones that were utilised as design drivers. Airflow velocity and density

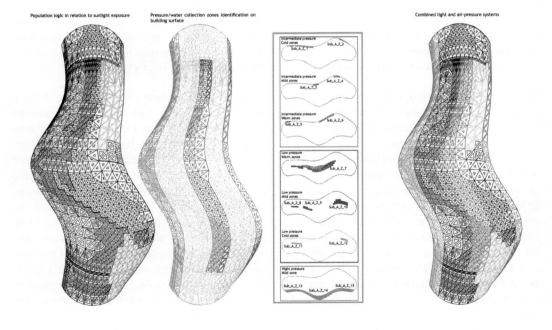

3.11

Final tessellation and distribution of frames over the double-curved surface of the building envelope (left); air-pressure zones and water-collection zones indicated on the envelope (centre); articulation of the envelope informed by the combined input parameters of light-exposure and air-pressure zones (right). MArch Dissertation of Juan Subercaseaux, February 2006.

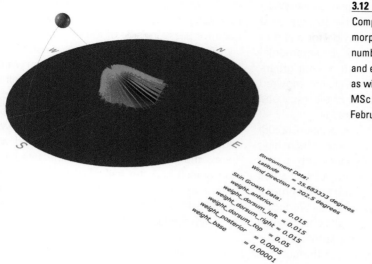

3.12

Computational setup of wind-driven morphology generation based on a number of system input parameters and environmental information such as wind direction and orientation. MSc Dissertation of Yukio Minobe, February 2009.

gradients were extracted, analysed, evaluated and fed back into the process of form-generation. In this process a distinction is made between prevailing winds associated with rain and those that are not. This serves the assessment of the presence or absence of rainwater, its distribution and its amount. This is of relevance not only to collecting rainwater to operate the pneumatic muscles, but also in assessing the distribution of openings. The direction of the wind, its velocity and the distribution of pressure zones can trigger the accelerated ventilation of the gridshell via the Venturi effect.

A parallel process concerned the overall form of the gridshell, as well as size and orientation of the frames relative to the sun path. Summer and winter solstice and equinox sun path and angles were assessed with regard to sunlight penetration and self-shading of the gridshell, both associated with the control of thermal gain of the gridshell, the ground surface and ultimately the enveloped space. Each geometric configuration of the gridshell with its specific tessellation pattern was then assessed with regard to an optimised rainwater collection and distribution layout so as to direct rainwater to the pneumatic muscles. The size of the water reservoir was determined by the amount

of pneumatic muscles fed by it, such that when all muscles are saturated with water the reservoir is emptied.

In the final stage of the process of evolving, the design was refined in such a way that the overall geometry of the gridshell was informed and constrained by form-finding experiments. The overall geometry was then elaborated through airflow analysis and aerodynamic criteria. The tessellation of the surface and the protocol for populating it with the parametrically defined frames was informed by the sunlight and self-shading analysis, while the air-permeability and thus the openable panels were distributed again in relation to airflow analysis. In a second move the airflow and sunlight inputs were negotiated, taking into account the air-movement resulting from thermal gain. This lead to a re-negotiation of the surface tessellation and distribution of openable panels and a further modification based on season-specific ventilation conditions, taking into account related amounts of precipitation and seasonally specific prevailing wind directions.

An interesting direction for a further development of this research could be to involve a specific building program to establish a range of environmental conditions that the system should cater for. The design and construction of a prototype for a greenhouse for specified plants would, for instance, provide for an interesting elaboration of this work. Environmental control remains a problem with current greenhouses that can only accomplish the required performance with a great deal of electrical and mechanical climatisation technology.

Yukio Minobe's MArch dissertation (2008) investigated the design of a complex branching system for ventilation embedded with a cast dome-shaped envelope. The project embarked from a detailed analysis of the environment-related shape of termite mounds reducing thermal impact, and the complex ventilation system of such mounds. The latter involved [i] upward airflows from the nest through the buoyancy effect; [ii] the lateral air distribution from the mound chimney via lateral connections towards surface conduits; [iii] airflow towards the negative pressure zone of the mound due to pressure differentials; [iv] suction from the negative pressure side of the mound.

The local scale of the project is established by the type of branching connections within the branching ventilation system, as well as the surface roughness of the inner surface of the branching network. Three different types of branching connections were analysed with regard to the airflow patterns associated with them: the flat section branch, the tilted section branch and the half-tilted section branch. Extensive computer fluid dynamics analyses identified the half-tilted section branch as the one with the least turbulent flow.

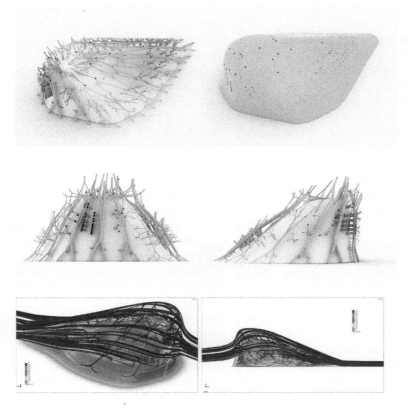

3.13

Digital model of the internal branching conduit morphology (top and centre) derived through a computational form-generation process based on iterative computational fluid dynamics simulation and evaluation (bottom). MSc Dissertation of Yukio Minobe, February 2009.

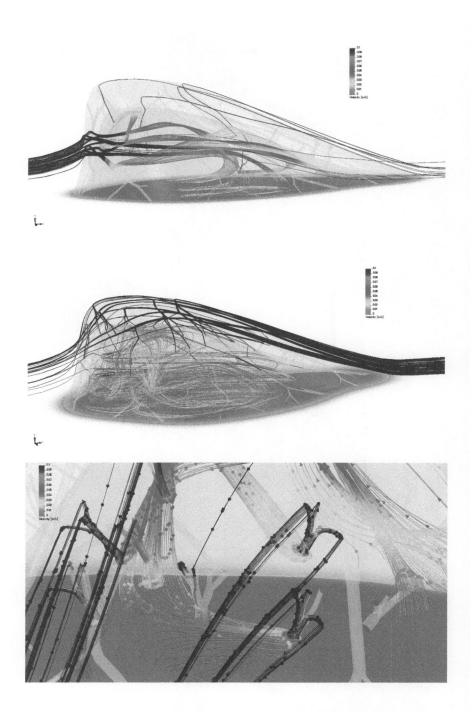

3.14

Illustration showing computational fluid dynamics analyses of the interrelation between airflow in the interior space (top and centre) and within the conduits (bottom). MSc Dissertation of Yukio Minobe, February 2009.

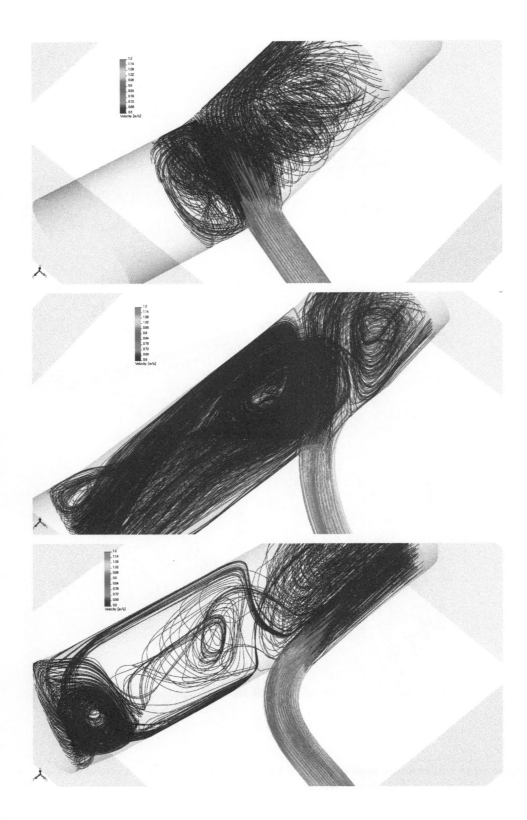

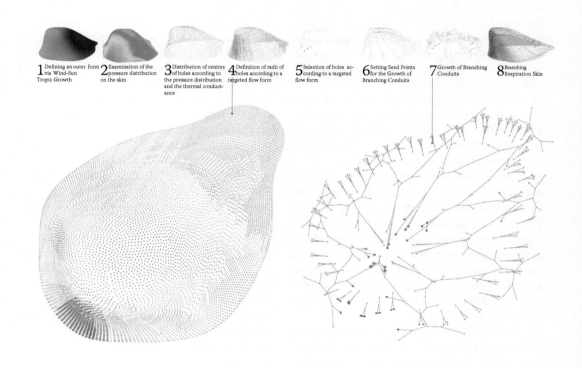

1 Defining an outer form via Wind-Sun Tropic Growth

2 Examination of the pressure distribution on the skin

3 Distribution of centres of holes according to the pressure distribution and the thermal conductance

4 Definition of radii of holes according to a targeted flow form

5 Selection of holes according to a targeted flow form

6 Setting Seed Points for the Growth of Branching Conduits

7 Growth of Branching Conduits

8 Branching Respiration Skin

3.15 (opposite)

Illustration showing computational fluid dynamics tests of different conduit bifurcation morphologies. MSc Dissertation of Yukio Minobe, February 2009.

3.16 (above)

Sequence of the morphogenetic design process indicating two key features: [i] the distribution of the inlet and outlet points for ventilation on the exterior of the volume; [ii] generation of the branching conduits. MSc Dissertation of Yukio Minobe, February 2009.

Following this study two algorithms were developed that articulate a branching ventilation network within the thickness of the material envelope of the volume: the centroid branching algorithm and the sphere-packing algorithm. These differ in their logic and in the branching pattern generated and thus needed to be analysed comparatively. The density of branching networks and the angles between branches were analysed for resultant airflow pattern.

Subsequently an algorithm was developed that articulates the overall orientation and articulation of a volume with regard to the sun path, deducing this principle from the termite mound. A specific site was selected to provide context-specific input including the sun path and prevailing wind directions. For this site a series of geometries for the global volume were derived. These volumes were analysed with regard to airflow utilising different branching ventilation patterns, with different numbers and locations of inlet and outlet points for ventilation.

Occasionally the computer fluid dynamics analyses resulted in improbable flow pattern. In these cases it was necessary to verify the result mathematically. In some cases it showed that the result derived from the computational analysis was incorrect; however, in most cases the results were reliable. Thus a context-sensitive iterative process of global form-generation, branching pattern generation and airflow analysis was established.

In one way one may argue that the reliance of the specific branching pattern with its inlets and outlets on the prevailing wind directions may imply that the resulting system is not robust enough to operate under strongly divergent wind directions. However, this may be solved by involving a greater range of wind directions in the setup of the wind and tropic algorithms and the definition of the solution space, or by investigating the possibility of opening and closing specific inlet and outlet points in a manner not unlike the previous research project, utilising material behaviour in response to environmental stimuli.

Further research questions will need to address material characteristics and their resulting impact on the thermal behaviour of a material construct, followed by physical tests on a construction scale. Furthermore, airflow pattern on various scales need to be taxonomised and related to a variety of uses of the interior spaces.

Typically two critical concerns are voiced vis-à-vis the research presented here. The first concern relates to the manufacturing and assembly costs of buildings made from parts that are all different in dimension. However, by and large it is now accepted that feasible production is possible owing to contemporary computer-aided manufacturing techniques. Because of the financial crisis of 2008–9, however, this concern has been repositioned; now, highly differentiated architectures are more often than not seen to stand for an exuberant capitalism out of control that does not consider expenditure or the lack of resources. Yet, the approach presented here may well be accomplished in a context of sparse material or technological resources, except those that drive the design process. The Emergent Technologies and Design programme has embarked on research to investigate this issue.

The second criticism, which is frequently voiced, is that the approach introduced here relies heavily on very specific knowledge, skills and tools. True as this may be, it needs to be seen within the context of the insufficiency of current answers to the problem of local, and eventually global, climate change. The question is whether architectural education and practice needs serious rethinking and repositioning. With this also comes the necessity of re-skilling and re-tooling. When seen in this context it may become more evident why first-principle knowledge in physics, computation and engineering is indispensable as a first step, and that more knowledge in this field may be required. In any case it is easy to imagine that this way of working may well soon become as ubiquitous as it is necessary.

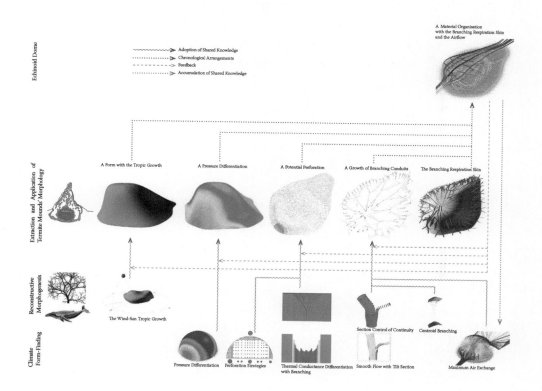

Echinoid Dome

Adoption of Shared Knowledge
Chronological Arrangements
Feedback
Accumulation of Shared Knowledge

A Material Organisation
with the Branching Respiration Skin
and the Airflow

Extraction and Application of
Termite Mounds' Morphology

A Form with the Tropic Growth   A Pressure Differentiation   A Potential Perforation   A Growth of Branching Conduits   The Branching Respiration Skin

Reconstructive
Morphogenesis

The Wind-Sun Tropic Growth

Climate
Form-Finding

Section Control of Continuity   Centroid Branching

Pressure Differentiation   Perforation Strategies   Thermal Conductance Differentiation
with Branching   Smooth Flow with Tilt Section   Maximum Air Exchange

3.17

Illustration showing computational fluid dynamics tests of different conduit bifurcation morphologies. MSc Dissertation of Yukio Minobe, February 2009.

Part 2
Research

Chapter 4
Fibres

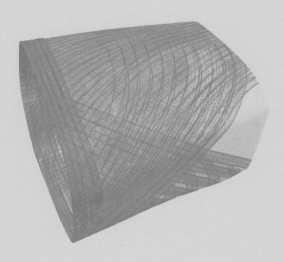

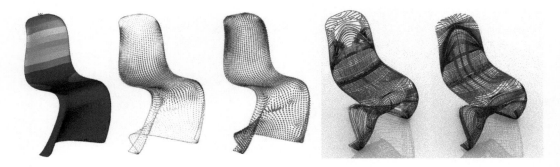

4.1

The illustration shows a first case study of differentiating the material make-up of the classic Panton Chair. A structural analysis of the chair being loaded by a person sitting on it and leaning on the backrest (left) is employed to identify the principal stresses (centre). The fibre layout matches the main stress distribution derived by algorithmically processing the principal stress vectors (right). MArch Dissertation of Christina Doumpioti, February 2008.

The high-level integration of form, structure and function inherent to living nature very often results from the astonishing versatility of fibrous systems. This is even more remarkable if one considers that most of these biological systems consist of a small range of materials only, as it suggests that nature organises material in a highly effective manner. Professor Dr George Jeronimidis, director of the Centre of Biomimetics at the University of Reading, posited:

> Biology makes use of remarkably few materials, and nearly all loads are carried by fibrous composites. There are only four polymer fibres: cellulose in plants, collagen in animals, chitin in insects and crustaceans and silks in spider's webs. These are the basic materials of biology, and they have much lower densities than most engineering materials. They are successful not so much because of what they are but because of the way in which they are put together. The geometrical and hierarchical organisation of the fibre architecture is significant. The same collagen fibres are used in low-modulus, highly extensible structures such as blood vessels, intermediate modulus tissues such as tendons and high modulus, rigid materials such as bone.
> (Jeronimidis 2004: 92)

As a result of their differentiated material make-up, fibre composites possess a number of properties that enable a highly specific and adaptable material distribution in response to the forces acting on them. Contrary to materials with homogenous internal structures and isotropic behaviour – that is to say, the same behaviour regardless of the direction of forces applied – natural composites are anisotropic. As a consequence, the material's structural capacity can be adapted in response to the force's direction and magnitude. By nature, fibres are most suited to carry tensile loads. Thus it is no surprise to discover that many natural fibres form the reinforcement of composite materials that function as membrane structures in biaxial tension, or they act as tensile elements in their own right. In addition, nature offers various examples of how fibrous structures can also carry compressive loads. Generally, fibres are prone to buckling and not suited to withstand compression forces, even if they have partial lateral support by being embedded in a composite matrix. However, several principles of how fibrous structures can perform in compression can be found in nature. The most expected strategy for increasing the compressive load-bearing capacity is probably reinforcing the fibres with high-modulus mineral phases. Another common strategy is prestressing the fibres in tension to such a degree that they are hardly ever exposed to compressive forces. In addition, there are natural strategies that increase the structural performance of

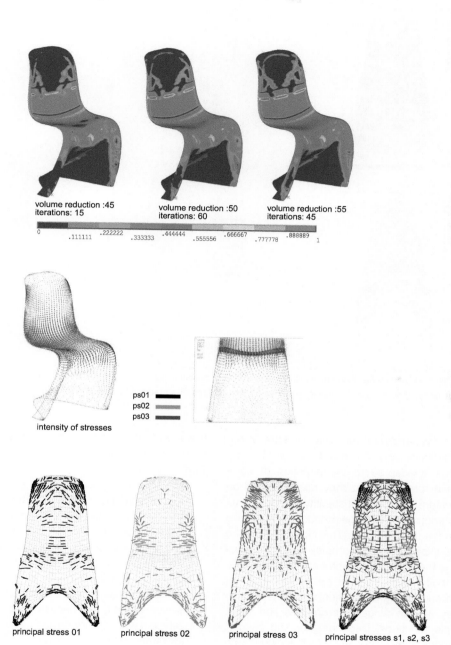

volume reduction :45
iterations: 15

volume reduction :50
iterations: 60

volume reduction :55
iterations: 45

0   .111111   .222222   .333333   .444444   .555556   .666667   .777778   .888889   1

intensity of stresses

ps01
ps02
ps03

principal stress 01

principal stress 02

principal stress 03

principal stresses s1, s2, s3

4.2

The illustrations show an iterative optimisation of the material distribution run over 60 cycles (top) and a related analyses of the three principal stresses (bottom) for the Panton Chair exposed to the load of a person sitting on it. MArch Dissertation of Christina Doumpioti, February 2008.

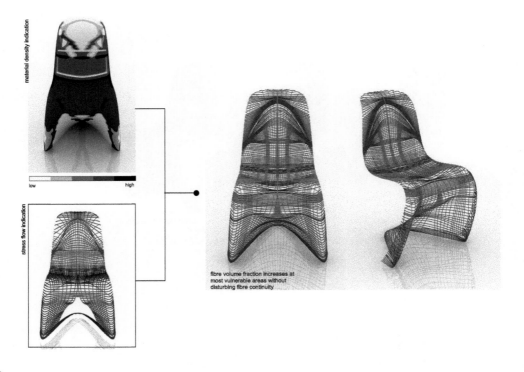

material density indication

low   high

stress flow indication

fibre volume fraction increases at
most vulnerable areas without
disturbing fibre continuity

4.3

The combination of material distribution and stress-driven fibre directionality (left) creates a differentiated material make-up on the given design of the case study Panton Chair. MArch Dissertation of Christina Doumpioti, February 2008.

fibrous systems by organising the fibre layout in a particular way. For example, the fibre orientation is adapted to the direction of compressive forces so that they no longer act on the system. Also, lateral stability can be significantly improved by a large number of cross links within the fibre network. This indicates that the critical aspect in most complex natural composites is the fibre organisation and layout, rather than their materiality. The same small number of material constituents, fibres and matrix, can display a wide range of properties and serve multiple functions. Depending on the specific conditions they grow in, which include both their positions and their function within a larger organic system, they can adapt their shape, topology and organisation.

Natural fibre composite structures emerge from processes of adaptive growth. In animal tissues, for example, this process is driven by fibroblast cells that produce the structural

framework of collagen fibres in constant feedback with the forces acting on them. As Scott Turner posits:

Fibroblasts are probably the commonest, but the least appreciated cells in the body. They weave so called connective tissue, a meshwork of fibrous protein threads that literally hold the body together ... They are also capable of restructuring their environment if it is necessary to regulate tension. Collagen meshworks are dynamic structures. New fibres are continually laid down (fibrogenesis), while old fibres are continually dismantled (fibrolysis). The meshwork architecture depends upon where and by how much these processes play off each other. Suppose, for example, a single collagen fibre is stretched more forcefully than fibroblasts can adjust to. If fibroblasts lay down another fibre in parallel to the first, each fibre can now carry half the load that previously had been carried by the single fibre. If two fibres do not suffice, three fibres might, and so on, up to as many fibres as necessary to bring the load on each fibre down to a level the fibroblast can handle. It works the other way too. If a fibre is too slack, so that the maximum pull of all the fibroblasts is not sufficient to tighten it to the preferred tension, the fibrolysis rate will kick up, pruning out the slack fibres to leave the load to be borne by the remaining fibres.

(Turner 2007: 32)

This process of growth under stress enables the remarkable versatility of natural fibre composites. The selective deposition of new material at the position and in the direction where it is needed is driven by the forces the organism experiences. Nature has derived multifaceted and numerous patterns of structural and functional fibre architectures in response to a specific set of mechanical conditions and requirements (Neville 1993). Investigating these remarkably resourceful and performative fibre structures has been a continuous concern of the Emergent Technologies and Design research programme. In the following paragraphs a project will be presented that takes this work a step further by not only investigating the organisation and layout of fibres, but also developing and employing a computational process of growth under stress

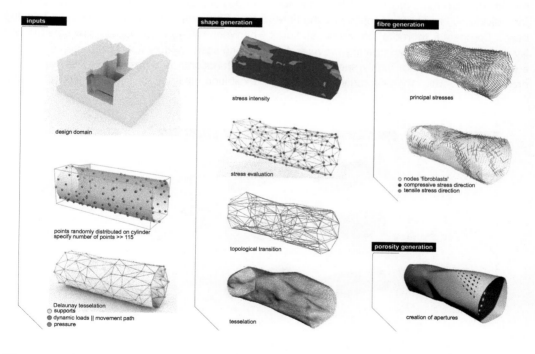

4.4

The drawing shows the processes underlying this research. According to a site-specific input (left) the overall shape (centre) and the specific distribution of fibres and surface openings (right) are derived in an integral feedback process. MArch Dissertation of Christina Doumpioti, February 2008.

for man-made fibre composite structures.

Christina Doumpioti's MArch dissertation (2007) aimed at developing a generic shape-finding and fibre-path generation method for tow-steered composite structures by transferring the underlying principles of natural adaptive growth into a computational design process. Tow steering is a manufacturing technique for high-end composite structures and is currently used in aerospace engineering and sailing technology. This production technology allows fabricating large-scale fibre composite structures, whereby each laminate is produced by combining layers of different fibre orientations, materiality and thickness. Most importantly, tow-steering technology allows for laying each fibre along an individual, digitally defined path. The fibre tows are fed off spools through a tensioning system to the tow placement head, which travels computer numerically controlled along a very thin layer of fibre mats laid onto a mould. The thin mats provide the base surface for individually laid fibres deposited by the fibre head. Compared to more conventional fibre lay-up technologies, tow steering provides for a production process of highly specific fibrous organisations. This manufacturing possibility enables the conception of large-scale, architectural fibre systems with highly differentiated fibre layouts that correspond with the structural and functional requirements of the system.

A computational process of adaptive growth was developed in order to exploit this manufacturing potential. This process consists of two interrelated sub-processes: one generates the particular shape of the overall system, and the other derives the fibre layout as a fibre reference pass for tow-steering manufacturing. Both sub-processes are interlinked within an ontogenetic process, which is informed by external forces and environmental influences acting on the system. In contrast to evolutionary adaptation taking place across generations of individuals, ontogenesis is the process of individual adaptive growth, in which stress acts as one of the main growth-promoting agents. As ontogenetic processes are always environment specific, the vehicle of a specific design project was used to develop and test the generic computational tool. This project's design intention is bridging between two existing buildings by constructing a long-span monocoque fibre composite shell that functions as a passageway as well as an exhibition space. Thus the objective of the

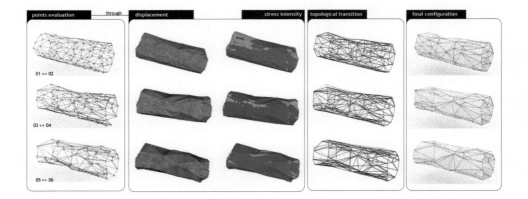

4.5

The project explores computational processes of stress-driven growth for both the overall shape and the fibre layout. The overall shape is derived through an iterative generation and tessellation process, in which surface nodes work as receptors for detecting local stress peaks, triggering a homeostatic growth process based on the recurring structural analysis. MArch Dissertation of Christina Doumpioti, February 2008.

4.6

The derived overall surface morphology is first established as a configuration of point connections. Subsequent processes of increasing tessellation are used to derive a surface definition suited for the fibre generation process. MArch Dissertation of Christina Doumpioti, February 2008.

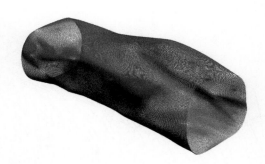

system's structural development is improving the load-bearing behaviour, minimising strain energy, levelling the magnitude of stress across the system and achieving a reduction of weight, while meeting the essential criteria of directional strength and stiffness. At the same time the fibre organisation has to respond to programmatic requirements as well as environmental influences.

The process of computational growth is based on transferring tow key principles of natural adaptive growth. In the process of generating the overall shape, points act as morphogen cells. Driven by an iterative algorithmic procedure, they self-organise into a particular pattern of point distribution. This serves as a base for defining a surface, from which new nodes are extracted that act as fibroblast cells during the fibre path generation process. Triggered by stress concentrations, they generate fibres in the direction of principal stresses in order to achieve a stress levelling across the entire system.

The ontogenetic process of the composite bridge structure is initialised by a first cycle of shape generation. Within a simulated environment of forces and other influences, the design domain is defined as a cylindrical geometry spanning 10 metres between two supports. Within this geometrically set search space, points are initially randomly distributed. Driven by a Delaunay algorithm, a tessellation

is derived by connecting the neighbouring points, while avoiding any intersection of edges between the vertices. For each vertices point a specific load and support condition is specified according to its location within the overall system. Subsequently the resulting structure is evaluated through a finite element analysis. For the key objective function of stress and strain levelling, this analysis calculates an outcome value for the defined set of material properties, for example density and elasticity. In the following step the vertices points with the lowest values of stress begin to act like attractors triggering surrounding points to migrate towards them, whereas the rate of attraction proportionally relates to the rate of proximity. In search of equilibrium of forces, the algorithm iterates through various cycles of structural analysis and point reconfiguration in accordance to the point values obtained each time until a relatively equal distribution of stress is reached.

For the fibre path generation, the generated overall shape is further analysed. By means of finite element analysis, the stress type, direction and magnitude are investigated. After defining a stress threshold value, the nodes displaying the highest stress concentrations are marked and defined as agents that organise the fibre structure between the nodes so that the fibres are laid in the direction of the largest principal stresses. They aim at maximising the system's load-bearing capacity through a fibre

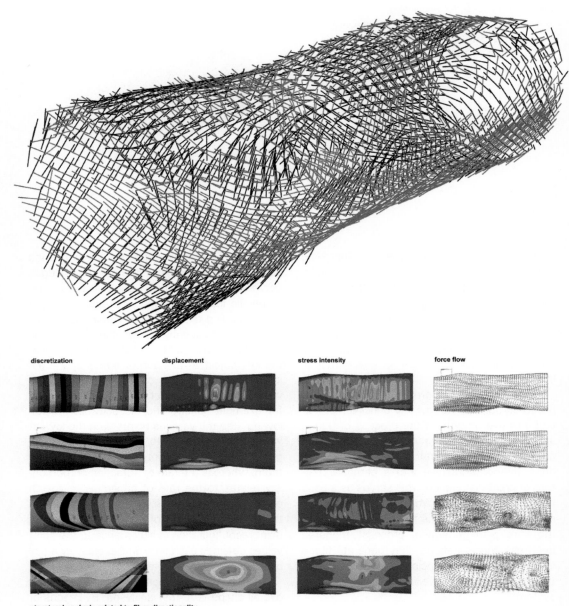

discretization displacement stress intensity force flow

structural analysis related to fibre directionality

4.7

The fibre layout is derived by a computational analysis of the force flow within the generated overall shape (bottom). Notating direction and strength, the vectors of the principal stresses (top) provide the critical input for algorithmically generating the layout of the fibres. MArch Dissertation of Christina Doumpioti, February 2008.

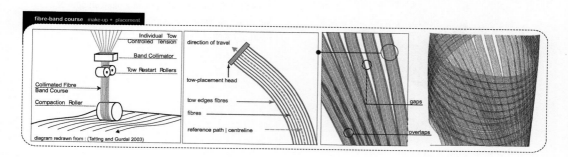

4.8

Computer numerically controlled steered-fibre lay-up manufacturing (left) is used to lay the fibres on the surface according to the computationally derived patterns. The tow placement head lays bands of multiple fibres (centre) on the surface, creating gaps between bands and overlaps of fibres in the process of building up the macro-fibre articulation (right). MArch Dissertation of Christina Doumpioti, February 2008.

4.9

This close-up view shows the differentiated fibre layout on one end of the prototype structure. Here the fibres are oriented not only according to the distribution of forces but also to prevent delamination at the edges. Thus the transversal tows are multiplied on both ends of the structure. MArch Dissertation of Christina Doumpioti, February 2008.

 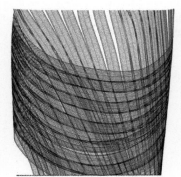 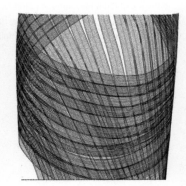

4.10

The illustration shows the incremental build-up of the macro-fibre articulation through computer numerically controlled steered-fibre lay-up manufacturing. MArch Dissertation of Christina Doumpioti, February 2008.

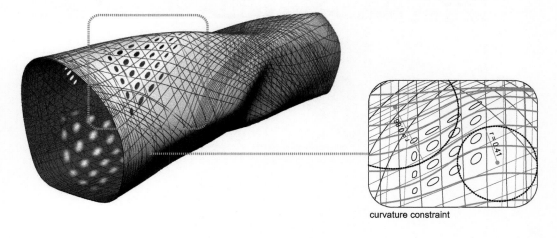

curvature constraint

4.11

Considering the curvature constraint of the steered-fibre lay-up manufacturing process, areas of little fibre density can be identified for the location of local surface openings. The fibres always flow around these openings in order to avoid any fibre discontinuity. MArch Dissertation of Christina Doumpioti, February 2008.

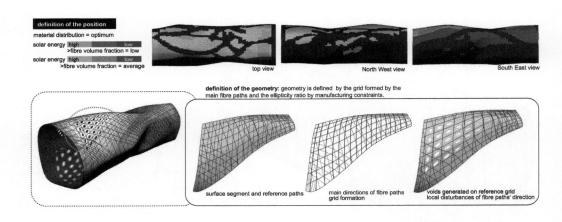

definition of the position

material distribution = optimum

solar energy [high] [low]
>fibre volume fraction = low

solar energy [high] [low]
>fibre volume fraction = average

top view

North West view

South East view

definition of the geometry: geometry is defined by the grid formed by the main fibre paths and the ellipticity ratio by manufacturing constraints.

surface segment and reference paths

main directions of fibre paths
grid formation

voids generated on reference grid
local disturbances of fibre paths' direction

4.12

The distribution of surface openings is informed by both fibre layout and environmental analysis. According to analyses of solar energy absorption and fibre density on the surface, openings are distributed within the grid occurring through main directions of fibre paths. MArch Dissertation of Christina Doumpioti, February 2008.

arrangement that at the same time minimises transverse stresses and shear between the fibres. The resulting structure displays a differentiated fibre layout in which each fibre's location and direction is directly related to the forces acting on it.

In addition to the structural requirements, another critical factor was included in the computational process of deriving the system's morphology. In order to achieve locally differentiated levels of porosity of the composite skin, the generation process is further elaborated by including environmental simulation cycles in dialogue with the structural analysis. Accordingly, the location and distribution of apertures is derived through a twofold process. First a structural analysis of the fibre path system allows for identifying skin areas with the least stress concentrations, that is to say areas where material can be removed without having a major impact on the overall load-bearing behaviour. Simultaneously a fibre volume fraction analysis indicates areas of little fibre density. Where the two areas overlap, there are possible locations for surface openings. In order to select which of these locations should subsequently be used to create openings, solar exposure analysis was employed to investigate the distribution and magnitude of incident solar radiation and light transmission to the system's interior. Furthermore, computational fluid dynamics enabled testing the impact of prevailing winds on the interior airflow patterns in relation to different distributions of surface openings. This iterative, computationally driven negotiation of design criteria such as structure, space, light and ventilation results in a highly differentiated fibre composite structure integrating a wide range of performance criteria.

The computational design process is also directly informed by the manufacturing method of steered fibre lay-up. The splines derived during the fibre path generation process can be directly employed to establish the related machine code for laying up the fibres. According to this information the applicator head of the tow placement machine traverses the surface and applies the fibres where needed. Approaching a surface area assigned to form an opening, the fibre paths are locally altered so that the fibres are not disrupted or cut. Rather than terminating abruptly, as is common in other fibre lay-up techniques, here the fibres follow the contours of the openings, which allows the forces to 'flow' around voids. In addition, the fibre layout on both ends of the prototype structure is further differentiated. Here the fibres are not only oriented according to the distribution of forces, but also to prevent delaminating at the edges. Thus the transversal tows are multiplied on both ends of the structure.

The entire bridge structure of the prototype proposal can be prefabricated off site. A mould with the particular surface articulation can be constructed from several pieces with a removable core. This allows for dismantling and removing the mould after the structure is manufactured through superimposed fibre courses laid up by the tow-steering application head. The finished one-piece monocoque shell is lightweight and easy to transport as long as the maximum size of the related loading space is considered.

In summary, this research demonstrates the enormous potential of combining the versatility of fibrous systems with new computational design and computer-controlled manufacturing processes. An interrelated development of material, structure and form in concert with novel design methods moves one step closer to the higher level functionality displayed by natural systems. In this process differentiation emerges through the intricate reciprocity between material make-up and environmental forces and influences that result in a structural articulation that cannot be reduced to its load-bearing capacity, but rather provides a robust and multifaceted range of performative capacities.

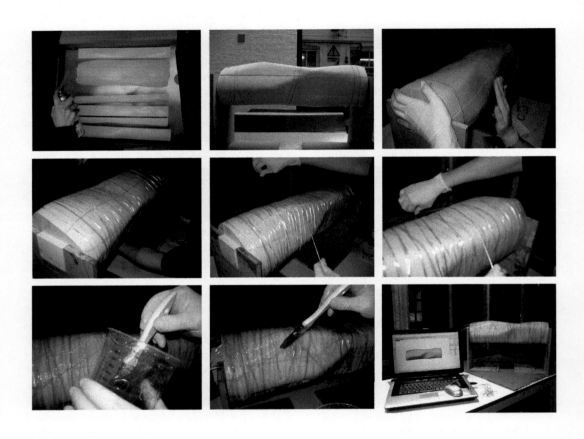

4.13

Based on the computationally derived data the fibre build-up process was manually tested on a scaled model using a CNC-milled mould. MArch Dissertation of Christina Doumpioti, February 2008.

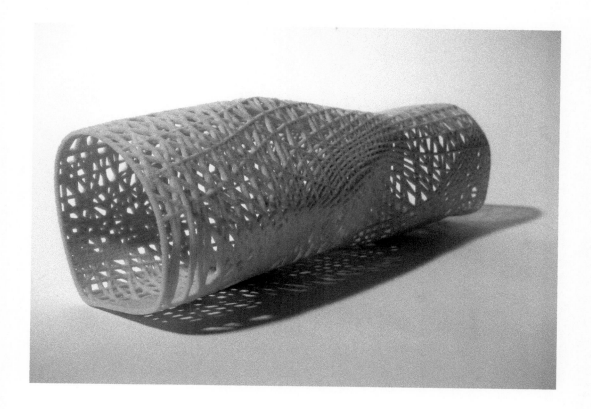

4.14

The photograph shows a three-dimensionally printed model of the prototype bridge structure. Owing to constraints in the fabrication process, the model displays the fibres at the wrong scale. However, the specific pattern of fibre distribution can be clearly perceived. MArch Dissertation of Christina Doumpioti, February 2008.

Chapter 5
Textiles

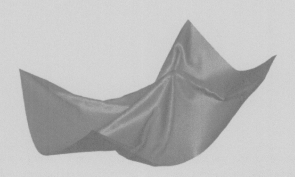

Textiles have been a dominant topic in architectural discourse, specifically related to the possible origin of architecture and therefore to the theoretical underpinnings of the development of architecture. Gottfried Semper (1803–79), for instance dedicated the entire volume one of his seminal *Style in the Technical and Tectonic Arts; or, Practical Aesthetics: A Handbook for Technicians, Artists, and Friends of the Arts* (Semper 1860) to the topic of 'Textile Art: Considered in Itself and in Relation to Architecture'. In the introduction to volume one Semper states as one of his key considerations 'the work as a result of the *material* used to produce it, as well as of the *tools* and *procedures* applied' (Semper 1860). This reads as if purposefully drafted to underpin a key aspect of the Emergent Technologies and Design approach.

In general a textile is a flexible material that consists of fibres and can be made in a variety of ways, including by weaving (interlacing of threads), knitting (loops of threads pulled through one another), crocheting (similar to knitting), knotting and also the pressing together of fibres, resulting in so-called felt. The actual characteristics of a textile therefore depend on the way it is made, the structure induced by this process and the characteristics of the thread(s) it is made from. Threads in turn also behave relative to the material and the way they are produced – reeling, knotting, drawing, twisting or spinning. With regard to textiles there are mesh formations with a continuous element of limited or unlimited length, there is plaiting or fabric production with passive or active warp, and there is half-weaving or weaving with passive

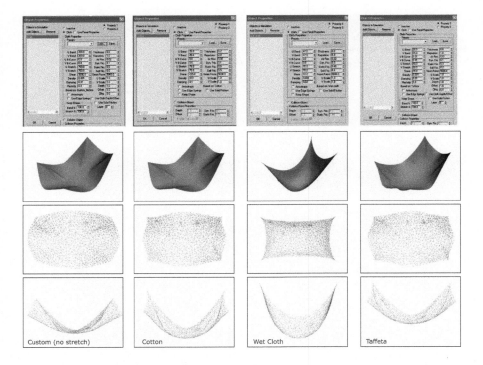

| Custom (no stretch) | Cotton | Wet Cloth | Taffeta |

5.1

Parametric setup and digital form-finding experiments for fabrics with different characteristics (from left to right): custom setting (no stretch), cotton, wet cloth and taffeta. The characteristics of the material can be defined through numerous numerical values, with the static parameters defining the geometric deformation of the material. An identical initial geometry with different material values results in different geometric articulations. Different material properties can be defined for each segment of a surface. MArch Dissertation of Arielle Blonder-Afek, February 2008.

or active warp (Seiler-Baldinger 1994). In addition, textiles can be manipulated in many ways: through gathering, ruffling, pleating, smocking, tucking, etc. (Wolff 1996). Each manipulation on each level of hierarchy from the thread, to thread interaction, to the production and manipulation of the textile changes its characteristics and related behaviour. So does a thread as part of a textile when pulled separately: it modifies the geometry of an entire region of the textile.

Due to the fact that all these methods and techniques are clearly defined, it is relatively easy to embark on a systematic and rigorous research with regard to the performative capacity of textiles. For structural performance there is a great wealth of references to be studied. Textiles have often been used to establish the specific geometries of shell structures, and less frequently served as textile reinforcement in resin-hardened shells.

Shell structures are surface-active structure systems (Engel 1999). Engel stated two of the key characteristics as follows: 'the potential of the structural surface to make forces change direction, i.e. to carry loads, is dependent on the position of the surface in relation to the direction of the acting force' and 'in surface-active structures it is foremost the proper shape that redirects the acting forces and distributes them in small unit stresses evenly over the surface' (Engel 1999: 212). This proper shape that is referred to here is often form-found through hanging models in the case of which also the definition of the form-active tension system applies. Such systems are established through

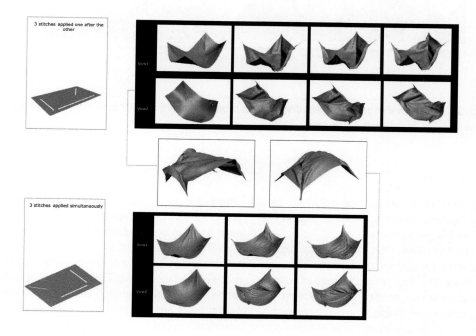

5.2

Introduction of fabric manipulation techniques, here specifically identical stitches applied in different sequences during the form-finding process. In one example the equilibrium state is found after each stitch, while in the other examples all stitches are implemented at once before finding the equilibrium state. MArch Dissertation of Arielle Blonder-Afek, February 2008.

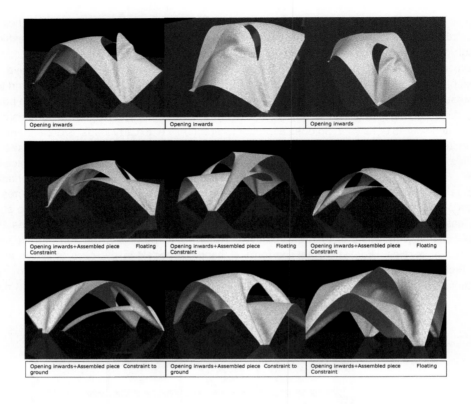

| Opening inwards | Opening inwards | Opening inwards |

| Opening inwards+Assembled piece   Floating Constraint | Opening inwards+Assembled piece   Floating Constraint | Opening inwards+Assembled piece   Floating Constraint |

| Opening inwards+Assembled piece   Constraint to ground | Opening inwards+Assembled piece   Constraint to ground | Opening inwards+Assembled piece   Floating Constraint |

5.3

Computationally form-found shell geometries with different kinds of openings resulting from the cut pattern of the fabric. MArch Dissertation of Arielle Blonder-Afek, February 2008.

hanging models, in which the funicular tension line evolves from the forces acting on the system, in this case gravity.

Heinz Isler, Frei Otto and others experimented with tensile-stressed forms resulting from textiles. This has led in the case of Isler to shell structures that result from hardening the hanging form and inverting it into a compression-stressed form. In any case these experiments were meant to explore the possibility of form-found lightweight shell structures that adhere strictly to the structural characteristic of shells that is the funicular tension line. In this case it is then necessary to avoid folds in the surface that would interrupt the shell action that is the particular stresses that can and cannot occur in a shell. What happens, however, when multiple criteria are used for form-finding, instead of an exclusively structural approach? When features such as folds occur, obviously the funicular tension line is interrupted and stress is no longer uniformly distributed within the thickness of the material surface. While Frei Otto had analysed patterns of folds in hanging fabrics, this has not led to direct speculations as to what such characteristics might contribute to the performative capacity of a material system. Whether or not one should refer to such a system as a shell is debatable with regard to the accurate structural definition. However, the primary question lies elsewhere: when the proper structural shell action is sacrificed locally, are the gains worth the extra effort that is required to re-establish structural stability?

In her MArch dissertation, Arielle Blonder-Afek (2007) commenced from a systematic study of Heinz Isler's experiments, while expanding the scope of form-finding with hanging fabrics. The intention was to utilise local features in the textile, such as folds, for purposes other than exclusively structural performance. Openings, folds and other features can thus be strategised and instrumentalised in an integral manner. Overall the dissertation comprised investigations into [i] combined utilisation of material and digital form-finding of form-active tension systems made from textiles; [ii] expansion of the formal repertoire of form-found textile systems driven by specified performance criteria; [iii] computational structural analysis feedback into the computational form-finding process; [iv] investigation of manufacturing strategies, in particular full-scale material form-finding as an integral part of manufacturing.

Initial sets of material experiments investigated techniques from garment production and fashion design, such as stitching over the fabric and pulling the stitch. This resulted in a complex curved surface with varied patterns of irregular folds.

In a second step the suitability of digital form-finding methods was investigated, not only with regard to deriving a global form, but also to implement specific local manipulations of the textile, established through material experiments.

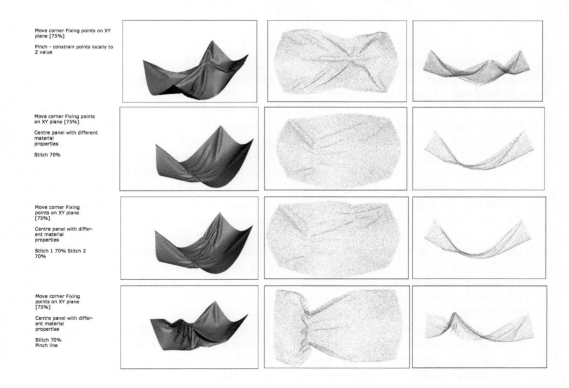

Move corner Fixing points on XY plane [75%]

Pinch - constrain points locally to Z value

Move corner Fixing points on XY plane [75%]

Centre panel with different material properties

Stitch 70%

Move corner Fixing points on XY plane [75%]

Centre panel with different material properties

Stitch 1 70% Stitch 2 70%

Move corner Fixing points on XY plane [75%]

Centre panel with different material properties

Stitch 70% Pinch line

5.4

Computational simulation of hanging surfaces with different additional manipulations, such as pinches and stitches. MArch Dissertation of Arielle Blonder-Afek, February 2008.

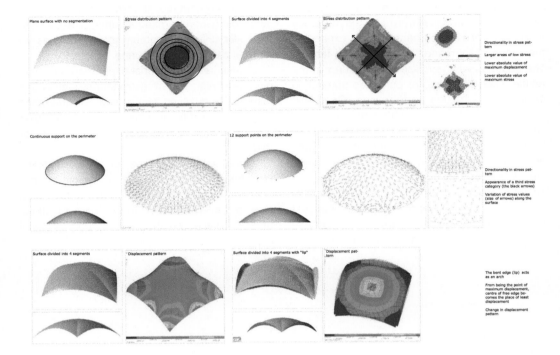

Two methods were combined: digital form-finding methods, and an iterative morphogenetic process that includes the following:

i   Form-finding of the overall geometry: based on the perimeter definition of the system and a distribution of desired volumes, a global geometry is derived by the hanging of a textile. In this stage the material of the membrane, its shape and the location of the principal anchoring points are defined.

ii Inducing primary articulation: a first set of modifications are applied. Initially overall manipulations are applied to the surface. Multiple designs were generated in this phase, all based on variation of the design output of the previous stage. The resulting individual geometries were then analysed and evaluated according to the specific performance criteria. Subsequently local manipulations are applied to the surface. Multiple designs with local variations are generated and assessed with regard to the criteria set for this stage.

The digital form-finding tool used was 'Cloth', an integrated application of 3DStudioMAX 9. This application includes two modifiers: 'Cloth' and 'Garmentmaker'. The cloth modifier is responsible for simulating the motion of cloth as it interacts with the environment, which may include collision objects and external forces (such as gravity). GarmentMaker is a specialised tool for creating 3D garments from 2D splines, analogous to the way real clothes are made by stitching together flat pieces of cloth. In the simulation the final shape is achieved when the fabric has reached its equilibrium state. Two parameter sets influence the simulation: [i] parameters related to the simulated configuration, and [ii] parameters related to the simulation tool itself.

The digital simulation offers a large number of variables, accessible through the user interface of the software. These parameters, which define the specific configuration of each simulation, can be categorised into two types: data describing the material behaviour (numerical input), and data describing the constraints. The manipulations are created through the user

5.5 (opposite)

Structural analysis of a form-found shell investigating the changes in stress pattern due to varying key systems parameters, such as the segmentation of the shell (top), the distribution of support points (middle) and the specific articulation of the free edge (bottom). MArch Dissertation of Arielle Blonder-Afek, February 2008.

5.6 (below)

Mesh preparation for the computational structural analysis (FEA) and structural analysis of different fabrics and their related morphologies resulting from the computational form-finding process (top to bottom): wet cloth, satin, spandex, cotton. MArch Dissertation of Arielle Blonder-Afek, February 2008.

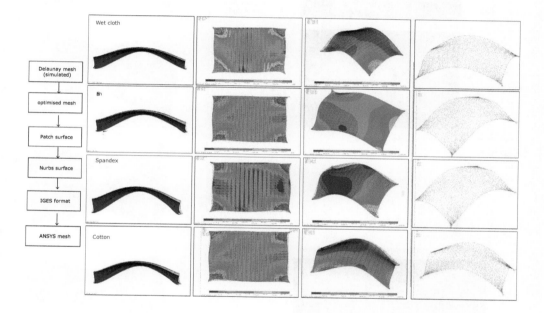

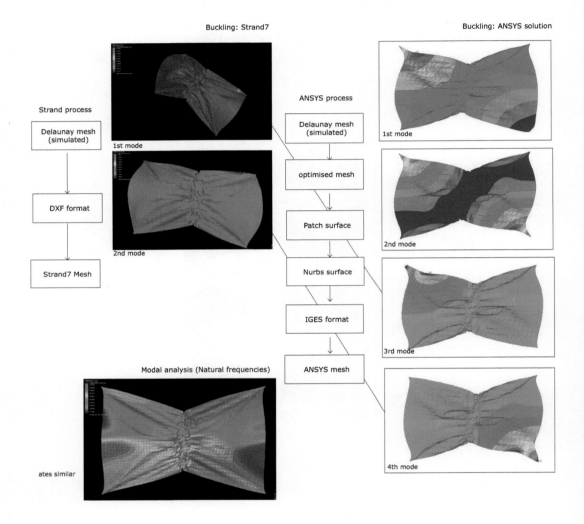

Buckling: Strand7

Buckling: ANSYS solution

Strand process

| Delaunay mesh (simulated) |

1st mode

2nd mode

| DXF format |

| Strand7 Mesh |

ANSYS process

| Delaunay mesh (simulated) |

1st mode

| optimised mesh |

| Patch surface |

2nd mode

| Nurbs surface |

| IGES format |

3rd mode

Modal analysis (Natural frequencies)

| ANSYS mesh |

ates similar

4th mode

5.7

Computational structural analysis: a specific shell geometry specified as a composite laminate is analysed for its buckling behaviour. The analysis was conducted in two different FEA software packages: Strand7 (left) and ANSYS (right). For each, the file to be analysed needed to be prepared in different ways, and the buckling analysis differs considerably. The first and second buckling modes of the Strand7 analysis appear similar to the third and fourth modes in ANSYS, with local buckling occurring at the free edges and close to the supports. The global buckling behaviour in the first and second buckling modes of the ANSYS analysis is missing from the first buckling modes solved by Strand7. This shows that FEA is sensitive to the software environment and the translation of the geometry of the surface into a mesh. MArch Dissertation of Arielle Blonder-Afek, February 2008.

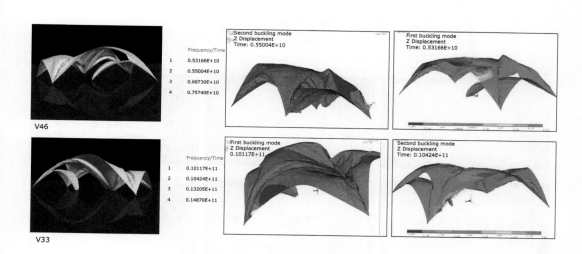

	Frequency/Time
1	0.53166E+10
2	0.55004E+10
3	0.68730E+10
4	0.75740E+10

V46

	Frequency/Time
1	0.10117E+11
2	0.10424E+11
3	0.13205E+11
4	0.14870E+11

V33

Second buckling mode
Z Displacement
Time: 0.55004E+10

First buckling mode
Z Displacement
Time: 0.53166E+10

First buckling mode
Z Displacement
0.10117E+11

Second buckling mode
Z Displacement
Time: 0.10424E+11

5.8

Computational structural analysis was used to analyse the buckling mode of two variants of a selected shell geometry with different openings. The opening plays an important role for the stability of the structure as it removes material from the load-conducting surface, but adds an additional support point. The buckling analysis reveals the superior capacity of solution V33, as it buckles only under a much higher load. The buckling behaviours of the two surfaces are slightly different, showing a local buckling on the first mode for V33, and a global one for V46. MArch Dissertation of Arielle Blonder-Afek, February 2008.

Model with theoretical overall thickness of 2 mm applied

Buckling value (1st mode): 0.914

Model with additional thickness in the legs

Buckling value (1st mode): 1.27

Model with theoretical overall thickness of 4 mm applied

Buckling value (1st mode): 4.444

Z Displacement (Static) Max: 5.5 (Absolute)

Z Displacement (Static) Max: 5.3 (Absolute)

Z Displacement (Static) Max: 1.5 (Absolute)

5.9

A digital model for the analysis was first set to an overall thickness of 2 mm. The analysis showed that the first buckling modes will appear around the legs of the structure. A second model was analysed, with a 3 mm different thickness for the legs. The addition of thickness around the legs raises the buckling value but keeps a similar pattern of displacement on the buckling, and similar values of displacement. If the overall thickness is increased to 4 mm, the buckling value rises substantially and the pattern of displacement changes as well. In parallel to the buckling analysis, a static analysis of displacement was done for all three models. Here, the pattern of displacement is identical in all three cases. The addition of thickness in the legs has only a slight influence over the maximum displacement value, while the thickness of 4 mm reduces the displacement value considerably. MArch Dissertation of Arielle Blonder-Afek, February 2008.

interface of the constraints. The parameters can be roughly categorised into three groups: parameters related to the membrane, parameters related to the constraints, and parameters related to the manipulations.

The group of parameters related to the membrane are first in the initial design process. The membrane has a specific size and shape. Material characteristics are then applied. The initial geometry of the membrane can be made out of an assembly of segments. The geometry of the segments is then to be defined. The geometry of the membrane (single or assembled) leads to the subsequent definition of the anchoring parameters, which define the way in which a membrane is initially constrained, before the application of the manipulations. The numbers of anchors, their location over the membrane and the type of anchoring have a critical effect on the curvature generated, and therefore are of great structural importance. The anchoring is actually the constraint applied on vertices of the mesh, tying it either to a specific location or to an external object. The displacements of the anchoring points, which define the ratio of the initial membrane to the hanging footprint, define the overall draping of the fabric. The manipulations are constraints applied to the membrane, in addition to the anchoring. The relevant parameters derive from the specific type of manipulation feature. Cuts, for example, require an input of orientation and

geometry, while stitches require the amount of pull and the spacing of the stitch. Timing and the sequencing of the manipulations regulate the three groups of parameters. The specified sequence of the manipulations and the time of their application during the draping process have a crucial effect on the final outcome, as the fabric self-organises at each step from the given constraints conditions. The interaction between the fibres and their response to external forces will change according to the starting state of the manipulation, whether a flat membrane, a membrane draped under gravity, or a membrane that has gone through additional manipulations.

For the analysis and evaluation of the individual surface geometries that result from the digital form-finding process, structural behaviour was chosen, since the application of specific features interrupts shell action. This was done with the aim to modify the overall or local geometry or to compensate for the loss of structural capacity through the local addition of material. This is added to by the fact that the structural behaviour of form-active tension systems is intrinsically related to the process of form-finding the surface. The stress pattern will obviously vary from geometry to geometry and one material to another. Yet, the choice of structural analysis software and the preparation of the file to be exported from one software to another can also have dramatic effect on the outcome of the analysis. Therefore comparative

		wet laminate	prepreg
Manufacturing constraints		[Technical] Assembly of impregnated segments → Fabric has to be assembled to final size prior to wetting → [Manipulation] Impregnation with resin	[Material properties] Curing in 70 degrees [Equipment] Large oven for curing (70-85 deg.)
Size implication		Width 5 to 10 mt	35 X 120 mt (largest oven built)
Labour		++++	+
Quality of laminate		+	++++
Environment		sensitive	non sensitive
Equipment		X	oven
Cost	$$	++	++++
Size of structure		W 5-10 mt L 30-50 mt	W 35 mt L 100-120 mt
Implementations		Disaster relief / military use in dry climates Intervention in existing buildings, of medium size	Large structures with temporary on-site oven Small-medium scale elements manufactured off-site
Future developement		A technique for a 'soft' assembly of wetted out segments, possibly by local uv curing resin on seams, activated by lamp	UV curing prepregs that do not necessitate oven curing.

analyses were undertaken in two different software packages: Strand7 and ANSYS. This comparison showed some different readings for the same initial surface geometry. Since it is shells that are being analysed, main focus was placed on buckling behaviour and modes. The structural analysis and evaluation was fed back into the form-finding process of the next generation of surfaces, thus enabling an evolutionary design setup (with a random factor feeding to promote mutation). In the following phase extensive comparative studies and development of geometries took place, deploying simultaneously physical and digital form-finding processes, and calibrating the latter based on measurements undertaken on the former.

In the final phase of the research an integral form-finding and manufacturing logic was elaborated, based on the production of large-scale surfaces. The prototypes were realised at the prototyping workshop of the UK branch of Gurit (SP Systems). Gurit supplied the facilities and the technical support, and sponsored the material. The physical testing was realised at the Centre for Biomimetics (Reading University) with the support of Professor Dr George Jeronimidis.

Two manufacturing processes were considered for the fabrication of composite shells through full-scale form-finding: [i] dry lamination with pre-impregnated fabric (prepreg or SPRINT), and [ii] wet lamination with dry-woven glass fibre fabrics. Following the evaluation of the potentials and disadvantages of both processes, it was decided with Gurit's expert advice to test the dry lamination process.

The resulting prototypes were physically load-tested with regard to their buckling behaviour. Because of the close relation between

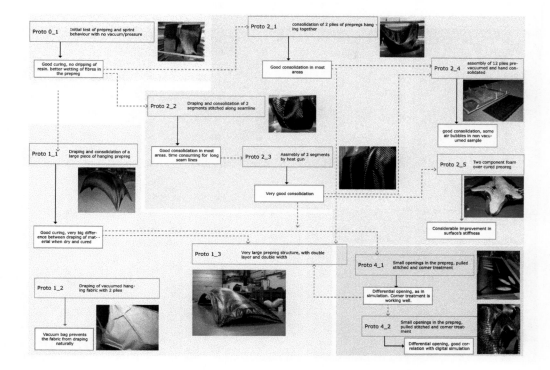

Proto 0_1 — Initial test of prepreg and sprint behaviour with no vacuum/pressure

Good curing, no dripping of resin. better wetting of fibres in the prepreg

Proto 2_1 — consolidation of 2 plies of prepregs hanging together

Good consolidation in most areas

Proto 2_4 — assembly of 12 plies pre-vacuumed and hand consolidated

good consolidation, some air bubbles in non vacuumed sample

Proto 2_2 — Draping and consolidation of 2 segments stitched along seamline

Proto 1_1 — Draping and consolidation of a large piece of hanging prepreg

Good consolidation in most areas. time consuming for long seam lines

Proto 2_3 — Assembly of 2 segments by heat gun

Proto 2_5 — Two component foam over cured preoreg

Very good consolidation

Good curing, very big difference between draping of material when dry and cured

Considerable improvement in surface's stiffness

Proto 1_3 — Very large prepreg structure, with double layer and double width

Proto 4_1 — Small openings in the prepreg, pulled stitched and corner treatment

Differential opening, as in simulation. Corner treatment is working well.

Proto 1_2 — Draping of vacuumed hanging fabric with 2 plies

Vacuum bag prevents the fabric from draping naturally

Proto 4_2 — Small openings in the prepreg, pulled stitched and corner treatment

Differential opening, good correlation with digital simulation

5.10 (above opposite)

Comparison of a wet lamination and a prepreg-based manufacturing process. On the basis of this comparison, it is possible to identify different specific uses for each method. The wet system would be ideal for on-site rapid manufacturing in cases where an oven for curing is not available. The dry process would be ideal for off-site manufacturing of elements of medium size that could fit in existing large ovens. It may also be feasible for on-site construction of large projects, where the erection of a temporary oven is possible, and quality is essential. MArch Dissertation of Arielle Blonder-Afek, February 2008.

5.11 (above)

Workflow of the production of various scaled and full-scale hardened fabric shells. MArch Dissertation of Arielle Blonder-Afek, February 2008.

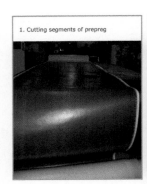
1. Cutting segments of prepreg

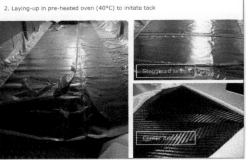
2. Laying-up in pre-heated oven (40°C) to initate tack

Staggered seams

3. Vacuuming the layup

4. Placing features

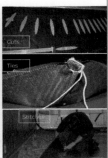
Cuts

Ties

Stitches

5. Hanging & curing

6. Inverting hardened shell

5.12 (above)

Manufacturing process of a prepreg fabric shell. MArch
Dissertation of Arielle Blonder-Afek, February 2008.

5.13 (opposite)

Full-scale prepreg carbon twill shell being inverted in
order to analyse the size limitations relative to the manual
inversion process and the self-load-bearing capacity.
MArch Dissertation of Arielle Blonder-Afek, February 2008.

the buckling behaviour of a structure and its natural frequencies, it is possible to undertake natural frequencies testing as a first indication of buckling behaviour. The measurement of natural frequencies is a non-destructive process that does not require physical contact with the structure it measures. This measurement is facilitated by the use of a laser Doppler vibrometer (LDV), an optical instrument that measures the velocity and displacement of vibrating structures that is the refraction of the laser beam from the surface, based on the Doppler effect, under excitation. The surface is excited by a gentle tap, making it vibrate in its natural frequencies. The information is transferred from the laser vibrometer into the computer, where it is recorded and processed. In this way an understanding of the buckling behaviour of such physical prototypes can be evaluated.

Overall, this research shows that there is potential in revisiting shell structures, particularly those that use textiles. It is the particular manipulations afforded by the use of textiles that opens up new avenues in formal articulation towards integral performative capacities

heretofore unexplored. While further research is pending, some key methods and tools for the generation, evaluation and manufacturing of such systems have been amply demonstrated, which leads to the insight that Semper's understanding of 'the work as a result of the *material* used to produce it, as well as of the *tools* and *procedures* applied' seems entirely suited to the approach and research introduced in this book.

Chapter 6
Nets

Nets are made from elements, or more specifically cables, that do not resist bending but can accept tensile forces. Nets are for that reason flexible mesh structures that are under tensile stresses. In architectural applications nets are frequently articulated as double-curved square meshes defined by geometric constraints. 'Net structures' take a significant role in the bearing of stresses (Bach *et al*. 1975). Nets belong, in the classification of Heino Engel, to form-active tension systems. Engel elaborated these systems as follows:

> The structure of form active systems in the ideal case coincides precisely with the flow of stresses … any change of loading or support conditions changes the form of the funicular curve and causes a new structure form.
>
> (Engel 1999: 58)

Form-active tension systems include cable nets, membrane systems including pneumatic systems and bending arches. In the Emergent Technologies and Design programme, these systems have been explored separately and in combination.

Due to the fact that it is the flow of stresses that determines the form of these systems, they are in turn directly suited candidates for form-finding. Frei Otto and his team developed physical form-finding methods for form-active tension structures to perfection, while at the same time undertaking extensive research into nets in nature and man-made applications (Bach *et al*. 1975). Based on this research, Frei Otto and Larry Medlin designed in collaboration with Rolf Gutbrod, and with Fritz Leonhard as lead engineer, the groundbreaking cable net roof for the German Pavilion at the World Expo 1967 in Montreal. This project majorly influenced the design of the world-famous cable net roofs of the Olympia Park and the Olympia Stadium in Munich built for the 1972 Olympic Games, designed by Behnisch and Partners in collaboration with Frei Otto. Most cable net roofs since are largely variations of these first large-scale pioneering projects that utilise cable nets in such a manner.

Nets can be planar or extend spatially. Three-dimensional net arrangements cannot simply be unrolled, and thus need to be made in a different manner than planar nets.

Current computational tools for form-finding planar nets are not very well suited for form-finding more complex spatially extended nets. Computational form-finding methods for nets and membranes exist in the form of dynamic relaxation, an iterative process which calculates and updates geometry step by step towards the eventual equilibrium state, yet requires careful modification for the purpose of form-finding complex spatial nets.

For the purpose of designing spatially extended nets, different methods need to be devised that may also hold the potential of integrating design and engineering methods. Spatial nets can for instance be articulated through a branching logic. Such a branching cable net was developed for the Emergent Technologies and Design End of Year Exhibition in 2005 at the Architectural Association. The net starts from a singular point at the floor and branches into three sets of cables that develop per pair along individual trajectories. This branching cable net is triangulated for the sake of enabling direction changes in the net and thus forms planar fields between the triangulations. These fields are populated with circa 800 tetrahedral components that are transparent and coloured in order to modulate the luminous environment of the exhibition space. The branching logic and direction of the cable net is of key importance with regard to orientating the components in a defined way towards the light source.

A second cable net was designed and built for the Emergent Technologies and Design End of Year Exhibition in 2008 at the Architectural Association as part of the MArch Dissertation of Sean Ahlquist and Moritz Fleischmann, delivered in February 2009. This net is defined by the network topology, which consists of computational springs through which form is generated by finding the equilibrium state of tension forces. The network topology is based on a 'ring' network method of association. Manufacturing and assembly constraints are embedded within this setup. Part of the potential for the network

6.1

The large cable-net roof of the Olympia Stadium built for the 1972 Olympic Games in Munich. Behnisch and Partners in collaboration with Frei Otto. Photos: Michael Hensel, 2005.

6.3 (below)

The photo shows a prototype of a differentiated cable-net structure built at the Architectural Association for the EmTech End of Year Installation in 2008. The installation was part of the MArch Dissertation of Sean Ahlquist and Moritz Fleischmann, February 2009.

6.2 (above)

The photo shows a full-scale triangulated cable net with differentiated and colour-coded cladding components built at the bar of the Architectural Association for the Emergent Technologies and Design End of Year Exhibition in 2005.

topology is to realise a specific architecture of multiple spaces defined by a single continuous boundary. Through a series of initial experiments a net based on an involuting cylinder is derived. The circular array of anchor points undergoes transformation into an elliptical array. It is then varied and tested to determine which end-nodes of the system attach to points along this elliptical array. A node is the point at which the springs connect. The spring, in the relaxed model, defines a physical distance between the nodes. The variable of switching nodes from being fixed to un-fixed was tested for various locations. This served to investigate the ranges of density in the resulting mesh and the number of required anchor points.

Fabrication is a matter of coordinating this information and qualifying it to the characteristics of the intended material. This logic is universal in the system. Whatever the formal outcome is, the method for sorting through the nodes for fabrication is the same for each result. The node identification is the most valuable information of the entire system. The next step is to understand the sequence of connecting the nodes. The selected cylinder topology is of particular interest because it describes a boundary and directionality. In a form-finding process, these spatial characteristics can also arrange structure. This possibility of organising space together with structure is a key characteristic of the installation. A membrane component serves to articulate the flow of views and space between the two meshes of the net installation. Compression elements exist in the computational model to push the surfaces

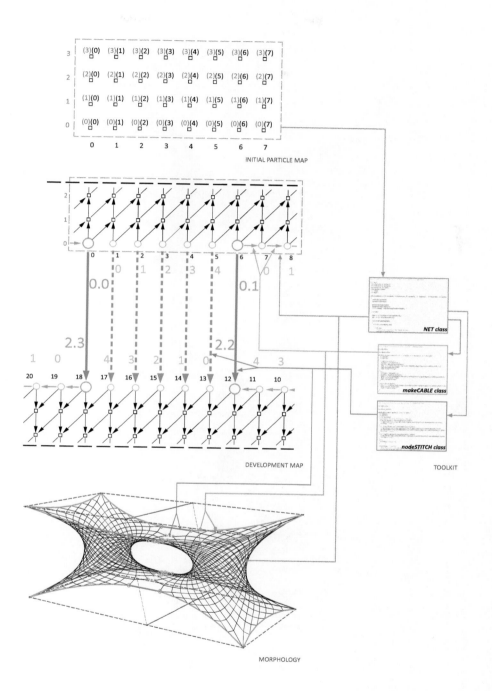

6.4

Computational form-finding setup: [i] definition of initial particle map (top), [ii] development map defining spring hierarchies (middle left), [iii] tool kit with scripts (middle right), and [iv] resulting case-specific morphology. MArch Dissertation of Sean Ahlquist and Moritz Fleischmann, February 2009.

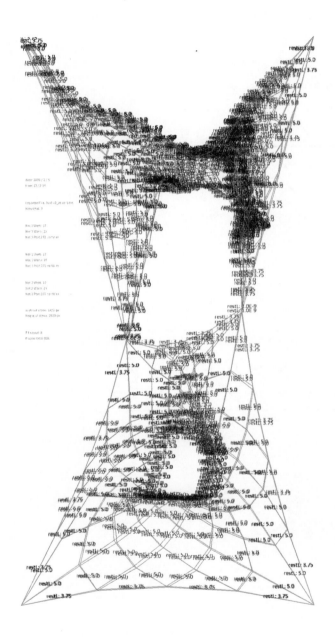

6.5

One instance of a computational cable-net simulation including annotation of differentiated rest length. MArch Dissertation of Sean Ahlquist and Moritz Fleischmann, February 2009.

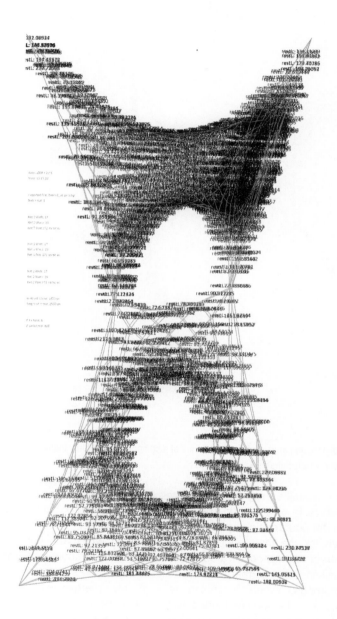

One instance of a computational cable-net simulation including annotation of differentiated rest length. MArch Dissertation of Sean Ahlquist and Moritz Fleischmann, February 2009.

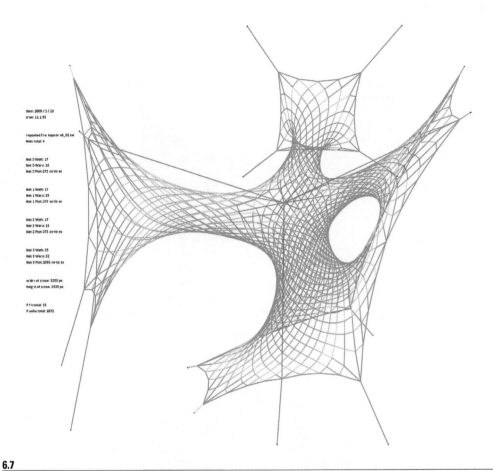

date: 2009 / 1 / 20
time: 11:1:52

imported file: kapoor v6_02.txt
Nets total: 4

Net 0 Weft: 17
Net 0 Warp: 15
Net 0 Pnot: 272 particles

Net 1 Weft: 17
Net 1 Warp: 15
Net 1 Pnot: 272 particles

Net 2 Weft: 17
Net 2 Warp: 15
Net 2 Pnot: 272 particles

Net 3 Weft: 33
Net 3 Warp: 32
Net 3 Pnot: 1056 particles

width of scene: 3000 px
height of scene: 2400 px

P f'x total: 15
P onfix total: 1872

6.7

Colour-coded force distribution analysis for one instance of a computationally form-found cable net. MArch Dissertation of Sean Ahlquist and Moritz Fleischmann, February 2009.

of the net apart in specified regions to modify spatial characteristics. In construction, they also serve as a device for post-tensioning.

The research for the installation focused on how to construct and associate a series of interconnected cylindrical nets that were comparatively autonomous. When beginning to associate multiple nets, the need for hierarchical arrangements arises, so as to manage a growing number of elements, arrays and variables. Thus the attention shifted to the topology of the spring networks, as opposed to discreet geometry, in turn requiring a computational method that is extensible to be able to facilitate the generation of topologically varied cellular pattern. The

cellular network was generated through a subdivision algorithm that was created in RhinoScript (see Chapter 1). Configurations were generated in which the complex net resulted in a branching arrangement. The latter is not directly coded in the script as a 'branching' function. It merely emerges because of a specific arrangement and accumulation of coincident points and edges. Recognising this relation in the process helps to qualify some of the geometric definition in the cellular framework mechanism of the system, and the subdivision algorithm that drives it. There are three main conditions that arise: [i] frames that associate with the context and create fixed anchor points; [ii] frames that

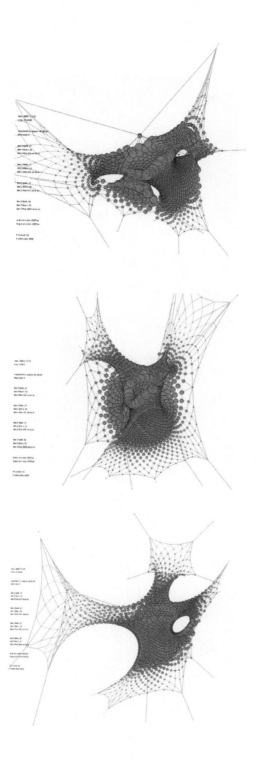

6.8

Combined computational form-finding simulation and visual density mapping for different cable-net configurations. MArch Dissertation of Sean Ahlquist and Moritz Fleischmann, February 2009.

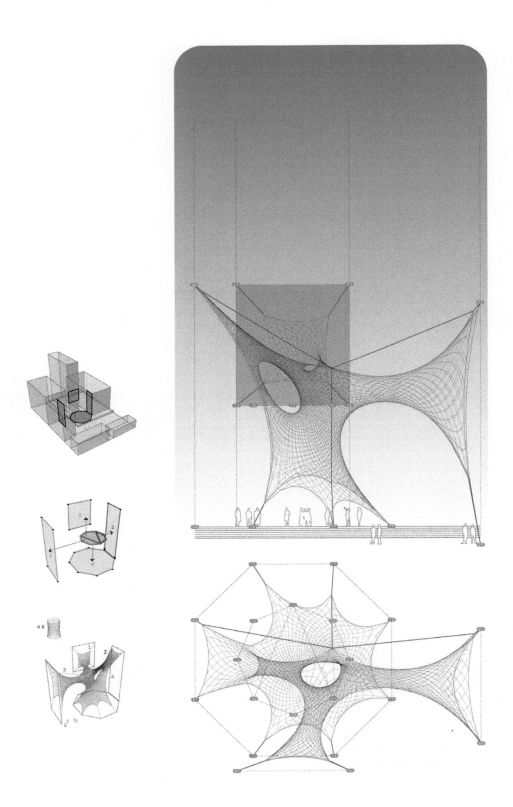

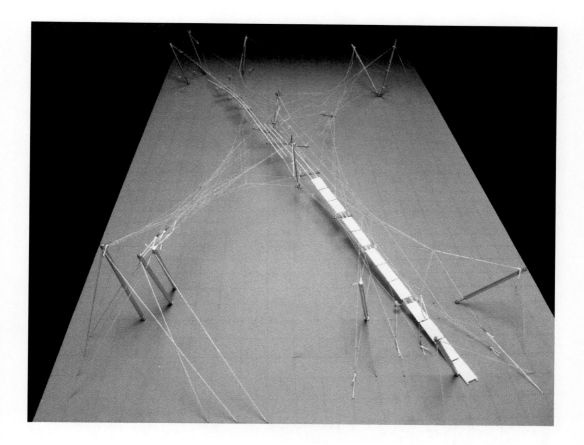

6.9 (opposite)

Prototype of a computationally form-found 3D cable-net. MArch Dissertation of Sean Ahlquist and Moritz Fleischmann, February 2009.

6.10 (above)

Bridge proposal based on a 3D cable-net. Studio Project: Sean Ahlquist, Moritz Fleischmann, Tomasz Mlynarski, 2008.

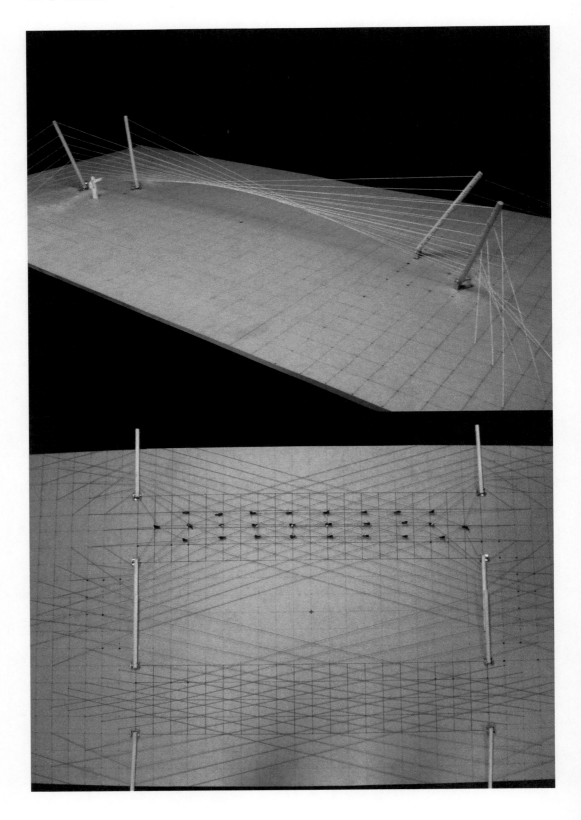

only define association between neighbouring nets; and [iii] frames that are a hybrid of both – association and location. This setup begins to expose the 'meta-spring' aspect of the system. Here, it expands beyond a device for connecting to anchor points. Instead, it becomes a larger network of springs which aids in controlling the overall form of the net.

Setting up design tests for such methods is a crucial element in their development. A second design elaborated through these methods was the design for a bridge with four cylindrical branches that constitute an inhabitable space at their intersection. This net too was utilised to act as a frame for an array of membrane patches to result in a greater degree of enclosure of the space of the bridge. Again this demonstrates the integration of spatial and structural aspects in the form-generation setup.

A second design for a net-bridge was developed in the studio and constructed at Hacienda Quitralco, in Chilean Patagonia, in 2008. The scheme consists of two sets of ropes that are interlaced and rotated in such a way that a hyperbolic paraboloid results with its arching curve along the long axis of the bridge. In order to address the unknown soil conditions, the arrangement of the four poles of the bridge was deliberately chosen to be asymmetrical to suit different arrangements. With the bridge not depending on a symmetric arrangement, poles could independently be shifted in location in response to given soil conditions. Once the design strategy was established, crucial solutions for low-soil-impact anchor-points for the tensioned ropes and integrating the decking into the scheme needed to be developed. Detailed scheduling of the assembly procedure and knotting and lashing procedures finalised the construction document. After purchasing rope, belt ratchets for tensioning and some essential tools in Santiago de Chile, the Emergent Technologies and Design group travelled to the remote site in Chilean Patagonia. Upon arrival all sixteen holes for the anchors and poles were dug; the poles and anchors were prepared and placed; and the holes were closed and the soil compacted. The distance between the poles on either side of the river is circa 20 metres and the distance between the furthest anchor points is circa 40 metres. The ropes and spacer-beams were assembled in a nearby barn, carried to the site and installed. Then the crucial pre-tensioning phase began, while the decking was prepared. After the decking was placed, the post-tensioning phase began. With the use of the belt ratchets and slipknots, the ropes were tensioned. Not all ropes could be tensioned simultaneously owing to the low number of available ratchets, which resulted in disequilibrium of tension in the overall system during the process of post-tensioning.

However, this was counteracted by careful sequencing of the post-tensioning process. As the tension increased, the knots securing the ropes began slipping and different knots needed to be deployed. Eventually the rope began to stretch more than expected, with its diameter dramatically decreasing, at the point of which the tensioning had to be stopped as the knots began slipping again. However, the tension at this stage was sufficient and the project completed two days ahead of schedule.

Research into complex spatial nets and also into the construction of such systems in a context with few anchoring options or lack of high-end technology is one of the key research areas of the Emergent Technologies and Design programme, as these systems have the potential to be used as supplementary architectural interventions in, for instance, climatic contexts where intermediary spaces between fully climatised interiors and fully exposed exteriors do not exist. With fast-to-assemble lightweight systems, such intermediary spaces can swiftly be provided together with an advanced passive environmental modulation capacity.

6.11 (opposite)

$^1/_{20}$ model of the net-bridge at Hacienda Quitralco in Patagonia, Chile. Design and Construction. Emergent Technologies and Design group 2007–08 in collaboration with Expedition Engineers, 2008.

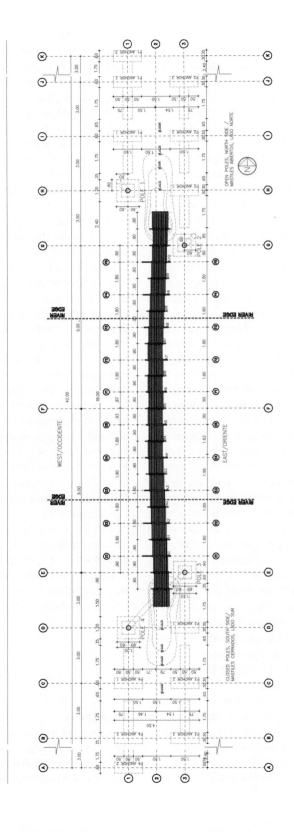

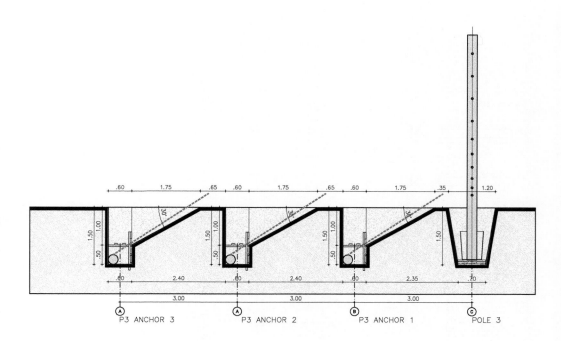

6.12 (opposite)

Construction drawings: plan of the net-bridge. Emergent Technologies and Design group 2007–08 in collaboration with Expedition Engineers, 2008.

6.13 (above)

Construction drawings: section of one pole and related foundations of tension anchors. Emergent Technologies and Design group 2007–08 in collaboration with Expedition Engineers, 2008.

WOOD/MADERA

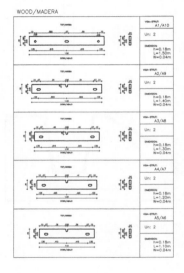
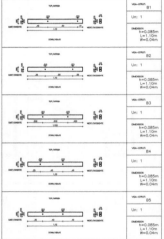
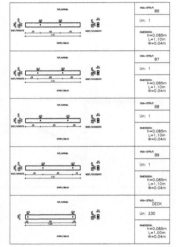

6.14

Construction drawings: specification of timber elements for the decking. Emergent Technologies and Design group 2007–08 in collaboration with Expedition Engineers, 2008.

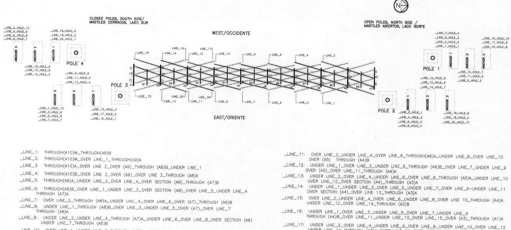

CLOSED POLES, SOUTH SIDE/
MASTILES CERRADOS, LADO SUR

WEST/OCCIDENTE

OPEN POLES, NORTH SIDE /
MASTILES ABIERTOS, LADO NORTE

EAST/ORIENTE

_LINE_1:   THROUGH(A10)M_THROUGN(A9)B

_LINE_2:   THROUGH(A10)M_OVER LINE_1_THROUGH(A9)A

_LINE_3:   THROUGH(A10)A_OVER LINE 2_OVER (A9)_THROUGH (A8)B_UNDER LINE_1

_LINE_4:   THROUGH(A10)B_OVER LINE 2_OVER (A9)_OVER LINE 3_THROUGH (A8)A

_LINE_5:   THROUGH(A9)A_UNDER LINE_2_OVER LINE_4_OVER SECTION (A8)_THROUGH (A7)B

_LINE_6:   THROUGH(A9)B_OVER LINE_1_UNDER LINE_3_OVER SECTION (A8)_OVER LINE_5_UNDER LINE_4 THROUGH (A7)A

_LINE_7:   OVER LINE_2_THROUGH (A8)A_UNDER LINE_4_OVER LINE_6_OVER (A7)_THROUGH (A6B)B

_LINE_8:   UNDER LINE_1_THROUGH (A8)B_OVER LINE_3_UNDER LINE_5_OVER (A7)_OVER LINE_7 THROUGH (A6)A

_LINE_9:   UNDER LINE_2_OVER LINE_4_THROUGH (A7)A_UNDER LINE_6_OVER LINE_8_OVER SECTION (A6) UNDER LINE_7_THROUGH (A5)B

_LINE_10: OVER LINE_1–UNDER LINE_3_THROUGH (A7)B_UNDER LINE_7_OVER SECTION (A6)_OVER LINE_9 THROUGH (A5)A

_LINE_11: OVER LINE_2_UNDER LINE_4_OVER LINE_6_THROUGH(A6)A_UNDER LINE_8_OVER LINE_10 OVER (A5) THROUGH (A4)B

_LINE_12: UNDER LINE_1_OVER LINE_3_UNDER LINE_5_THROUGH (A6)B_OVER LINE_7_UNDER LINE_9 OVER (A5)_OVER LINE_11_THROUGH (A4)A

_LINE_13: UNDER LINE_2_OVER LINE_4_UNDER LINE_6_OVER LINE_8_THROUGH (A5)A_UNDER LINE_10 OVER LINE_12_OVER SECTION (A4)_THROUGH (A3)A

_LINE_14: UNDER LINE_1_UNDER LINE_3_OVER LINE_5_UNDER LINE_7_OVER LINE_9–UNDER LINE_11 OVER SECTION (A4)_OVER LINE 13_THROUGH (A3)A

_LINE_15: OVER LINE_2_UNDER LINE_4_OVER LINE_6_UNDER LINE_8_OVER LINE 10_THROUGH (A4)A UNDER LINE_12_OVER LINE_14_THROUGH (A2)B

_LINE_16: UNDER LINE_1_OVER LINE_3_UNDER LINE_5_OVER LINE_7_UNDER LINE_9 THROUGH (A4)B_OVER LINE_11_UNDER LINE_13_OVER LINE_15_OVER (A3)_THROUGH (A1)A

_LINE_17: UNDER LINE_2_OVER LINE_4_UNDER LINE_6_OVER LINE_8_UNDER LINE_10_OVER LINE_12 UNDER LINE_14_THROUGH (A3)A_OVER LINE_16_OVER (A2)_THROUGH (A1)B

_LINE_18: OVER LINE_1_UNDER LINE_5_UNDER LINE_7_OVER LINE_9_UNDER LINE_11 THROUGH (A3)B_OVER LINE_13_UNDER LINE_15_OVER LINE_17_THROUGH (A1)A

_LINE_19: OVER LINE_2_UNDER LINE_4_OVER LINE_6_UNDER LINE_8_OVER LINE_10_UNDER LINE_12 OVER LINE_14_UNDER LINE_16_THROUGH (A2)A_OVER LINE_18

_LINE_20: UNDER LINE_1_OVER LINE_3_UNDER LINE_5_OVER LINE_7_UNDER LINE_9_OVER LINE_11 UNDER LINE_13_THROUGH (A2)B_OVER LINE_15_UNDER LINE_17_THROUGH (A1)M

6.15

Construction drawings: net layout and related assembly constructions. Emergent Technologies and Design group 2007–08 in collaboration with Expedition Engineers, 2008.

6.16

Construction process of the net-bridge at Hacienda Quitralco in Patagonia, Chile. Emergent Technologies and Design group 2007–08 in collaboration with Expedition Engineers, 2008.

6.17

Views of the completed
net-bridge. Design and
Construction. Emergent
Technologies and
Design group 2007–08
in collaboration with
Expedition Engineers,
2008. Photo Credits: Defne
Sunguroğlu, 2008.

Chapter 7
Lattices

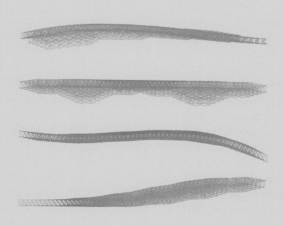

7.1

The photo shows the Multihalle Mannheim designed by Carlfried Mutschler and Frei Otto in 1975. Engineering: Ove Arup Consulting Engineers. Photo: Michael Hensel, 2006.

In its most generic definition the term 'lattice' refers to a structural organisation described by an array of points repeating periodically in three dimensions. For example, in crystallography the crystal structure is defined by a number of unit cells specifying atom positions that are organised in particular lattice structures. In the field of construction 'lattice' most generally refers to structures made by crossing laths or thin strips that form a specific network. Owing to the relative simplicity of constructing lattices from repetitive linear elements, a large number of research projects within the context of the Emergent Technologies and Design programme have been investigating lattices' potential to articulate performative material systems. In the following paragraphs two exemplary projects will be explained: the first project aimed at developing an adaptable gridshell based on a continuous rectangular lattice; the second project explored a discontinuous triangular lattice configuration based on a *kagome* organisation.

The MA dissertation of Jordi Truco and Sylvia Felipe aimed at advancing the research on gridshells through the investigation of alternative form-finding and construction methods. The term grid- or lattice-shell was described by Edmund Happold and Ian Liddell, two of the leading engineering pioneers of this field, as follows:

> The term lattice shell is used to describe a doubly curved surface formed from a lattice of timber laths bolted together at uniform spacing in two directions. When flat, the lattice is a mechanism with one degree of freedom. If it were formed of rigid

members with frictionless joints, movement of one lath parallel to another would evoke a sympathetic movement of the whole frame causing all the squares to become similar parallelograms. This movement causes changes in length of diagonal lines through nodes. It is this property which allows the lattice to be formed into the double curved shape of the shell.
(Happold and Liddell 1978: 60)

The Multihalle in Mannheim was constructed in 1975 as the first complex large-scale gridshell. The collaborative work of Frei Otto, Carlfried Mutschler and the engineers Edmund Happold and Ian Liddell, working for Ove Arup at the time, the shell was geometrically developed as an inverted thrust form using hanging

net models. The actual construction method on site in Mannheim was equally innovative, as the entire shell was constructed as a regular rectangular timber lattice, which was subsequently jacked up on strategic points, finding by itself the specific shape of its 60 metre span roof.

The work of Truco and Felipe focused on developing a type of gridshell that would find its form on site neither by raising the grid from the ground, as in the example of the Multihalle Mannheim, nor by lowering it from scaffolds, as in the example of Shigeru Ban's Pavilion for the Expo Hannover. Rather, the structure was developed in such a way that a layered gridshell with uniform grid layout made from elastic members becomes globally defined through local manipulations of actuators that regulate the distance between the members of the layered lattices. Unlike the use of significant lifting

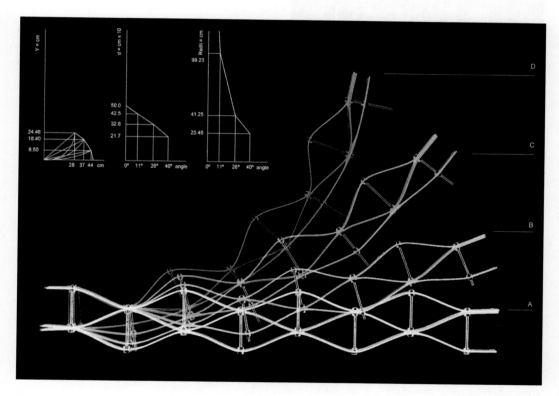

7.2

Basic element of the HybGrid gridshell system demonstrating the capacity for parametric shape-change. MA Dissertation of Jordi Truco and Sylvia Felipe, October 2003.

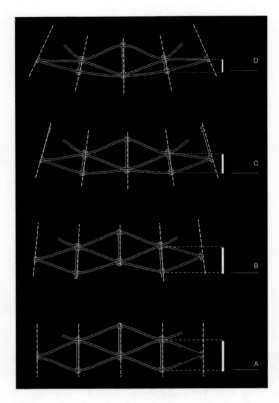

7.3

Different element states corresponding with four actuator settings. MA Dissertation of Jordi Truco and Sylvia Felipe, October 2003.

forces induced at a small number of points only, as in Mannheim, or the step-by-step removal of a supporting scaffold, as in Hannover, this cumulative actuation does not act on the system from outside but rather becomes an integral part of the reconfigurable material system of the lattice. This novel approach towards gridshell constructions was developed in collaboration with Buro Happold, the leading structural engineering consultancy for gridshells that was involved in developing both the Mannheim and the Hannover buildings.

An initial set of experiments was based on a simple element consisting of an upper, centre and lower chord connected by spacer elements. Changing the setting of these spacers, in this case threaded rods, allows for changing the curvature of the element. For example, incrementally reducing the distance between the mounting points of the actuators on one layer causes the lattice element to bend. This relation between spacer setting and resulting geometry was parameterised and used for the articulation of a larger lattice system. The production of the next set of test models was quite simple, as there was no need for differentiation in the configuration of the grid during fabrication and assembly processes. Nevertheless, once the assembly had been completed the test model demonstrated the system's ability to generate formal and structural differentiation by changing the relative distances between these strips through local actuation of the spacer elements placed between the layered strips. The parameterisation of the local behavior then allowed computing of the overall shape in both an analogue and a computational manner. Through a large number of subsequent tests, the system's physical behaviour was calibrated with a custom-written software tool that enables computational generation of different system configurations based on a set of defined input values as well as boundary conditions. The design of the system implied the design of the software,

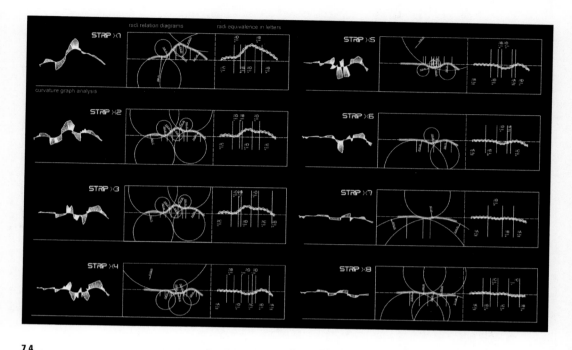

7.4

Curvature definition and associated actuator settings for eight element strips. MA Dissertation of Jordi Truco and Sylvia Felipe, October 2003.

so that the limits, the rules and the ranges of the system are parametrically defined in relation to the maximum and minimum curvature radii at local and global levels. The software can respond to desired changes in the global configuration, the size and location of required internal spaces and other performance criteria.

Once a particular configuration is defined, the computational process derives the required local position of all local actuators, their unique address and the particular spacer setting for achieving the specified shape. This enabled the construction of a full-scale prototype built at the Architectural Association School of Architecture in July 2003. Initially constructed as an entirely flat and regular grid, the structure raised into its structurally stable, double-curved shape by incrementally actuating the local spacer elements. As the actuator settings can be altered to adapt to a different computationally derived configuration at any point in time, there is no division between form-finding and adaptation of the form in use, as form-finding continues each time a change to the building is activated. This extends the idea of form-finding from shape optimisation for a single minimum energy configuration under stress, towards a dynamic structural system. It extends the research on gridshells by the possibility of combining multiple configurations or equilibrium states in a structural system with a control system that produces complex global transitions between forms from very simple local rules.

Matthew Johnston's MArch research aimed at investigating a *kagome* lattice system with a particular focus on both quantitative and qualitative aspects of interrelated structural and acoustic performances through vibration behaviours. A kagome lattice is characterised by a specific arrangement of laths. These form interlaced triangles, six of which form a hexagon between them. This arrangement is related to tri-hexagonal tiling.

Through the use of digital, physical, and

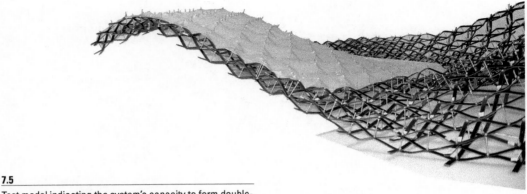

7.5

Test model indicating the system's capacity to form double-curved surfaces. MA Dissertation of Jordi Truco and Sylvia Felipe, October 2003.

mathematical models, ray trace and vibration tests, the relations between rigidity, mass and attenuation characteristic, as well as shape, curvature, and volume of the lattice, were investigated.

An initial set of experiments explored inter-laced arrangements that possess strength and flexibility through both their material characteristics and their geometrical configuration. A particular kagome lattice system was developed as a result of these initial investigations, which offers possibilities of adapting to structural and acoustic requirements by changes to the lattice morphology. A kagome tri-directional weave establishes the organisational logic for the two layers of the lattice system. Three linear elements join the two layers at alternating connection nodes, with increasing distance in one segment length of each of the triangular connection nodes. One of the layers allows for rotation and the other for rotation and sliding within a given range. In addition, several long element strips are overlapped across two connection bars in each of the three weaving directions. On large-scale physical models it was observed that this arrangement generally tends to stiffen movement within the system but does not act to inhibit it. If the element strips are shorter and

only pass between each of the connection bars, they can be conceived of as discontinuous segments. The physical test models also showed that each triangular connection node with three connection rods has a concave type of distortion, whereas the interstitial triangles between those with rods are convex. Through this curvature induced by the rods, a certain amount of torsional distortion also occurs across the width of the woven strips. Another behaviour which was observed relates to the weakness of the structure when a lateral force is applied. As a force is introduced, the elements tend to fold together, which can be compensated for by changing the material thickness or adding more rods along the periphery. Normal to the lattice's surface, the system generally has a high load-bearing capacity when uniform forces are applied. Under local forces and disturbances, the structure is generally weaker. In addition to the system's capacity to fulfil structural requirements, its ability to respond to acoustic requirements through alterations to the surface local and global curvature, as well as dampening properties, was of critical importance.

The kagome lattice demonstrates the potential for integrating multiple functional requirements within one system. For example, the conception of its structural capacity is not limited to its ability to carry its self weight, as well as resolving applied forces per se, but rather to the manner in which the forces are dispersed through a combination of material characteristics, friction and geometrically determined factors. The kagome lattice is a complex system, not only in its geometric definition but in the manner in which it disperses energy. This energy may take the form of acoustic waves, vibration induced by human activity, or seismic movement, and the manner in which this energy is dampened, dispersed or otherwise redistributed through the structure is influenced by a number of key factors. Material characteristics affect the ability of the structure to disperse energy, which has been introduced through local bending of the strips. For example, in test models constructed from black styrene, the material became white in areas where introduced forces, externally applied or internally induced, began to exceed the bending capability of the material, with breaking occurring in some cases. There is a degree of damping, which can be related to both the material utilised and the geometric articulation of the lattice, through which the energy is distributed in direct dependency

to the actual configuration and redundancies of the lattice. Friction is another critical constituent of the system. The friction taking place within the rod-to-strip and the strip-to-strip joints is an instrumental manipulation through which energy can be dissipated and/or redistributed. The relatively large number of connection rod intersections and overlapping strips give rise to this factor.

The parametric definition of each of the kagome lattice elements enables the strategic differentiation of the system's morphology. Through altering the surface connection distances in a differential manner, that is to say with differing distance between the upper layer and the lower layer, localised curvature variations in the sinusoid surface elements are possible, as well as intermediary degrees of curvature change that allow for both varying degrees of single direction or double direction curvature of the overall system. Through selective node manipulations it is possible to articulate differential rigidity in the lattice, which in turn enables multiple resonance possibilities. Resonance can be defined in terms of mass, rigidity and time. As the kagome lattice has relatively little mass, the structure has, generally speaking, an

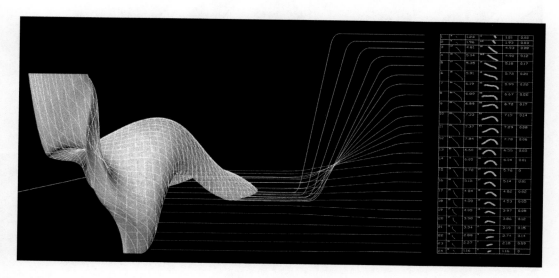

7.6

Digital model containing all construction information and spacer settings of the HybGrid prototype. MA Dissertation of Jordi Truco and Sylvia Felipe, October 2003.

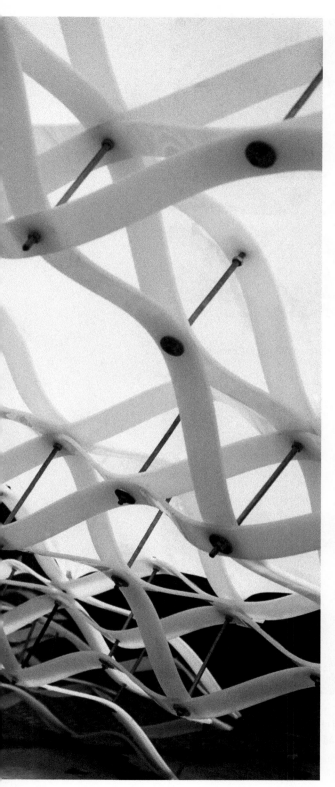

7.7

Close-up view of full-scale HybGrid prototype.
MA Dissertation of Jordi Truco and Sylvia Felipe,
October 2003.

7.8

Close-up view of full-scale HybGrid prototype. MA Dissertation of Jordi Truco and Sylvia Felipe, October 2003.

7.9

Full-scale HybGrid prototype built for the EmTech End of Year Exhibition at the Architectural Association in 2003. MA Dissertation of Jordi Truco and Sylvia Felipe, October 2003.

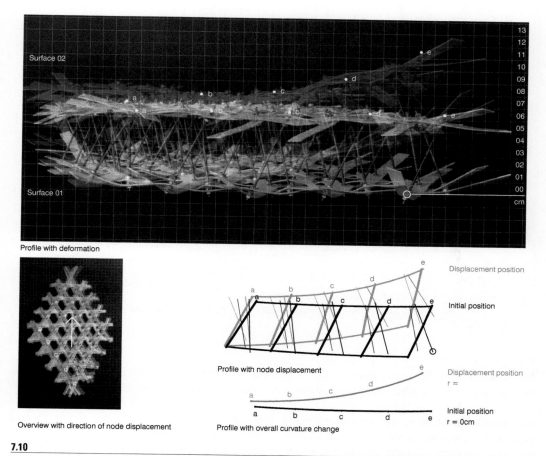

Surface 02

Surface 01

Profile with deformation

Overview with direction of node displacement

Displacement position

Initial position

Profile with node displacement

Displacement position
r =

Initial position
r = 0cm

Profile with overall curvature change

7.10

Basic element of the kagome lattice system demonstrating the logic of the shape-change of the system. MArch Dissertation of Matthew Johnston, February 2005.

inherently high-resonance frequency. In regard to rigidity and time, it was observed in several test cycles that nodes or areas of nodes with higher degrees of rigidity exhibit a higher magnitude of vibration. They also exhibit vibration with a greater duration after the influence of a force has been stopped, owing to the clusters' rigidity having a lower capacity to disperse vibration.

Vibration testing was a means for cross-checking issues raised by the computational, physical, and mathematical models established during the system development. The computational model and ray trace tool addressed aspects of acoustic performance, while vibration testing looked into both acoustic and structural performance aspects and repercussion. Elaborate

vibration tests were conducted at the laboratories of Reading University. The tests focused on response frequencies, lattice support, material and geometric aspects and response, attenuation and damping characteristic. The testing was undertaken with a kagome lattice without a continuous skin and initially investigated direct contact vibration transmission. At first two differing regions of the lattice were isolated and tested individually. In a second step the entire extract, comprising three regions, was tested with particular focus on airborne vibration. Testing with direct transmission provided information which has structural implications, while testing concentrating on airborne transmission offered information having acoustical

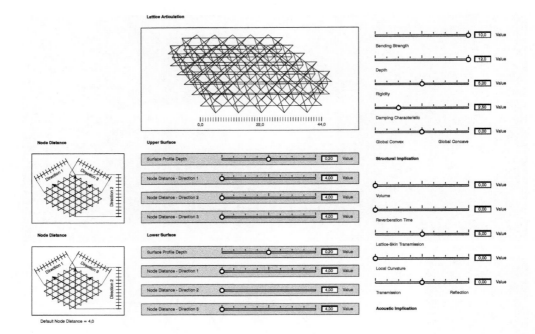

7.11

Parametric definition of the upper and lower layer of the kagome lattice system in relation to the implications for structural and acoustic performance for each system configuration. MArch Dissertation of Matthew Johnston, February 2005.

implications. In order to get a more complete picture of the lattice's behaviour, a laser vibrometer was used to read the amplitudes of lattice resonance in comparison to frequencies of the source vibrations. Visual observations of lattice responses were made with the use of the stroboscope. Taking readings from only one node already showed that there were several levels of response, depending upon the precise position, proximity to the connection rods, and distance from the source. Two main response modes were observed. The first was a bouncing-type mode of response. This behaviour depends on the type of support, and began to provide insights into system manipulations related to lattice support methods. Additionally, lateral and longitudinal means of support were investigated. The second was a bending-type mode of response. This behaviour depends on stiffness, and began to provide insights into the relation between stiffness, damping characteristic and attenuation. Additionally, material and geometric changes were investigated as they relate to stiffness. Multiple membrane modes were also observed and relate to aspects of stiffness, attenuation and the transmission and/or reflection of acoustic energy. These behavioural aspects were then organised to establish highly specific performance profiles in order to prepare for applications of the kagome lattice that are highly specific to the related structural and acoustic context.

In summary, it can be said that the EmTech research on lattices demonstrates their capacity to form adaptable as well as performative material systems. However, it also needs to be stated that, despite the appealing logic of constructing from simple linear members, the complexity in structural organisation and behaviour rises exponentially when introducing the necessary curvatures in plan and section to form larger-span shell-like structures.

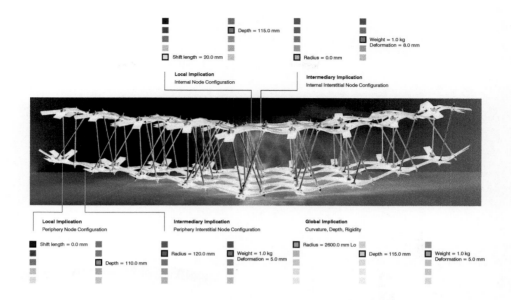

7.12

Parametric system characteristics of the kagome lattice and their specific relation to peripheral and internal node configurations. MArch Dissertation of Matthew Johnston, February 2005.

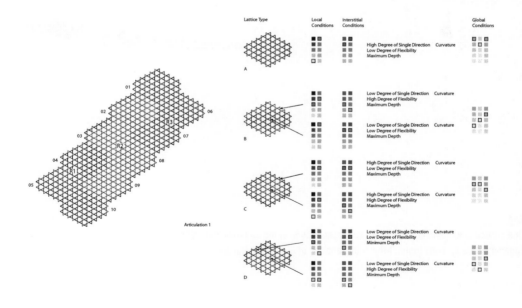

7.13

Parametric system characteristics of a kagome lattice, and identification of particular characteristics and the implication of their modification with regard to the local, meso- and global scale articulation of a lattice. MArch Dissertation of Matthew Johnston, February 2005.

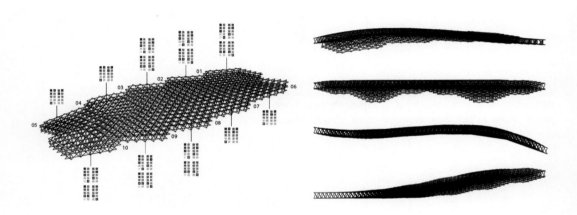

7.14

One particular kagome lattice system and identification of the underlying specific system parameters (left) and four varied kagome lattice systems (right). MArch Dissertation of Matthew Johnston, February 2005.

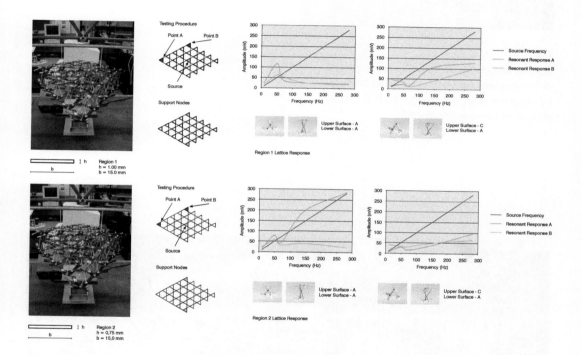

7.15

Vibration tests and direct contact transmission analysis of two different configurations of a kagome lattice system at the laboratories of the Centre for Biomimetics at Reading University. MArch Dissertation of Matthew Johnston, February 2005.

7.16

Close-up view of a kagome lattice system prepared
for vibration tests at the laboratories of the Centre for
Biomimetics at Reading University. MArch Dissertation
of Matthew Johnston, February 2005.

7.17

Vibration tests of a kagome lattice system at the laboratories of the Centre for Biomimetics at Reading University.
MArch Dissertation of Matthew Johnston, February 2005.

7.18
Setup for a vibration test of a kagome lattice system at the Centre for Biomimetics at Reading University.
MArch Dissertation of Matthew Johnston, February 2005.

Chapter 8
Branches

Branching patterns appear in great abundance in natural systems, ranging from overall plant morphologies, to respiratory and vascular systems of organisms, to rivers and climatic phenomena such as lightning strikes. Natural branching systems generally provide for energy efficiency in the distribution of other materials. Such patterns are self-similar, which implies that 'each piece of a shape is geometrically similar to the whole' (Mandelbrot 1982: 34), whether they are dispersive or convergent. Nevertheless, there are also differences in the specific patterns that occur in natural systems. Both self-similarity and differences between different branching patterns derive from the rate and ratio of bifurcations that characterise a particular branching pattern. Discerning the differences between diverse types of branching patterns seems initially not an easy task to tackle. Yet, as Philip Ball stated:

> in recent years, scientists have developed tools for assessing in a mathematically precise way the generic features of different branching patterns, and by doing so, have been able to provide clear and unambiguous criteria for distinguishing one such form from another. These tools have played a crucial role in allowing us to understand how branched forms grow, because only through them do we have a definite quantifiable means of determining how close a given physical or biological model comes to reproducing the form observed in reality.
> (Ball 1999: 111)

He continued to elaborate that:

> For branching patterns in particular, attempts to provide mathematical descriptions of shape and form unfold along rather different lines than we are used to in classical geometry. Such models are in fact more properly regarded as prescriptions rather than descriptions – they do not provide geometrical labels of shape like 'circle' or 'octahedron', but instead sets of rules, called algorithms, for generating characteristic but non-unique forms.
> (Ball 1999: 128)

For the visualisation and simulation of plant growth, developmental algorithms are frequently utilised, and a great wealth of literature is available on this topic.

Lindenmayer-systems, or so-called L-systems, are a specific variant of a formal grammar – iterative parallel rewriting systems that are utilised for the purpose of plant growth modelling in theoretical biology, developed by the Hungarian biologist Aristid Lindenmayer (1925–89). L-systems are particularly suited to model the growth of branching geometries. A recursive

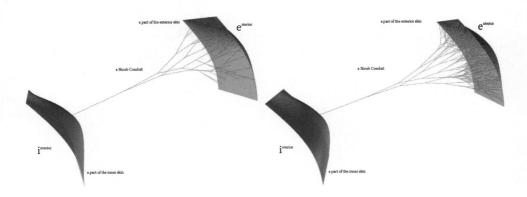

8.1 (opposite)

Two different runs of the centroid branching algorithm with a lower number of generations (left) and a higher one (right). A higher number of generations leads to a greater number and density of daughter branches. MArch Dissertation of Yukio Minobe, February 2009.

8.2 (above)

Echinoid dome generated by combined wind- and heliotropism with a medium-density branching ventilation system generated by deploying the centroid branching algorithm. MArch Dissertation of Yukio Minobe, February 2009.

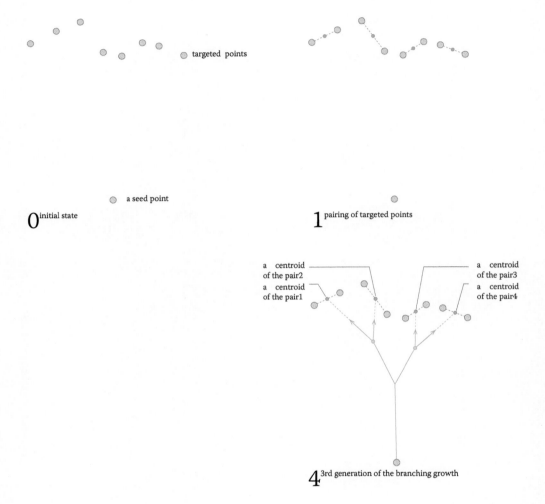

targeted points

a seed point

0 initial state

1 pairing of targeted points

a centroid of the pair2

a centroid of the pair1

a centroid of the pair3

a centroid of the pair4

4 3rd generation of the branching growth

8.3

The centroid branching algorithm defines the growth direction of branches by calculating a centroid of each cluster of points per growth generation, which is designated as an attractor for a seed point to converge upon the targeted points. This serves the purpose of evolving branching systems between defined starting and target points on the inside and outside of a material surface. MArch Dissertation of Yukio Minobe, February 2009.

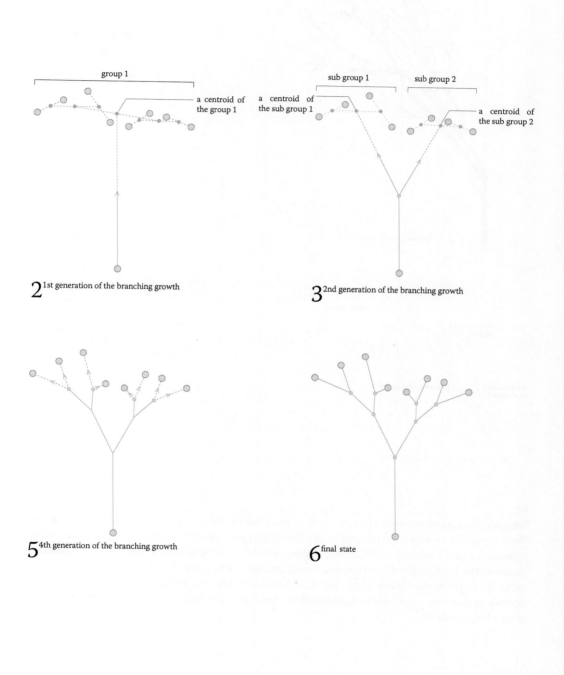

group 1

a centroid of
the group 1

2 ¹ˢᵗ generation of the branching growth

sub group 1   sub group 2

a centroid of
the sub group 1

a centroid of
the sub group 2

3 ²ⁿᵈ generation of the branching growth

5 ⁴ᵗʰ generation of the branching growth

6 final state

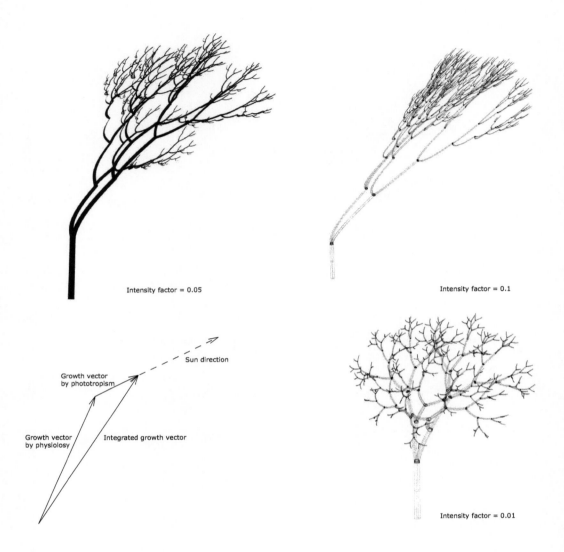

Intensity factor = 0.05

Intensity factor = 0.1

Sun direction

Growth vector
by phototropism

Growth vector
by physiolosy

Integrated growth vector

Intensity factor = 0.01

8.4

Tropism governs the growth of plants in response to an environmental stimulus, depending on the direction of the stimulus.
'Phototropism', for instance, is the response to light, 'heliotropism' with regards to sunlight, while 'gravitropism' is the
response to gravity. Integrating such responses in growth models for branching systems allows for context-sensitive
growth models. The illustrations result from experiments in modelling tree growth involving phototropism. By adding a
vector directing to the sun to an existing growth vector, following Murray's law, the branches grow towards the light.
Significantly such models can integrate multiple extrinsic stimuli into a phenotypic expression. Natural Systems Research
of Yukio Minobe 2007–08.

process evolves self-similar forms that, when a stochastic logic is introduced, can vary the geometry as well as the topology of each individual output of the process. In 'context-specific' L-systems (see, for instance, Jirasek, Prusinkiewic *et al.* 2000), this process can incorporate a variety of influences, such as the simulation of gravitropism and phototropism, opening these processes to potentially be informed by performance criteria by utilising performance-related stimuli as an input to an informed growth process. L-systems and algorithmic growth solutions have been frequently written about and deployed by the Emergent Technologies and Design programme. Two examples are introduced below.

Yukio Minobe pursued algorithmic procedures in the definition of branching patterns in his MArch dissertation. In order to evolve a branching ventilation system between the inside and the outside of a cast shell structure, and between determined start and end points of the branching systems on the inside and outside of the material surface, he developed two different types of algorithms: a centroid branching algorithm and a close sphere packing algorithm.

Centroid branching algorithms are deployed to adjust the growth direction of each growth step. Predefined endpoints are treated as attractors, attracting a tip point of new branches, so that branches can eventually reach the attractor. This type of attractor-based branching algorithm serves to define a growth direction at each growth step, depending on distances between attractors and a grown point. This algorithm utilises centroids of targeted points as attractors. Initially, a centroid per each pair is calculated, which forms an end cluster of branches. By calculating a centroid of all centroids and designating this centroid as an attractor in this growth step, the growth direction is defined. In subsequent steps, a group of points are divided into two and the same procedure is applied, thus defining the next growth direction. The final growth direction is defined by connecting the last evolved point with a specified target point on the inside or outside of the material surface.

In this approach, the branch length needs to be defined and, depending on that length, the branching angle will be defined too. Therefore this algorithm defines the geometry of the branching pattern related to the branch length, to be negotiated to match specific circumstances to do with the physics of a branching network for ventilation purposes (see also Chapter 3). The branch length can be adjusted in each growth step and for each cluster. This makes it possible to modify the branch length for each growth step according to required airflow conditions within the branching network.

Pavel Hladik's master dissertation (2006) focused on physical and digital form-generation and form-finding processes for branching systems that are linked to structural and environmental performance criteria, as well as to material and manufacturing constraints. Physical form-finding methods and techniques devised by Frei Otto and his team at the Institute for Lightweight Structures in Stuttgart were utilised and modified for the purpose of this research and, more specifically, to gather empirical data from material experiments to inform the computational logic for the digital form-generation and form-finding process. In these experiments, woollen threads with a certain amount of slack form branching patterns when dipped into water, owing to the surface tension of water, resulting in minimal path branching patterns with a specific structural behaviour and capacity.

Stochastic L-systems were utilised for the form-generation process and implemented in an associative modelling environment (Generative Components from Bentley Systems). Implementing L-systems in an associative environment enables the possibility of deploying self-organising processes in combination with easy modifiability through a shared parametric logic. The physical experiments delivered the data to establish the range of permissible parametric variation of a model. From these experiments geometric logics to define associative models and an L-system setup were extracted. In this setup, the length of the branches is specified and thus the density of the overall branching pattern. Likewise, the allocation of starting points for the growth is crucial. Moreover, certain geometric logics based

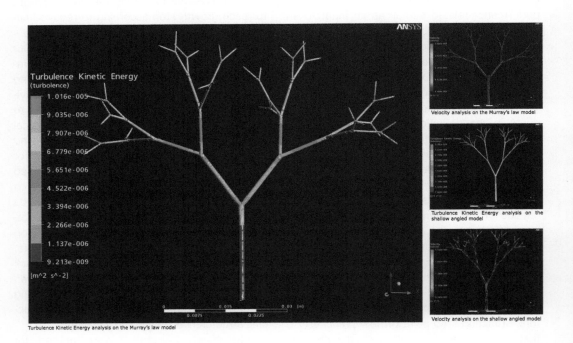

Turbulence Kinetic Energy analysis on the Murray's law model

Velocity analysis on the Murray's law model

Turbulence Kinetic Energy analysis on the shallow angled model

Velocity analysis on the shallow angled model

8.5 and 8.6

In order to evaluate the flow of a fluid through a branching model, computational fluid dynamics were used.
Two different models were tested; the first is modelled according to Murray's law, while the second is characterised
by shallow branching angles. Murray's law is a formula that relates radii of daughter branches to the radii of parent
branches. This is used to model the circulatory and respiratory system, but also the branching of xylems in plants.
The purpose of the formulae is to identify the optimum radius that requires minimum energy expenditure of a life form.
Criteria for analysis were pressure differences and velocity, as well as turbulent kinetic energy. Natural Systems
Research of Yukio Minobe 2007–08.

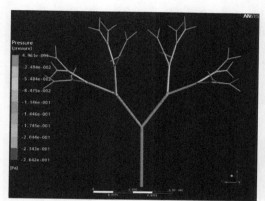

Pressure analysis on the Murray's law model

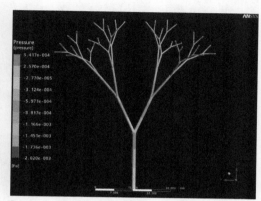

Pressure analysis on the shallow angled model

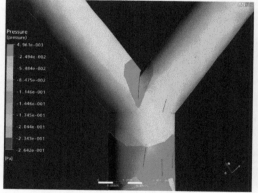

Detail of pressure analysis on the Murray's law model

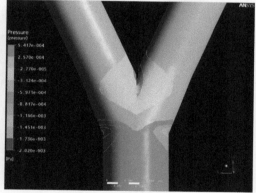

Detail of pressure analysis on the shallow angled model

A

fig. 01, ex 01, dry threads

fig. 02, ex 01, threads influenced by surface tension of water

fig. 03, ex 02, level 2 threads of II. degree of slack, front view

fig. 04, ex 02, level 2 threads of II. degree of slack, left view

fig. 05, ex 03, level 3 threads of III. degree of slack, front view

B

fig. 07, ex 04, thick 4 ply threads dipped into water, front view

fig. 08, ex 04, thick 4 ply threads dipped into water, left view

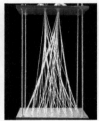

fig. 09, ex 05, threads dipped into water, 4 base 'trunks', topological change from others, front view

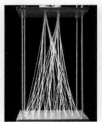

fig. 10, ex 05, threads dipped into water, 4 base 'trunks', left view

fig. 11, ex 06, threads with configuration of ex 05, II. degree of slack, front view

C

fig. 13, ex 07, 2 ply threads, co-joining of threads, bases oppposite each other, front view

fig. 14, ex 07, 2 ply threads, co-joining of threads, bases opposite each other, left view

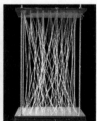

fig. 15, ex 08, threads dipped into water, bases connected according to the random function run in excel, front view

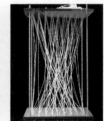

fig. 16, ex 08, threads dipped into water, bases connected according to the random function run in excel, left view

fig. 17, ex 09, threads dipped into latex, threads in two layers, 2. layer oriented - fig 02 page 14, top view

8.7

The form-finding method for branching systems developed by Frei Otto and his team, based on woollen threads with slack that are dipped into water and form branching configurations owing to the surface tension of water in the threads, was examined for geometric rules that can be embedded in an associative digital process and model. MA Dissertation of Pavel Hladik, 2006.

on material choices can be embedded. With the intended use of bent wood, this pertains to the curvature of each bent element, relative to its length, which is also extracted from physical experiments. Initially, the starting, intermediary and end points derived from the L-system serve as a scaffold for the distribution of these elements. However, since the continuity of the curvature between the pieces and the associated stress distribution is not yet embedded, this needed to be solved in a subsequent stage. In order to inform this stage, a series of assemblies of branching structures were constructed from bent laminated wood. Key constraints are the type of wood, the dimensions of layers in a laminate, the dimensions of the laminate, the distribution of butt joints, and also constraints pertaining to manufacturing such as distribution of clamping points in the lamination process.

The following sets of digital modelling experiments embedded these constraints. The curvature of the bent elements was articulated in an associative model, in which the curves are controlled by the rotation of tangency points and the connection angles between elements deduced from the physical models. The first set examined the areas in which elements of different branching structures coincide in a certain density within one plane, so that the resulting behaviour of the structural system tends to shift from that of a vector-active system to that of a surface-active system in a similar way to the 'lattice' of a gridshell (Engel 1999). The second set of experiments examined the structural interaction between converging branching elements of different branching structures. In these areas the stresses from the 'lattice' are split into clearly defined vectors, while these elements collaborate in bearing the stresses resulting from self-weight and dynamic loads. The third set of experiments investigated the overall structural performance of the collaborating multiple branching systems. The structural behaviour was analysed by means of the finite element method (ANSYS).

Different logics were deployed to generate and analyse branching patterns. One set of experiments utilised, for instance, spiral phylotaxis as an underlying logic for a branching system

that was implemented through L-systems in an associative modelling environment. The generated branching pattern was subsequently elaborated to comprise the dimensions of the laminated elements and their relation to one another. From this setup ensued a design study for a context-specific structure. This implied that relevant parameters of the site needed to be embedded with the generative setup of the associative model, pertaining to [i] the available space for construction, [ii] the articulation of the ground plane in relation to the distribution of the starting points for evolving the branching system, [iii] the structural behaviour that is associated with the evolved specific branching structure, and [iv] environmental modulation criteria, such as the density of the lattice that results from the collaborating branching elements and the related sunlight penetration and shading patterns. The structural and environmental performance of each branching configuration is directly related to the type of branching logic and the key parameters that define and constrain the L-system used to evolve each configuration.

The transition from a vector active system to a surface active lattice type system was not initially intended, but emerged as a possibility because of the research undertaken. This shifts the reductive mode of designing and engineering with reference to singular structural types to one in which different types of collaborative systems can emerge from different setups in the generative mode of the design. What may start as a singular type as a motive can thus proliferate towards an unanticipated potential.

Consequently the subsequent research examined the ramifications of different logics and different parametric variations of branching system articulation, distributions and densities. For this purpose the interrelation of an iterative generative process facilitated by L-systems in an associative modelling environment became a powerful test bed. However, a more comprehensive systematic study is still pending. There is definitely much scope in elaborating the algorithmic procedures of the generative process with the purpose of enabling a greater hierarchical differentiation of collaborating branching

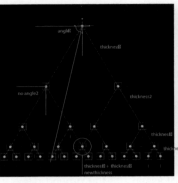

8.8

Geometric rules were extracted from the physical form-finding experiments and implemented in an associative modelling environment (Generative Components of Bentley Systems). MA Dissertation of Pavel Hladik, 2006.

systems, exploring, for instance, the possibilities of nested form-finding, in which a branching macro-system is inhabited or rearticulated by branching meso- and micro-systems. Again this process can be driven by specified performance criteria. A more integral approach to form-generation and performance analysis would be useful to enable a more direct feedback. This line of inquiry would benefit from converging with the research into fibrous materials (see Chapter 4) in order to strategise and accomplish fabrication processes that ensure greater fibre continuity with a branching system in order to improve on its structural capacity. This can involve different strategies for working with natural fibrous materials, such as wood, as well as artificial fibrous composite materials. An extensive foundation for research into the relation between branching and fibre directionality has been laid by Claus Mattheck, who investigated among other natural systems branches of trees and the stress pattern associated with the branch geometry and the fibre directionality (Mattheck 1998). The integral understanding and utilisation of direction-specific morphological features, such as branches, in collaboration with direction-specific material characteristics (anisotropy) has been deployed in traditional building methods; however, there is still an enormous unexplored potential in instrumentalising this towards a positive take on anisotropy and the associated variable behaviour that ensues from it. Some steps have been taken to rethink the potential of anisotropy as an opportunity for technical innovation (Wagenführ 2008). However, on a broader scale this is not yet recognised as an opportunity for architectural design, let alone being considered as an alternative approach to industrial logics and preferences in manufacturing.

In principle this method of form-generation can be utilised for other systems, some of which are elaborated in this book. Likewise it can be of interest in the utilisation of branching logics, pattern and type of connectivity for the distribution of features and the overall articulation of other systems. The Emergent Technologies and Design programme has therefore intensified the analysis of natural branching systems. Extensive studies of respiratory systems of insects and vascular systems of plants were undertaken, as well as of the branching logic of river systems. Further research and experimentation with the findings is pending, but clearly some potent possibilities have already been formulated.

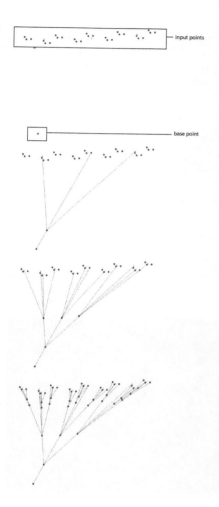

input points

base point

8.9

Three individual branching systems derived by implementing an edge-rewriting L-system algorithm in an associative modelling environment (Generative Components of Bentley Systems). MA Dissertation of Pavel Hladik, 2006.

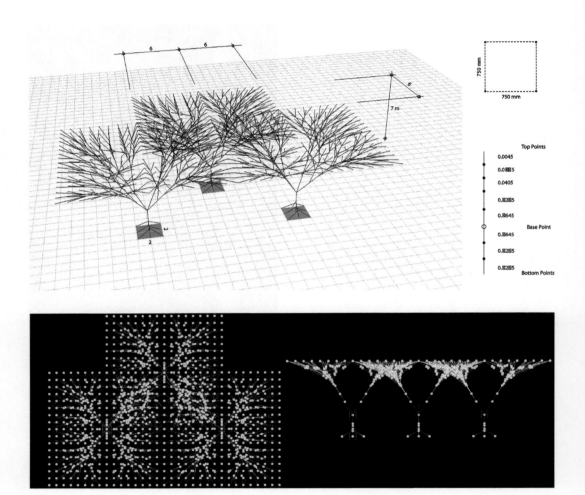

8.10

Three related branching systems derived by implementing an edge-rewriting L-system algorithm in an associative modelling environment (Generative Components of Bentley Systems). MA Dissertation of Pavel Hladik, 2006.

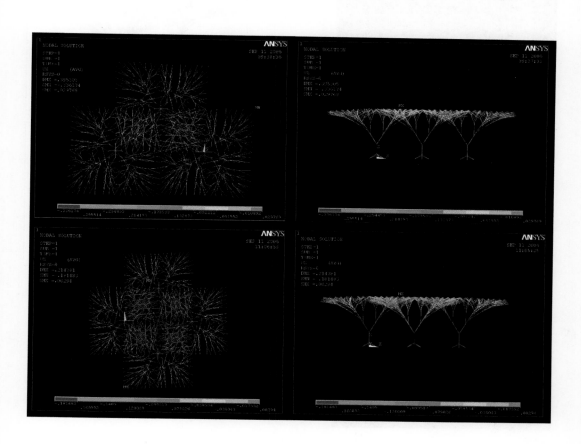

8.11

Computational finite element analysis (FEA in ANSYS) of branching systems investigating stress pattern associated with self-weight. MA Dissertation of Pavel Hladik, 2006.

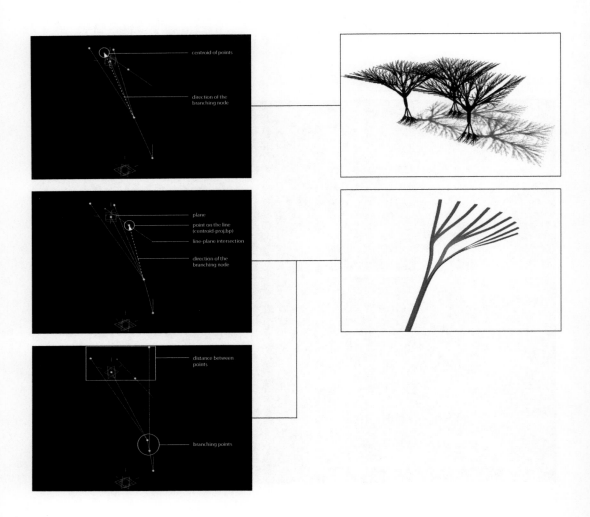

8.12

System hierarchies and detailing of a branching system derived by implementing an edge-rewriting L-system algorithm in an associative modelling environment (Generative Components of Bentley Systems). MA Dissertation of Pavel Hladik, 2006.

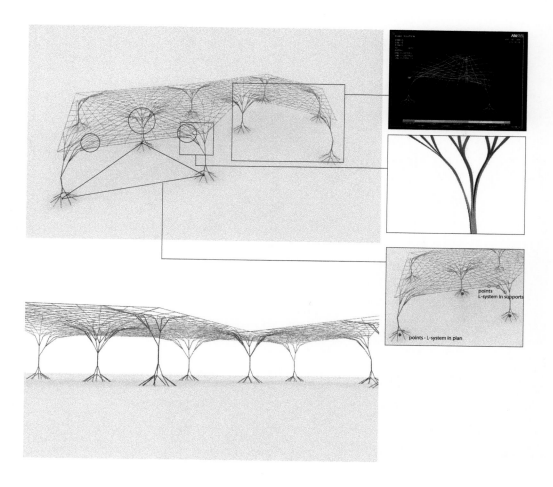

8.13

Branching system with a transition from a vector-active to a surface-active system derived by implementing an edge-rewriting L-system algorithm in an associative modelling environment (Generative Components of Bentley Systems) and driven by stress analysis (FEA in ANSYS). MA Dissertation of Pavel Hladik, 2006.

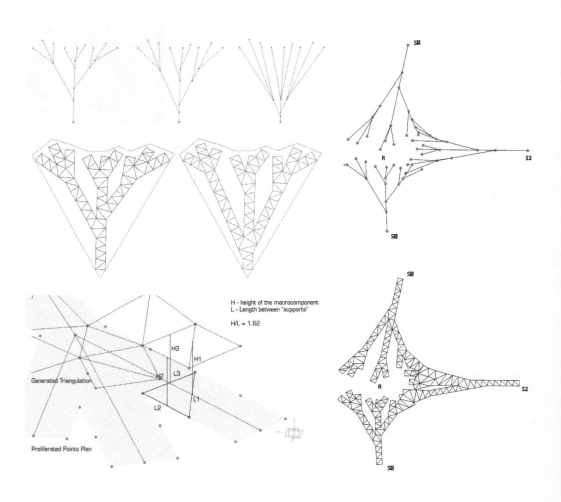

H - height of the macrocomponent
L - Length between "supports"

H/L = 1.62

Generated Triangulation

Proliferated Points Plan

8.14

Rules for a site-specific proliferation of a branching system generated by an edge-rewriting L-system algorithm in an associative modelling environment (Generative Components of Bentley Systems). MA Dissertation of Pavel Hladik, 2006.

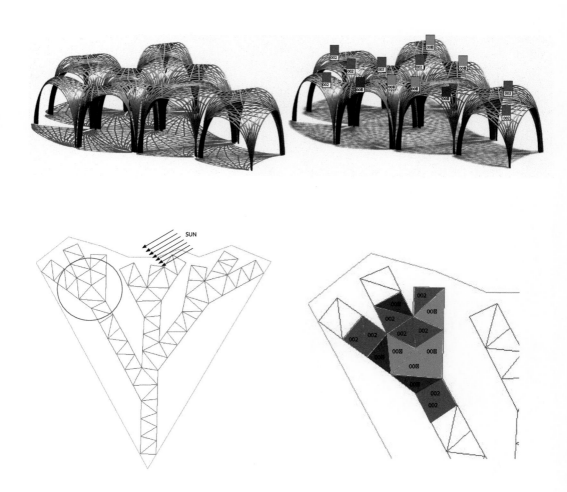

8.15

Site-specific proliferation of a branching system generated by an edge-rewriting L-system algorithm in an associative modelling environment (Generative Components of Bentley Systems). The density of the lattice resulting from the branch interweaving is analysed with regards to sunlight penetration and self-shading. MA Dissertation of Pavel Hladik, 2006.

Chapter 9
Cells

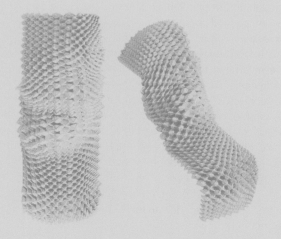

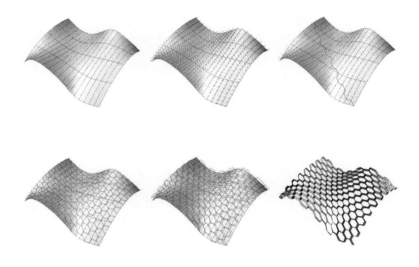

9.1

The illustrations shows six steps of the algorithmically driven generation of honeycomb cells on a double-curved surface. MA Dissertation of Andrew Kudless, October 2004.

Cells are the basic elements of all systems in living nature. The process of cellular differentiation underlies most natural systems' capacity for functional integration and adaptation. In the Emergent Technologies and Design programme multifaceted cell research has been conducted over a number of years, ranging from in-depth investigations in the field of cellular solids to the development of cell-based pneumatic structures. In the following paragraphs two exemplary research projects will be explained.

The field of cellular solids is remarkable as it is emblematic for a paradigm shift in material science. Until recently material research was conducted in a material-specific manner. For example, metallurgists studied metals and polymer scientists studied plastics. By nature, this material-specific approach did not investigate more general properties that traverse a particular material category and are shared by a wide range of different materials. However, over the last few decades an increasing number of trans-material researches have been conducted focusing on certain characteristics that are common to a wide variety of materials,

regardless of whether they are natural or man-made. One particularly interesting trans-material area of investigation and experimentation is cellular solids. In their seminal book *Cellular Solids: Structure and Properties*, L. J. Gibson and M. F. Ashby state that the fascination with cells has, of course, a long history in science, yet the rigorous investigation and classification of cell characteristics across different materials is a relatively recent phenomenon:

> The structure of cells has fascinated natural philosophers for at least 300 years. Hooke examined their shape, Kelvin analyzed their packing, and Darwin speculated on their origin and function. The subject is important to us because the properties of cellular solids depend directly on the shape and structure of the cells. Our aim is to characterize their size, shape and topology: that is the connectivity of the cell walls and of the pore space, and the geometric classes into which they fall. (Gibson and Ashby 1999: 15)

Digital (left) and physical (right) models of five different honeycomb cell morphologies that were produced during the development process of the honeycomb-deriving algorithm. MA Dissertation of Andrew Kudless, October 2004.

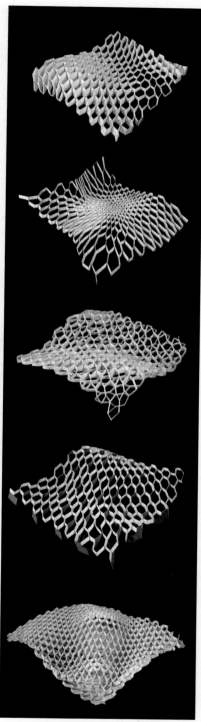

9.3

Physical model of a cylindrical arrangement of a differentiated honeycomb morphology. MA Dissertation of Andrew Kudless, October 2004.

In the most basic definition cellular solids can be described as assemblies of cells. Gibson and Ashby describe cellular solids as being made up of an interconnected network of solid struts or faces. These struts or faces are understood as the edges and faces of cells. A simple cellular solid is a two-dimensional array of packed polygons filling a plane. These cell assemblies very much resemble the hexagonal cell patterns produced by bees. Thus Gibson and Ashby call such two dimensional cellular solids *honeycombs*, whereas they refer to the more common, three dimensional packing of polyhedral cells as *foams*.

The MA dissertation of Andrew Kudless focused on the development of cellular solids systems. The research aimed at providing an architecture-specific background to the geometric, mechanical, and morphological properties and processes of honeycomb cellular solids with the ambition of developing a novel honeycomb structure made from readily available stock material, in which each cell can be different in size, shape and orientation. Owing to manufacturing constraints, up to now any industrial application of honeycomb systems required a regular cell pattern. The ability to differentiate the honeycomb morphology brings it much closer to the remarkable versatility found in natural systems, in which irregularity is the key to functional integration and adaptation while regularity is just a highly unlikely anomaly.

> Cells come in many shapes and sizes. Two-dimensional arrays (honeycombs), if regular, are assemblies of triangles, squares or hexagons. Many man-made honeycombs, and some naturally occurring ones, are regular; but in nature there are frequent deviations from regularity caused by the way in which the individual cells nucleate and grow, and the rearrangements which take place when they impinge.
> (Gibson and Ashby 1999: 49)

As a consequence this research is based on the hypothesis that a differentiated honeycomb cellular solid provides the material and technological innovation required for a higher-level integration of multiple-performance criteria as observed in natural cellular solid systems. The integration of form, growth and behaviour exemplified in natural cellular solids is remarkable. However, for architects to exploit this level of integration new design and production methods need to be developed. Hence the first critical task was abstracting the geometric and material properties of cellular solids into industrial manufacturing logics. As a starting point for this development, existing man-made cellular solids and the related fabrication processes were studied. One of the most widely used industrial cellular solids is honeycomb sandwich panels. They are used in the aerospace industry, where high strength to weight ratio is of critical importance, but also in architecture, for example as the core of facade panels or lightweight wall partitions. Because of the fabrication processes of these panels, they have relatively stringent constraints relating to the amount and type of curvature that can be achieved. Furthermore, the amount of variability in cell sizes, depth and orientation across any one panel is limited, producing a relatively homogeneous performance capacity across the entire system despite potentially heterogeneous requirements. Through the investigation of design and production processes not normally associated with honeycomb structures, it became possible to expand the amount of morphological differentiation and related performance capacity.

The manufacturing approach developed in this research combines three industrially common, yet usually unrelated, techniques to form hybrid production logics. The first addresses the cutting of non-uniform strips that form the cell walls of the honeycomb in their final folded state. Large-scale CNC laser or plasma cutting machines can be used for the production of irregular strips. They are then folded with braking machines. If these production logics become an integral part of a computational form-generation process, the assembled honeycomb can expose a greatly increased range of properties as compared to standard honeycomb systems that are fixed to one global cell size and only a limited range of curvature. The

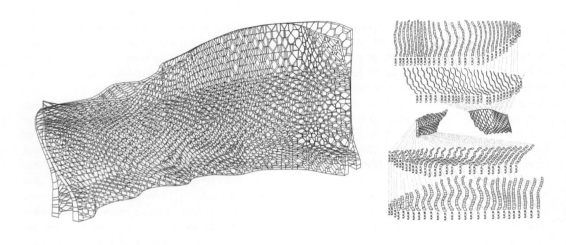

9.4

Exploded axonometric view of the honeycomb morphology prototype showing the double-layered structure and a detailed view of the folded strips from which one construction module is made. MA Dissertation of Andrew Kudless, October 2004.

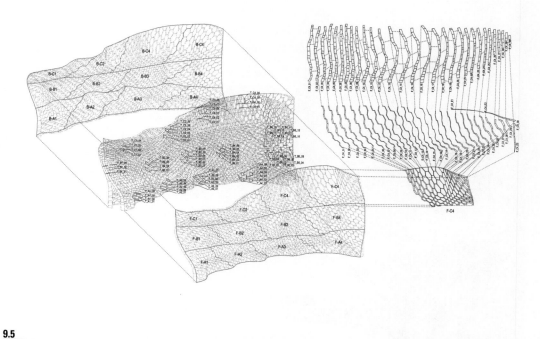

9.5

Digital model of the double-layered honeycomb cell structure constructed as the EmTech End of Year Installation 2004. The illustration shows the three-dimensional model (left) and the unfolded cut patterns of the individual strips (right). MA Dissertation of Andrew Kudless, October 2004.

9.6 (left)

Assembly process of the full scale prototype built up of modules each consisting of a number of differentiated honeycomb cells. MA Dissertation of Andrew Kudless, October 2004; EmTech End of Year Installation 2004.

9.7 (opposite)

Photograph of the double-layered honeycomb cell structure constructed as the EmTech End of Year Installation 2004.

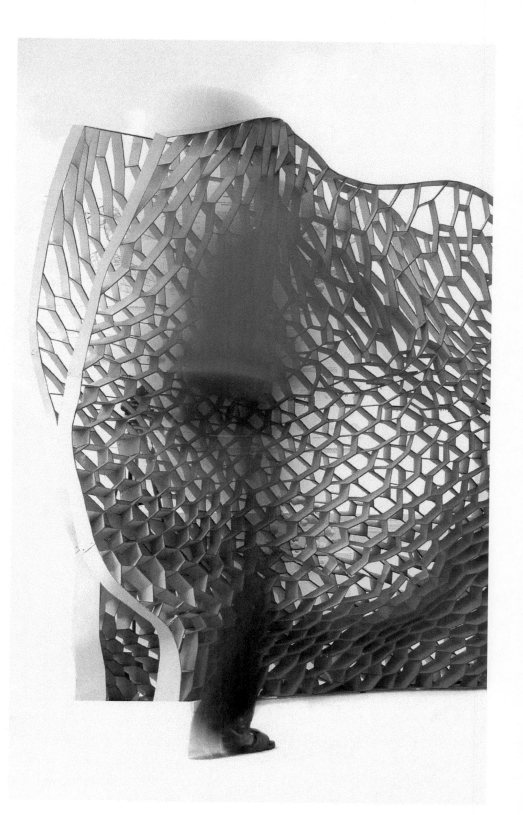

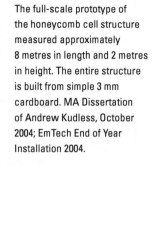

9.8

The full-scale prototype of the honeycomb cell structure measured approximately 8 metres in length and 2 metres in height. The entire structure is built from simple 3 mm cardboard. MA Dissertation of Andrew Kudless, October 2004; EmTech End of Year Installation 2004.

development of a computational tool capable of unfolding a high degree of morphological differentiation while remaining within the constraint space defined by the production methods to be used required the consideration of three critical aspects.

First, all generated cells need to remain hexagonal and tangential with the adjacent cell walls in order to ensure topological continuity. The twist resulting from the deviating angles of the fold lines normal to an underlying guide surface needs to remain within limits given by the twisting capacity of the material to be used. In this research a large number of experiments were conducted for testing the limits of local curvature and its effect on cell wall twisting on various physical models. Second, as all the folded material strips, of which the overall system consists, are cut from planar sheet material, the computational generation of elements needed to be linked to the constraints of the related production technique, namely two-dimensional cutting of limited size, and the specific material properties, for example the folding behaviour. For this project, the parameters of the laser cutter were explored to provide an alternative system-specific way to quickly fold cardboard strips. Usually the material is scored on the side opposite the direction of a fold to facilitate the fold. A variation of the speed and power settings of the laser cutter would easily achieve such scores. However, for the production of this system scores were needed on both sides to allow the strips to be folded in both directions. Thus the third variable, frequency, in laser-cutting machines was used produce a perforated fold line. Varying the frequency, which is the number of pulses of light that penetrate the material per inch (ppi), enables specifically perforated fold lines. The third important point is the anticipation of required assembly logistics through labelling all elements and inherently defining the construction sequence by the uniqueness of each pair of matching cell walls.

Based on these aspects, a honeycomb-deriving algorithm was developed in constant feedback with additional series of physical tests. The resultant computational generation process comprises the following sequence. In order to define the eventual vertices of the honeycomb strips, points are digitally mapped across a surface that is defined by the designer and remains open to geometric manipulations. The parametrically defined correlation of point distribution and geometric surface characteristics can also be altered. By connecting the distributed points, an algorithmic procedure derives the required folded strip lines. Looping this algorithm across all points then forms the honeycomb mesh, and this procedure is repeated across an offset point distribution to generate a system wireframe model. Honeycomb structures are usually prone to deformation under coplanar shear stresses. That is why most industrial applications of honeycomb structures rely on external skins. In order to add considerable structural capacity, particularly in terms of shearing, a second layer of honeycomb cells is generated in such a way that it is generally aligned in the opposite direction to the first layer; yet, it provides shared cell walls at every second interval. All defined honeycomb strips are automatically unfolded, labelled and nested in a subsequent step in order to prepare for production.

This integral form-generation and fabrication process derives a double-layer honeycomb system in which each cell can be unique in shape, size and depth, allowing for changing cell densities and a large range of irregularly curved global geometries. The resultant differentiation in the honeycomb has considerable performance consequences, as the system now carries the capacity for adaptation to specific structural, environmental and other forces not only within the overall system, but locally across different sub-locations of varying cell size, depth and orientation. Embedding the possibilities and constraints of material and production technology of man-made cellular solids, the form-generation technique and its parametric definition becomes per se the main interface of negotiating multiple performance criteria.

The combined MSc research of Amin Sadeghy and MArch research of Mehran Gharleghi aimed for a similar level of functional integration through morphological differentiation. In addition, they aimed for including

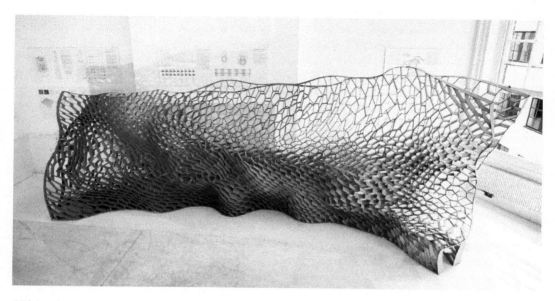

9.9 (above)

Photograph showing the algorithmically derived honeycomb prototype in which each cell is unique in shape, size and depth allowing for changing cell densities and double-curved global geometry. MA Dissertation of Andrew Kudless, October 2004; EmTech End of Year Installation 2004.

actively responsive elements within a system of pneumatic cells that form a multi-performative, self-regulating envelope. A large number of initial tests were conducted physically and digitally in order to develop a basic cell type consisting of two main elements. The first element consists of four cone-shaped pneumatic bodies that have one common centre. These elements are assembled by creating a large triangular seam at the top point where four of the elements meet and linear seam lines where the truncated cones touch. The resultant, structurally stable component has four openings, into which a second element type is mounted: a double cone pneu that can swivel around its central axis in order to close or open the component's surface. The rotating movement is actuated by the contraction and expansion of pneumatic muscles triggered by internal pressure changes. For example, exposure to direct sunlight may increase the internal pressure exerted on the membrane of the components. Once this pressure change is detected by a pressure-sensitive valve, the local air management units open a pressure-release valve that actuates the pneumatic muscle and the component locally opens. Both the feasibility of construction and the system's structural capacity as well as the functionality of these responsive elements were tested in a large number of computationally derived and physically fabricated test models. In addition, a functional full-scale prototype of the system was constructed by an expert manufacturer for non-standard pneumatic structures.

The system's inherent capacity of adapting both the static overall component configuration and the responsive field of local elements to specific environmental influences was further developed through the prototypical exploration of a responsive pneumatic envelope situated on a site in Iran. Set within the harsh climate of an arid region, the project attempts to modulate the interior climate by controlling solar penetration and employing natural ventilation as a means of passive cooling. Taking macro- and micro-climatic features of the chosen site into consideration, the proposal projects the system spanning between existing buildings. As a responsive skin, the system provides a climatic envelope for a large courtyard otherwise fully exposed to the harsh outside climate. The envelope's global morphology is derived through a process of negotiating multiple performance criteria in direct relation to the system's material properties and capabilities. The critical criteria belong to the following four categories: [i] spatial quality and height limits; [ii] assembly and manufacturing constraints that had to be coordinated with the complicated boundary condition and the isoparametric-curve-based ordering system of the building envelope; [iii] structural performance and load-bearing capacity in terms of self-weight but also wind loads; [iv] environmental modulation, with a particular emphasis on enabling strategic cross ventilation during different seasons and different times of the day. Another important environmental aspect is the regulation of direct sunlight and shading.

All four criteria informed an iterative computational form-generation process based on continual feedback with digital simulation and analysis tools. For example, solar analysis enabled the digital simulation of patterns of varying sun exposure over the day and for different seasons. This enabled a highly specific articulation of the openings in relation to their individual orientation towards the sun and potential self-shading as well as direct light transmission through the system. Shading plays a significant role in this prototypical proposal. For the pneumatic system, two ways of modulating the transmission of sunlight were developed. The first strategy utilises the fact that any pneumatic structure requires constant air supply owing to diffusion on the molecular level as well as manufacturing deficiencies. Based on local sensors measuring the sunlight intensity, smoke can be added to the air supply of each pneu, which changes the affected area from transparent to translucent. While this increases the ratio of indirect light considerably, the openings would still allow direct sunlight to enter the building. Thus a self-shading strategy for the opening areas was developed. Through a series of digital experiments, the shading behaviour of the components was investigated and, through a limited number of geometrical manipulations, for example height and radii

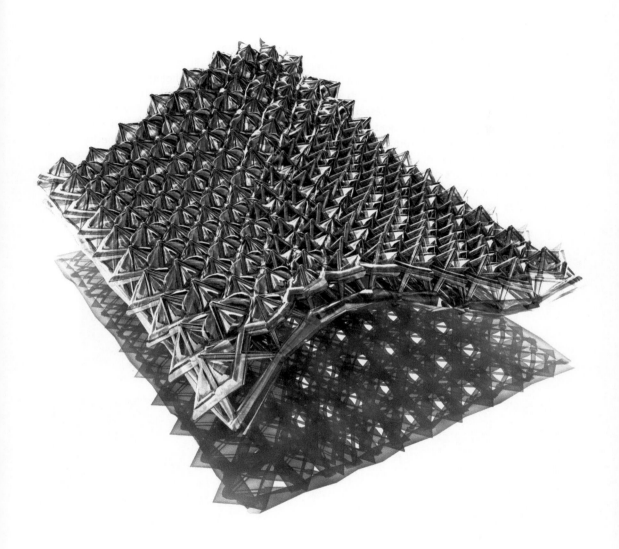

9.10

Digital model of a pneumatic component system indicating the differentiated articulation and related shadow patterns.
MSc Dissertation of Amin Sadeghy, October 2008; MArch Dissertation of Mehran Gharleghi, February 2009.

variations, the elements were articulated in such a way that the opening areas are shaded during the critical times of the day.

The resultant data provided a first input for the development of a site-specific envelope articulation. This was further informed by structural analysis and the analysis of the enclosure's thermodynamic behaviour, resulting from temperature and thus pressure differences, as well as the interaction with the outside wind. With regard to the latter, a number of experiments indicated that the initial global morphology would suffer from a lack of cross ventilation during specific times of the day, leading to a lack of fresh air within the envelope. Based on this data, which included both detailed local analysis of components in different states of closure and simulations on the scale of the entire structure, the system's morphology was further modified in a number of additional form-generation cycles using cellular automata algorithms.

The continued development of the envelope's morphology resulted in considerable cross ventilation throughout the day. In addition, the solar gain during peak periods in summer time was reduced by evolving a surface geometry with a high degree of self-shading. Global shading analyses revealed that the majority of the surface area, in fact more than 80 per cent, is shaded during the most critical days in summer.

Both projects demonstrate the remarkable level of functional integration facilitated by the high level of differentiation possible in cellular structures. Morphological changes to cell elements that are based on the same underlying dataset, including the key material, geometric- and manufacturing-related constraints, enable a high level of integral performance. Further research on such pluripotent cellular configurations seems to be most promising for the future.

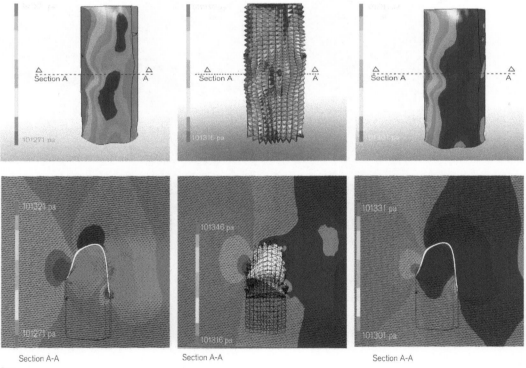

9.11

Computational fluid dynamics analysis of the pneumatic component system's application as an adaptable roof structure between existing buildings demonstrating the system's capacity to modulate local airflow. MArch Dissertation of Mehran Gharleghi, February 2009.

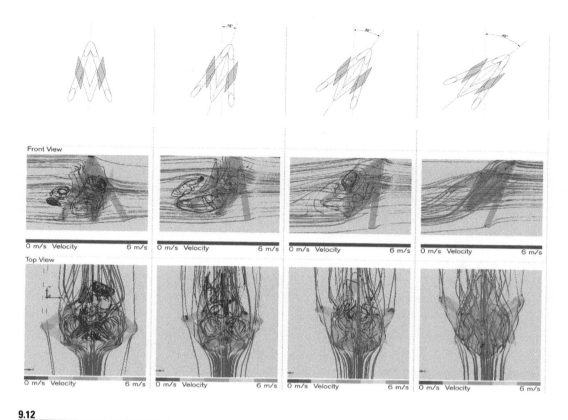

9.12

Computational fluid dynamics analysis of the changing modulation of airflow in different opening states of the adaptable pneumatic component. MArch Dissertation of Mehran Gharleghi, February 2009.

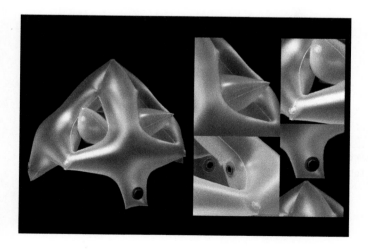

9.13

Photograph showing one full-scale pneumatic component with four adaptable openings (left) and close-up photographs of the prototype's details including openings, seams, joints and valves. MSc Dissertation of Amin Sadeghy, October 2008; MArch Dissertation of Mehran Gharleghi, February 2009.

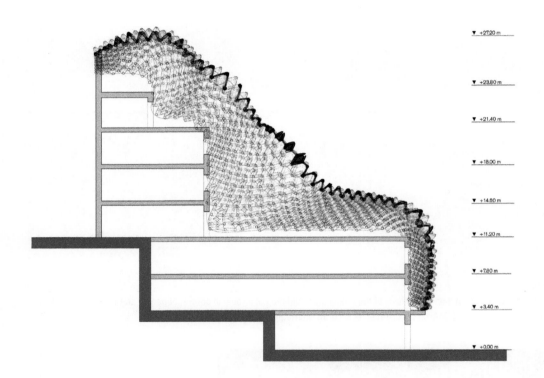

▼ +27.20 m

▼ +23.80 m

▼ +21.40 m

▼ +18.00 m

▼ +14.60 m

▼ +11.20 m

▼ +7.80 m

▼ +3.40 m

▼ +0.00 m

9.14

Section of the pneumatic component system's application covering the terraced courtyard between existing buildings.
MArch Dissertation of Mehran Gharleghi, February 2009.

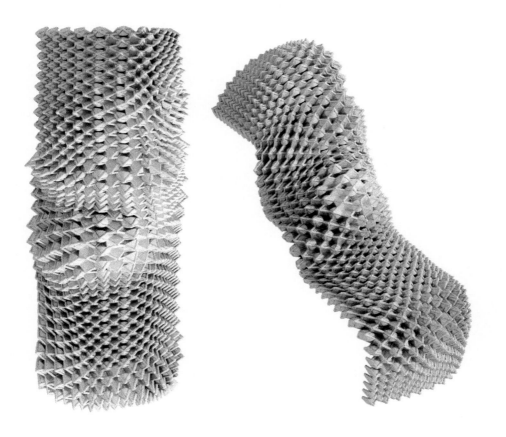

9.15

Rendering of the differentiated articulation of the pneumatic component system derived through the integration of multiple design criteria including ventilation, shading and structure. MArch Dissertation of Mehran Gharleghi, February 2009.

Chapter 10
Mass components

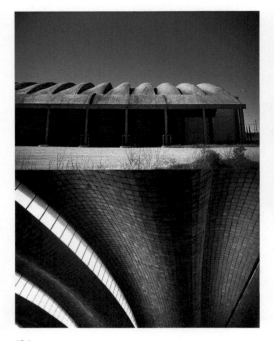

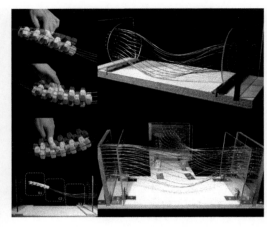

10.1

The ADF Wool Warehouse in Juanicó (Uruguay, 1992–94) designed by Eladio Dieste displays one of his key inventions: the Gaussian vaults. The interior view (bottom) demonstrates how double-curved surfaces may be used to modulate light conditions inside of the built volume. Photo credit: Defne Sunguroğlu.

10.2

Initial physical modelling studies served to deduce the behaviour of the combination of bending rods and bricks and the possibility of self-stabilisation of such a system. In addition, the parameterisation of the slender bending rods under torsional buckling was worked out. MSc Dissertation of Defne Sunguroğlu , October 2007.

The dimensions of bricks as a building element related from their first use until today to the size and weight that can be moved by the bricklayer with one hand while the other hand remains free to use tools, such as the trowel, thus enabling feasible and fast ways of construction. Hence bricks are one of the oldest quasi standardised building elements known to man. They have been used since circa 7,500 BC. Evidence of this was found in the Neolithic town of Çayönü in south-eastern Anatolia, and also in Jericho in Palestine and Catal Hüyük in Western Turkey. The latter is thought to have had up to 8,000 inhabitants. These Neolithic settlements provided a fertile context for the development of town planning, architecture, agriculture, technology and religion (Gates 2003). Charles Gates wrote with regard to the use of brick in Jericho during the Pre-Pottery Neolithic phases A and B, circa 8,500 to 6,000 BC:

Spread over an area of ca. 4ha, the PPNA settlement has yielded both houses and a fortification wall. The houses are round, and made of sun-dried mud bricks with a distinctive rounded top ('hog backed', or 'plano-convex') ... Jericho in the subsequent PPNB featured new architectural forms, possible indicators of social changes. House builders abandoned the round house in favour of the rectangular rooms arranged around a central courtyard. Construction used a different form of air-dried mud brick: 'cigar-shaped' bricks with finger impressions across the top to key in the mud mortar. (Gates 2003: 18–19)

Early bricks were hand-formed and sun-dried. Fired bricks only began to emerge circa 3,000 BC in the Middle East, when it was discovered that firing bricks can improve on a variety of characteristics, such as hardening and an increase in mechanical strength, as well as making bricks moisture-proof, thus making it possible to construct with bricks in much harsher climates. The particular ability of bricks to store thermal energy, given their considerable mass, could be utilised to modulate the interior of buildings, with the brick releasing the stored thermal energy during the night.

Bricks became widely used in ancient Egypt, the Indus Valley and also Rome. The Romans introduced the use of bricks to large parts of the Roman Empire, because of the use by the Roman legions of mobile kilns for firing bricks. In consequence, it was possible to build a much greater number of permanent lasting

constructions everywhere and to accelerate the development of large engineering constructions, such as aqueducts, cisterns and wide-span arches, enabling a feasible and far-reaching expansion of architectural possibilities.

It is not possible to separate the history of the brick from the history of mortar. The improvement of the latter made possible radical innovation in the field of brick construction. Brick can, of course, be laid dry, but in order to accomplish improved structural performance bricks need to be bonded to one another through the use of mortar, which also serves to compensate for tolerances in brick dimensions resulting from moisture loss in the firing process. While different types of mortar were used by the ancient Egyptians, Mesopotamians and Romans, it was the development of so-called Portland cement as one of the main constituents of mortar that led to new possibilities in brick construction.

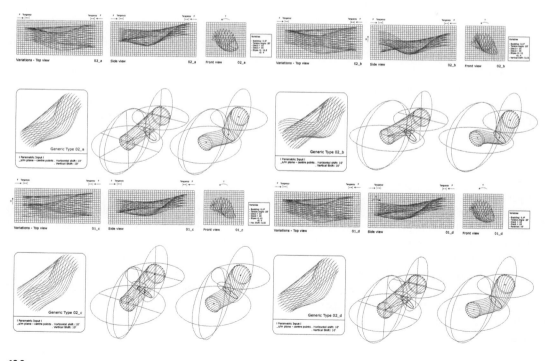

10.3

Parametric definition and digital modelling of the slender rods in different torsional buckling configurations. MSc Dissertation of Defne Sunguroğlu, October 2007.

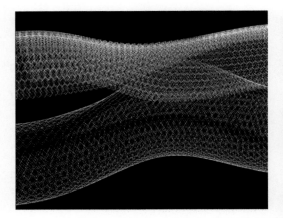

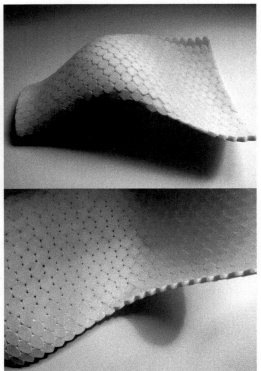

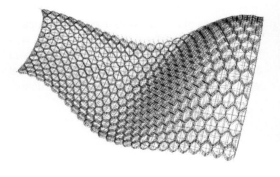

10.4

Parametrically defined digital model of one specific double-curved surface configuration, resulting from the interaction of bending rods and bricks. MSc Dissertation of Defne Sunguroğlu, October 2007.

10.5

Rapid prototype model of one specific double-curved surface configuration: the representational model serves to check the correct geometric definition of all elements. MSc Dissertation of Defne Sunguroğlu, October 2007.

This significant development commenced in the 1820s with the work of Joseph Aspdin utilising hydraulic limes for the production of cement. It was later completed by his son, William Aspdin, who is credited with the invention of Portland cement. The mortar made with this type of cement displayed two characteristics that were of major advantage: high fire resistance and a much reduced setting time, leading to high structural strength in a short time span. These possibilities were soon realised by the Catalan architect Rafael Guastavino (1842–1908), a contemporary of Antoni Gaudí. Guastavino developed the traditional principle of low-arch Catalan vaults into a new method of construction with layered ceramic tiles bound with mortar, the

so-called 'Gustavino tile' or 'Tile Arch System', patented in 1885.

Remarkably, exposed brickwork even survived the whims of Modernism. Ludwig Mies van der Rohe used bricks extensively, praising the simplicity of the brick that enabled a great wealth of expression, while highlighting the discipline that is necessary to master the material. A major development with regard to the use of bricks can be attributed to the work of Eladio Dieste (1917–2000), the Uruguayan architect and engineer, who stated that brick 'is a material with unlimited possibilities completely ignored by modern technology' (Dieste 1997). Dieste combined the use of brick with reinforcing and pre-stressing methods imported from concrete construction. Besides his daring cantilevering barrel vaults and free-standing arches, it is his Gaussian vaults that are remarkable and of importance to the research described below. These Gaussian vaults are shells made of only one layer of brick. They utilise a catenary arch in a double-curved arrangement that resists buckling behaviour, based on the careful geometric definition of the vault.

Dieste posited the importance of geometric articulation of these structures as follows:

> The resistant virtues of the structure that we make depend on their form; it is through their form that they are stable and not because of an awkward accumulation of materials. There is nothing more noble and elegant from an intellectual viewpoint than this; resistance through form.   (Dieste 1997)

Dieste's barrel vaults deploy reinforcement and pre-stressing methods. The cross section works in compression with pre-stressing cables running outside the brick surface from one side of the cross section to the other, fixing the distance between the two sides. The free-standing vaults, too, are reinforced and pre-stressed, and deploy arch action in the cross section and pre-stressing within the shell, using a steel mesh inside a layer of concrete sprayed on the outside of the surface. The steel mesh helps avoid flexural tensile stresses in the longitudinal direction. The aforementioned Gaussian vaults develop this relation between form action, reinforcement and pre-stressing further.

Used in this way, the combined formal and structural repertoire of bricks is far from exhausted. This becomes even more interesting if one returns to the question of the environmental modulation capacity of bricks. The utilisation of their thermal mass has been explored since the early days of the use of brick. To this was added the use of domes in the hot climate of the Middle East for the sake of self-shading to reduce thermal impact. Likewise,

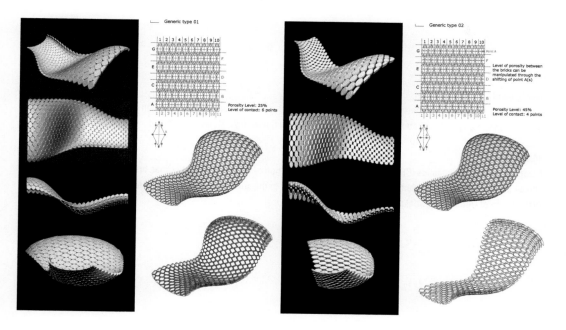

10.6

Parametric variations of brick and opening dimensions of one specific double-curved surface configuration. MSc Dissertation of Defne Sunguroğlu, October 2007.

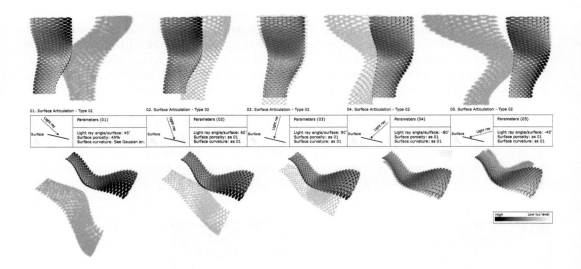

01. Surface Articulation - Type 02   02. Surface Articulation - Type 02   03. Surface Articulation - Type 02   04. Surface Articulation - Type 02   05. Surface Articulation - Type 02

Light ray	Parameters (01)
Surface	Light ray angle/surface: 45°
	Surface porosity: 45%
	Surface curvature: See Gausian an.

Light ray	Parameters (02)
Surface	Light ray angle/surface: 60°
	Surface porosity: as 01
	Surface curvature: as 01

Light ray	Parameters (03)
Surface	Light ray angle/surface: 90°
	Surface porosity: as 01
	Surface curvature: as 01

Light ray	Parameters (04)
Surface	Light ray angle/surface: -50°
	Surface porosity: as 01
	Surface curvature: as 01

Light ray	Parameters (05)
Surface	Light ray angle/surface: -45°
	Surface porosity: as 01
	Surface curvature: as 01

High   Low lux level

10.7 (above)
Self-shading and shading pattern analysis of one specific double-curved surface configuration at five different times on 21 June relative to a specific location. MSc Dissertation of Defne Sunguroğlu, October 2007.

10.8 (opposite)
Computational fluid dynamics (CFD) analysis of a selected portion of a double-curved porous brick surface. The analysis shows airflow conditions resulting from airflow perpendicular to the surface and the resultant turbulent flow. MSc Dissertation of Defne Sunguroğlu, October 2007.

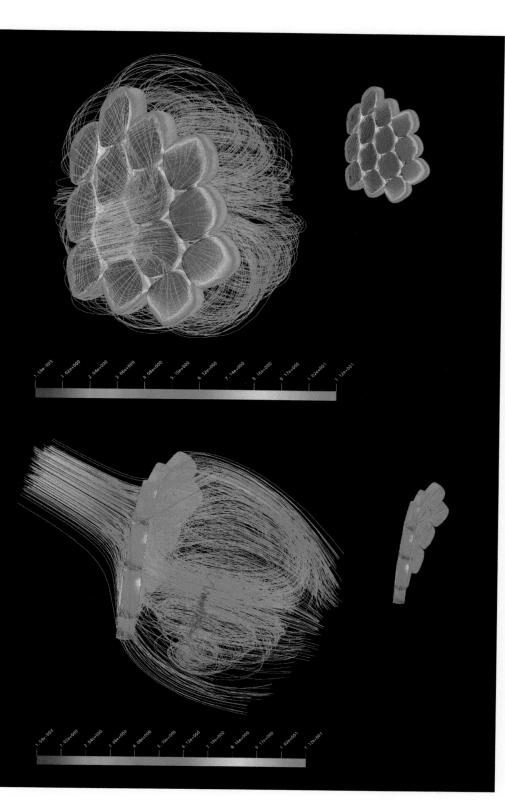

the inverse is possible: the mass can be oriented towards the sun path in such a manner that more surface area is exposed and more thermal energy can be collected. Moreover, constructing screen walls with openings, such as the Islamic *mashrabīyas*, *shanashils*, or *jalis*, or the more contemporary Brazilian *Cobogós*, enables an integral combination of functions. Hassan Fathy posited:

> The mashrabīya has five functions. Different patterns have been developed to satisfy a variety of conditions that require emphasis on one or more of these functions. These functions involve: (1) controlling the passage of light, (2) controlling airflow, (3) reducing the temperature of the air current, (4) increasing the humidity of the air current, and (5) ensuring privacy. Each mashrabīya design is selected to fulfil several or all of these functions. In the design, it is the sizes of the interstices (spaces between adjacent balusters) and the diameter of the baluster that are adjusted.   (Fathy 1986: 47)

Fathy continued to elaborate these functions in detail. Interestingly, this portrays a multifunctional architectural devise that is perfectly suited for associative modelling and environmental analysis. The question is then how to bring all the capacities of brick together into an integral systematic approach.

In her MSc dissertation, Defne Sunguroğlu pursued exactly this question. Her work embraces Eladio Dieste's recognition of the importance of geometry as the means to provide structural capacity, while extending this interest by a crucial question: is it possible to further elaborate the scope of formal articulation of brick systems, while informing the design process by an integral relation between structural and environmental performance criteria? The research focused initially on structural means to elaborate the geometric repertoire of brick systems. The use of mortar was relinquished and different means of pre-stressing were explored to accomplish double-curved

brick surfaces. These included utilising bending rods to instrumentalise torsional buckling as a means of pre-stressing synclastic brick surfaces – an approach thus far considered a no-go area in structural engineering – as well as using cable nets as a means of pre-stressing anticlastic, and more specifically hyperbolic paraboloid, brick surfaces. The work commenced with a large number of scaled physical models to investigate the complex interaction between the pre-stressing system and the bricks as a stabilising compression system. This needed to be considered in a variety of scales ranging from the local interaction from brick to brick and rod or cable to brick, to neighbourhoods of components and perimeter behaviour, to the assessment of an overall system. Based on these studies, computational modelling in an associative modelling environment commenced. The latter served multiple purposes. One purpose was to examine different brick geometries and the resulting interaction between bricks within the system, as well as the formal possibilities and manufacturing processes and tolerances that ensued from this. Another purpose was to accelerate the modification of system arrangements to analyse environmental modulation capacities, investigating related airflow, self-shading and light penetration patterns. The arrangement of the bricks within the system was thus pursued in such a manner that openings are allowed between the bricks, without reducing the coherence of the structural system or its load-bearing capacity. This implied the modification of the brick geometry in such a way that sufficient contact area between the bricks exists, while sufficient opening sizes are also possible to facilitate an environmental exchange between both sides of a brick surface, and when used as an envelope between an inside and an outside.

An extensive study of the environmental performance range of different system configurations through computer fluid dynamics simulation and analysis made it possible to relate the articulation and orientation of the system in relation to the context-specific, prevailing wind directions as well as the direction and angle of the sun path. The analysis of the performative capacity of the differentiated brick surface

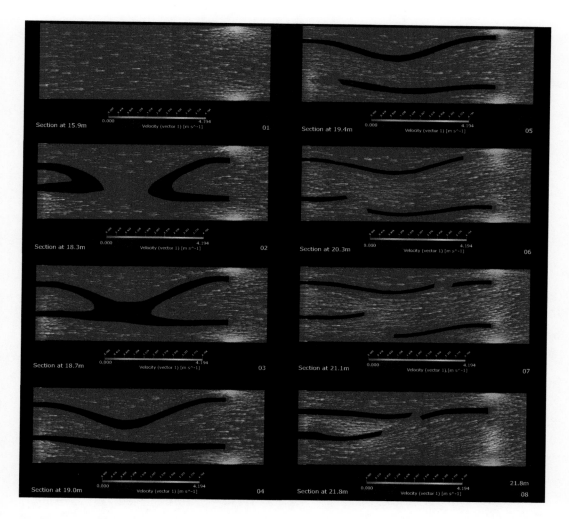

10.9

Computational fluid dynamics (CFD) analysis of airflow in various sections of a complex double-curved brick surface. The analysis investigates the overall system with regard to accelerating and decelerating airflow. MSc Dissertation of Defne Sunguroğlu, October 2007.

10.10

Rapid prototype model of a hyperbolic-paraboloid surface that results from a combination of a cable net with bricks as compressive elements. MSc Dissertation of Defne Sunguroğlu, October 2007.

was conducted both on the local scale of a small region of individual bricks and on the larger scale of entire surface assemblies. (Compare with Yukio Minobe's work discussed in Chapter 3.)

One difficulty that presented itself with regard to this research is that developing the mathematics to calculate the structural performance of a system of this degree of complexity seems to be dependent on empirical data gained from a full-scale construction. For the latter, however, it is important to get the dimensions of the elements, bricks and rods or cables, as well as perimeter details, edge cables and anchors, correctly calibrated. It is therefore necessary to develop a set of functional models that gradually increase in size in order to establish criteria for the assessment of the dimensions of the elements. The work thus far has progressed to the construction of a $1/10$ scale model. What must be considered here, however, is the manufacturing of the bricks. The degree of symmetry with a given configuration of a system determines the amount of repetition of brick geometries. The less symmetry there is, the more the system converges towards bricks all having individual shapes. For the construction of smaller-scale models this is less significant since rapid prototyping can be used as a means of producing the brick-like compression elements and the degree of variation of the elements can be resolved. At a larger scale, however, when the elements must converge onto the actual mass of bricks to be used, this presents a significant technical difficulty. This is added to by the fact that no mortar will be used, so that the system can remain adjustable in the construction process. This requires a significant reduction in tolerances of the brick dimensions resulting from the firing process. Defne Sunguroğlu has commenced PhD studies that focus on addressing and solving a variety of questions associated with the development of the system, including the manufacturing of highly varied brick geometries. Another area of research is the actual material make-up of the brick, deploying, for instance, fibre-reinforcement in case of a required higher stress-bearing capacity, or the introduction of a higher degree of porosity of the material to decrease weight and to alter the environmental performance range of the bricks. The amount, shape and orientation of the pores would also need to be examined with regard to the structural capacity of a brick.

While the production of bricks implies a rather high carbon footprint, the integral performance of a complex brick system, as outlined by this research, might suggest a great reduction of the carbon footprint of the built environment, with a system that is finely calibrated to the context and that fulfils a multitude of performance criteria in a passive manner. In any case, this research indicates that the Emergent Technologies and Design approach can serve the revision of everyday building materials, elements and processes. It will remain interesting to follow this line of research and the particular research project discussed above.

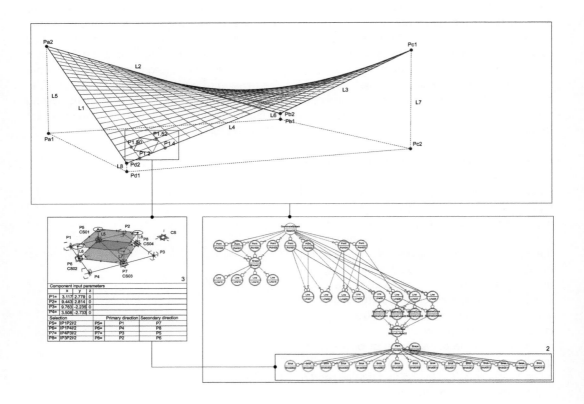

10.11

Associative logic of a hyperbolic-paraboloid arrangement: the digital model serves to determine the geometry of the bricks within a system with two-axial symmetry for the production of a $^1/_{10}$ model. MSc Dissertation of Defne Sunguroğlu, October 2007.

10.12

Setup for the construction of a ¹/₁₀ model of a hyperbolic-paraboloid surface arrangement, combining a cable net with bricks. MSc Dissertation of Defne Sunguroğlu, October 2007.

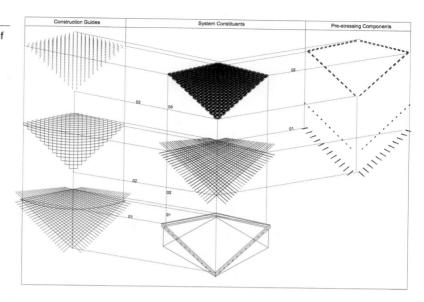

10.13

Geometric definition of the overall ¹/₁₀ model of a hyperbolic-paraboloid surface arrangement, and the geometric definition of the bricks relative to this setup. MSc Dissertation of Defne Sunguroğlu, October 2007.

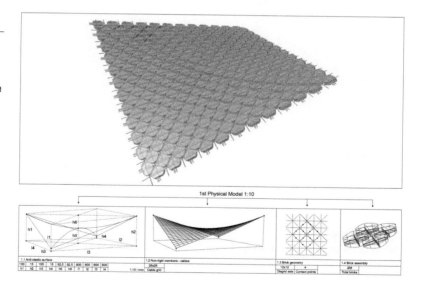

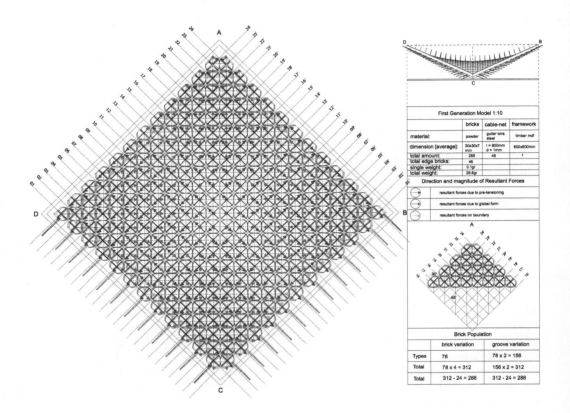

10.14 (above)

Specification of all elements of the ¹/₁₀ model of a hyperbolic-paraboloid surface arrangement, and a schematic elaboration of the interaction between the structural elements overlaid on the plan view. MSc Dissertation of Defne Sunguroğlu, October 2007.

10.15 (opposite)

Views of one of the two constructed ¹/₁₀ models. This model elaborates the interaction between cable-net and bricks, calibrating the stresses within the system. MSc Dissertation of Defne Sunguroğlu, October 2007.

Chapter 11
Casts

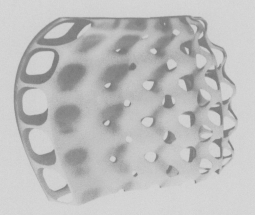

The research interest of Gabriel Sanchiz Garin's MSc dissertation (2007) originated in the context of Diploma Unit 4 at the Architectural Association, where the groundwork was laid. The inquiry started with a fascination with the research collaboration of the biologist Johann-Gerhard Helmcke and Frei Otto within the context of the Biology and Building workgroup that focused on, among other issues, the shells of diatoms and the skeletons of radiolaria. This interdisciplinary research was driven by an interest in lightweight natural structures and related autoformative processes in nature, based on the hypothesis that these offer direct potentials as analogous models for technical constructs and thus for architectural design.

Diatoms are unicellular or colonial algae. The cell is encased by a morphologically highly differentiated silicified cell wall. Radiolaria belong to marine planktonic protozoa and feature a chitinous capsule and siliceous porous spicules. These shells and skeletons form owing to a hardening at the periphery of cell walls or, as Helmcke and Otto put it, 'pneus'. Ulrich Kull described these processes as follows:

> Living organisms can produce such structures only when their cells secrete materials which can be deposited in a crystalline pattern … Simple multicellular animals are often soft constructions consisting of small numbers of rigid pneus; their stability is the result of a pneu-within-pneu structure known as hydroskeleton … Rigid pneu constructions can be found in animals that have a skeleton. If the outer, enveloping pneu is rigid, the animal has an exoskeleton such as, for example, the integument of an insect. If the rigid pneu lies within the animal, they form an endoskeleton such as the bone structure of vertebrates. Both endoskeletons and exoskeletons can be found in unicellular organisms such as radiolarians (endoskeleton), foraminifers, and diatoms (exoskeleton).
>
> (Kull 2009: 46–7)

The initial phase of the material system development focused on producing a skeletal framework articulated through the interstitial spaces left between pressurised pneus. Typically a first series of experiments explored ways of casting plaster between air-filled balloons to achieve the typical shape of the mineralised skeletons between pneus that occurs in the formation of radiolarian skeletons and the shells of diatoms. Based on different cushion arrangements four-, five- and six-armed cast configurations were produced and became the basic elements of the material system. Each of these elements is parametrically defined as the relation between pneu organisations and internal pressure by which aspects such as the volume, shape and thickness of each element can be varied.

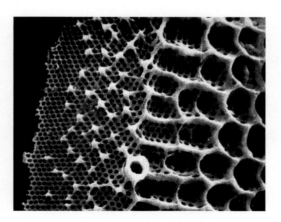

11.1

The microscopic photography shows a diatome structure as researched by Johann-Gerhard Helmcke and Frei Otto. Diatomes are unicellular or colonial algae with a highly differentiated cell wall impregnated with silica. The porous mass of the cell encasements of diatoms provides interesting principles for the development of differentiated, performative cast walls.

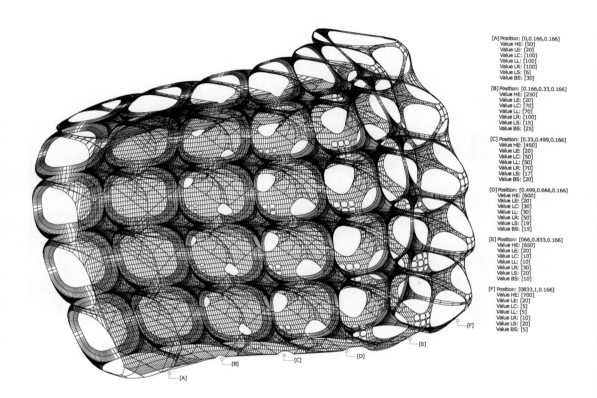

[A] Position: [0,0.166,0.166]
  Value HE: [50]
  Value LE: [20]
  Value LC: [100]
  Value LL: [100]
  Value LR: [100]
  Value LS: [6]
  Value BS: [30]

[B] Position: [0.166,0.33,0.166]
  Value HE: [250]
  Value LE: [20]
  Value LC: [70]
  Value LL: [70]
  Value LR: [100]
  Value LS: [15]
  Value BS: [25]

[C] Position: [0.33,0.499,0.166]
  Value HE: [450]
  Value LE: [20]
  Value LC: [50]
  Value LL: [50]
  Value LR: [70]
  Value LS: [17]
  Value BS: [20]

[D] Position: [0.499,0.666,0.166]
  Value HE: [600]
  Value LE: [20]
  Value LC: [30]
  Value LL: [30]
  Value LR: [50]
  Value LS: [19]
  Value BS: [15]

[E] Position: [066,0.833,0.166]
  Value HE: [650]
  Value LE: [20]
  Value LC: [10]
  Value LL: [10]
  Value LR: [30]
  Value LS: [20]
  Value BS: [10]

[F] Position: [0833,1,0.166]
  Value HE: [700]
  Value LE: [20]
  Value LC: [5]
  Value LL: [5]
  Value LR: [10]
  Value LS: [20]
  Value BS: [5]

11.2

The illustration shows the digital system definition based on manipulation-components constituted by the interaction of various pneumatic bodies within a cast system. A specific cast system morphology with varying degrees of porosity can be achieved through parametric changes to the component proliferation and associative adaptation to a mould's shape and curvature. Diploma Project of Gabriel Sanchiz Garin, AA Diploma Unit 4, Unit Masters: Michael Hensel and Achim Menges, 2006.

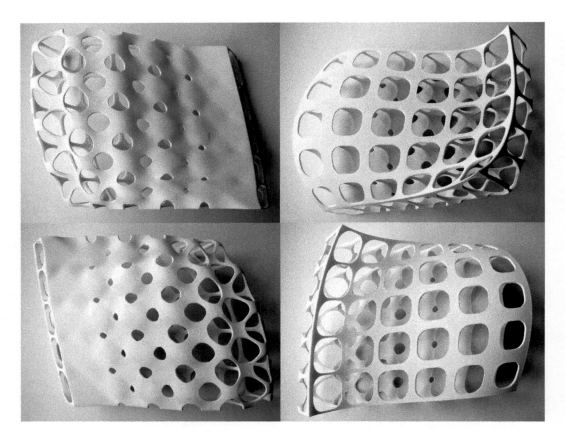

11.3

The four photographs show morphological study models produced with selective laser sintering rapid prototyping processes. Different morphologies can be derived through computational processes based on the findings of empirical tests investigating the skeletal framework articulated through the interstitial spaces left between compressed pneumatic containers. Diploma Project of Gabriel Sanchiz Garin, AA Diploma Unit 4, Unit Masters: Michael Hensel and Achim Menges, 2006.

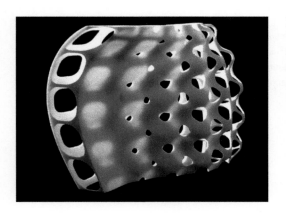

11.4

The photograph of a rapid prototype morphological test model shows the interstitial spaces and resulting porous structure inherent to the cast system. Diploma Project of Gabriel Sanchiz Garin, AA Diploma Unit 4, Unit Masters: Michael Hensel and Achim Menges 2006.

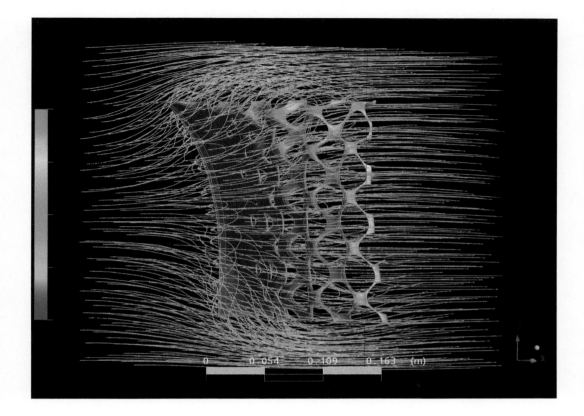

11.5

The computational fluid dynamics (CFD) analysis indicates the cast system's performative capacity to modulate airflow through regional and local porosity gradation. The influence of porosity on airflow along and across the system can be modulated through changes to the pneumatic cells' parametric setting. Diploma Project of Gabriel Sanchiz Garin, AA Diploma Unit 4, Unit Masters: Michael Hensel and Achim Menges, 2006.

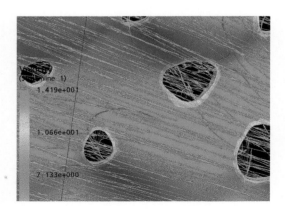

11.6

A local analysis of airflow patterns by means of computational fluid dynamics (CFD) enables the understanding of the system's morphology in relation to aerodynamic behaviour. The findings of the computational analysis informed the subsequent construction of a prototype. Diploma Project of Gabriel Sanchiz Garin, AA Diploma Unit 4, Unit Masters: Michael Hensel and Achim Menges, 2006.

11.7

A five-axis CNC machine was used to mill the macro formwork for casting a prototype structure from a solid high-density styrofoam block. The undulations on the mould's surface define the location of the pneumatic cells used in the casting process. Diploma Project of Gabriel Sanchiz Garin, AA Diploma Unit 4, Unit Masters: Michael Hensel and Achim Menges, 2006.

Based on this setup, a series of digital models of such systems were derived. Secondary and tertiary levels of articulation were developed using a series of meso- and micro-pneus to further subdivide the interstitial space between macro-pneumatic cushions. Another series of experiments focused on how it might be possible to gain porosity in the cast material itself by using wax pebbles that could be melted away.

A list of casting materials that feature different thermal characteristics was established. Physical experiments and digital analysis served to establish the possible range of light and airflow modulation relative to morphological features such as the size and density of pores and other characteristics of the material system.

Subsequently a range of manufacturing approaches were tested, resulting in the production of a full-scale prototypical portion of the material system that integrated computer-aided manufacturing processes and pneumatic form-finding as a construction method. A cast form was milled on a five-axis CNC machine from high-density polystyrene blocks, from which first a fibreglass form and later a form cast from plaster were produced. Air-pressured cushions were distributed into the form and inflated, and then concrete or other materials were cast into the interstitial spaces between the pneumatic units and the mould.

A second approach focused on strategising a mould that would respond to the casting process and would therefore deploy material self-organisation. After several experiments with fabric moulds, a rigid frame with an equally rigid back panel was made. The back panel supports an inflatable formwork, with pneus placed between two layers of rubber sheet. The concrete was then cast between the two layers of rubber sheet to fill the space between the pneus. An acrylic inlay in the frame allowed visual control of the casting process and the proper filling of the space between the pneus. The resulting cast is characterised by double-curvature, controlled porosity, and density and mass of the poured material. The result in this case is a network of close-packed spherical voids that are connected at their interface. This is due to the deformation of the touching area of the pneus, which flattens and results in a circular opening between the spherical voids. In this way porosity on a macro-level is accomplished so that an inside and an outside is not separated by the porous surface, but instead direct contact between the inside and the outside is facilitated. This surface can absorb thermal energy and release it to the airflow between inside and outside enabled by the porosity, and the double-curvature can be utilised for thermal exposure or self-shading.

In a modified application, it is possible to articulate a poche wall with cavities that are neither connected with one another nor connect the two sides separated by the surface. This type of cavity wall can perform in similar ways to the one with the connective network of spherical voids while, however, not permitting direct ventilation. It is also possible to accomplish a gradient between the two types, which gradually changes from a connective network of spherical voids with inside–outside connectivity, via decreasing diameter of the circular connections towards a surface with disconnected pockets.

The already existing so-called 'bubble-deck' system utilises spherical pneus to accomplish lighter-weight cast concrete surfaces. SANAA's 2006 project for the School of Management

11.8

The photograph shows the setup of producing a full-scale prototype. The different pneumatic components were parametrically defined as the relation between pneu organisation and internal pressure by which aspects such as shape, volume and thickness of each element can be varied. Diploma Project of Gabriel Sanchiz Garin, AA Diploma Unit 4, Unit Masters: Michael Hensel and Achim Menges, 2006.

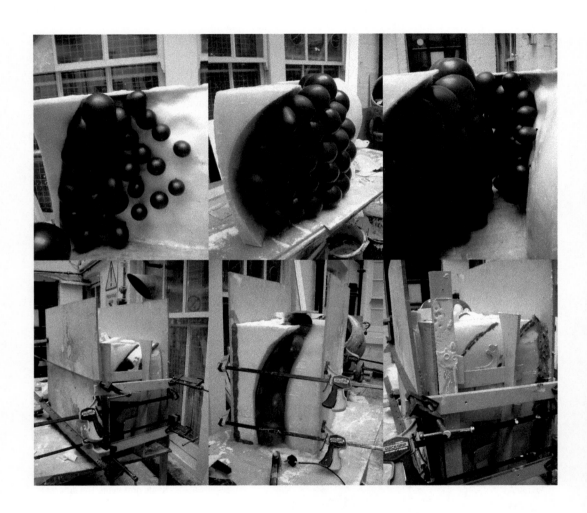

11.9

The two halves of the formwork, each equipped with an array of pneumatic components, are assembled to form the cavity space in which the system is cast. Diploma Project of Gabriel Sanchiz Garin, AA Diploma Unit 4, Unit Masters: Michael Hensel and Achim Menges, 2006.

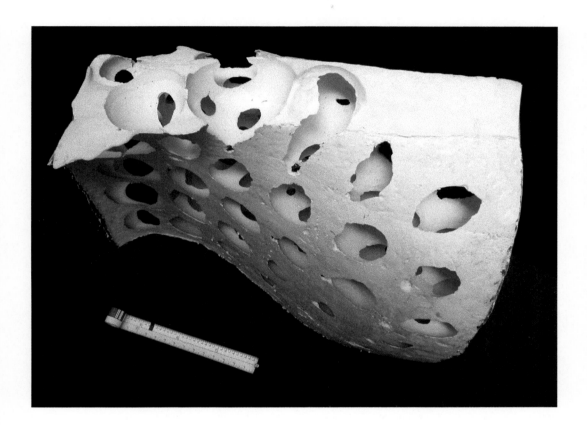

11.10

The photograph of the first full-scale prototype demonstrates the system's capacity to provide different degrees of porosity and a transition from a closed cavity cell configuration to an open, skeletal articulation. Diploma Project of Gabriel Sanchiz Garin, AA Diploma Unit 4, Unit Masters: Michael Hensel and Achim Menges, 2006.

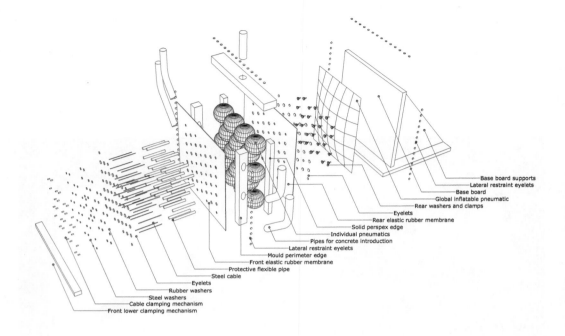

Base board supports
Lateral restraint eyelets
Base board
Global inflatable pneumatic
Rear washers and clamps
Eyelets
Rear elastic rubber membrane
Solid perspex edge
Individual pneumatics
Pipes for concrete introduction
Lateral restraint eyelets
Mould perimeter edge
Front elastic rubber membrane
Protective flexible pipe
Steel cable
Eyelets
Rubber washers
Steel washers
Cable clamping mechanism
Front lower clamping mechanism

11.11

Based on the findings of the first research phase, a second method for producing a cast system with varying porosity and density is developed. The illustration shows that this entailed changing from a CNC milled formwork to a formwork that acquires its specific shape through a larger pneumatic body included in the mould setup. MSc Dissertation of Gabriel Sanchiz Garin, October 2007.

and Design in Essen, Germany, is perhaps the most published architectural work to feature the bubble-deck system. In this case the main purpose of the system is, as mentioned, the improvement of structural performance through the reduction of weight. In contrast, Gabriel Sanchiz Garin's research foregrounds the relationship between mass and its selective removal towards an integral structural and environmental performance. The research was therefore taken forward by a speculative design for a double-layered shell structure cast over a pneumatic formwork. Both layers exhibit a varied porosity based on interconnected spherical void networks. Extensive computational fluid dynamics analysis served to investigate the airflow and exchange from the inside to the interstitial space between the two layers and the outside. Such simulations must take into consideration the global form of the shell and the

potentially varying distance between the layers and their thickness, as well as the size, density and distribution of the spherical void network.

This was simulated for airflow perpendicular as well as parallel to the double-layered shell. Since a small modification in connectivity can trigger rather dramatic changes in the airflow and exchange patterns, it was realised that extensive multi-level analysis must remain an integral part of the methodological setup of the form-finding and materialisation process. Further research needs to focus on the capacity for storing thermal energy, which can be highly varied by means of a non-uniform thickness of the material surface, as well as the effect of the removal of mass by means of the spherical void network. Overall, this will require a rather advanced level of thermodynamics analysis and multi-scalar computational fluid dynamics analysis. However, the obviously difficult empirical elaboration of this system to the extent that it can be varied in a rigorous instrumental manner and that the resulting conditions can be accomplished within selected ranges promises great potential for an environmentally heterogeneous modulation of space. The need for such heterogeneity was already recognised by Frei Otto:

> If we bear in mind the natural inequality of individuals and the different individual demands on the organic and inorganic environment caused by this inequality, it becomes clear that we will never succeed in finding those conditions which provide every human being with an optimum environment because 'some like it hot'.
>
> (Otto 1971: 27)

While this does not seem to be a surprisingly radical thought, it nevertheless runs entirely contrary to the standards of interior environment specifications on which contemporary practice operates. To continue lamenting this problem is ineffectual. Instead, energy might be invested to locate existing architectures and architectural elements that might shed light on a possible way forward. The above described research does this, commencing from a biological model and converging onto an architectural potential. Likewise, it may be possible to commence from a discussion of the perforated Islamic screen walls discussed in Chapter 3, 'Material systems and environmental dynamics feedback'. These are multi-performative systems with a distinct environmental and cultural relevance. Articulation as an ornamental

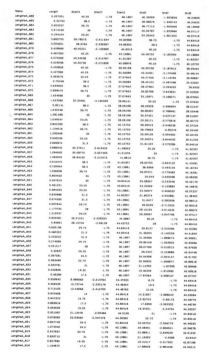

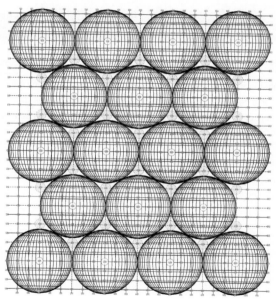

11.12

The definition of the system's shape is based on the parametric definition of system's variables such as the configuration, size and internal pressure of the pneumatic cells and the pneumatic formwork. The illustration shows the notation of the parametric information required for the fabrication process. MSc Dissertation of Gabriel Sanchiz Garin, October 2007.

11.13

The photographs show the setup for the production of a second full scale prototype based on the interaction of local pneumatic cells and the pneumatic formwork. The information required for the fabrication process is directly transferred from the computational definition. MSc Dissertation of Gabriel Sanchiz Garin, October 2007.

pattern and performative capacity are indivisible in these examples. However, this question warrants some analysis as to the range of environmental provisions offered by these screen walls, without relying on established and still relatively narrow so-called comfort ranges that do not truly operate on a paradigm of heterogeneity. If these screen walls were elaborated in two ways – first by utilising them as envelopes instead of localised panels, and second if the dimensions of the openings and balusters were to be varied more – would their articulation and performative potential be so different from the cast system elaborated above? The answer might be that they would not differ a great deal.

Hassan Fathy described part of the performative capacity of these screen walls, called 'mashrabīya', as follows:

> At eye level, the balusters of the *mashrabīya* are set close together with very small interstitial spacing both to intercept direct sunlight and to reduce dazzle of contrasting elements in the pattern. But to compensate for the accompanying dimming effect, the interstices are much larger in the upper part of the *mashrabīya* ... This arrangement permits reflected light to brighten the upper part of the room, while an overhang ... prevents direct sunlight from entering ... To provide airflow into a room, a *mashrabīya* with large interstices will ensure as much open area in the lattice as possible ... Where sunlight considerations require small interstices and thus sufficient airflow is not provided, an open, large interstice pattern can be used in the upper part of the *mashrabīya* near the overhang ... If this solution still does not provide sufficient air movement due to small interstices required to reduce the glare, the dimensions of the *mashrabīya* can be increased to cover any size opening, even to the point of filling up the entire façade of a room ... [and so on].
>
> (Fathy 1986: 47–8)

And so the question might arise as to whether the wheel is being reinvented here. There is of course an element of rediscovery. More important, however, is the realisation that there are many variables that can be activated in a complex parametrically defined system and that a system can be brought into contact with rather different context-specific environmental conditions and dynamics. Most significantly, contemporary computational methods and tools accelerate a rigorous systematic understanding and utilisation of the data gained from equally accelerated empirical studies. This implies that it does not take generations of people to develop a system small step by small step. Instead, skilled designers can undertake the development of multiple systems extensively and concurrently. At this point it is then crucial to shift the prevailing understanding of function as one-way causalities towards multiple concurrent performative capacities. Here biology comes back into the discussion, offering a new paradigm for the purpose at hand.

11.14 (above)

The full-scale prototype shows the interstitial spaces resulting from the distribution of interacting pneumatic cells. MSc Dissertation of Gabriel Sanchiz Garin, October 2007.

11.15 (opposite)

The digital analysis shows the local undulations in relation to the datum plane given by the mould frame and the elastic membrane in which the pneumatic cells are contained. MSc Dissertation of Gabriel Sanchiz Garin, October 2007.

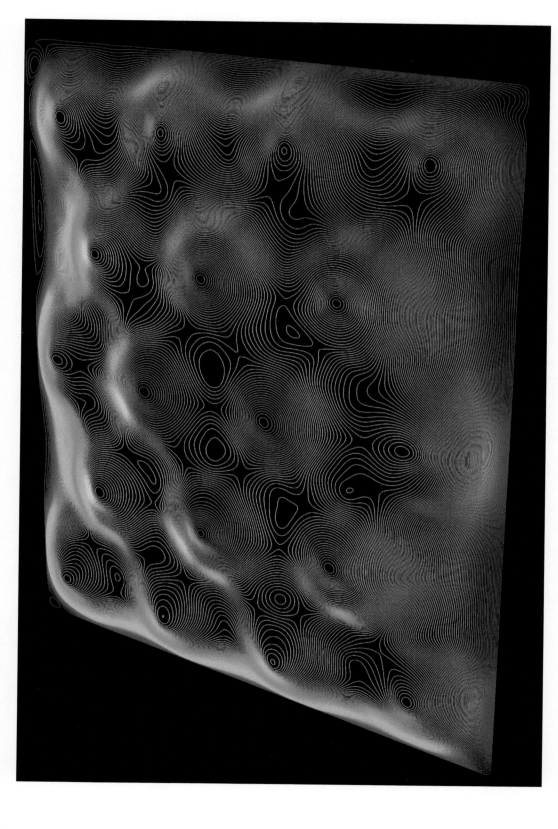

Chapter 12
Aggregates

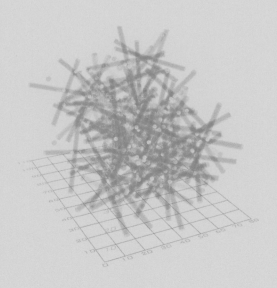

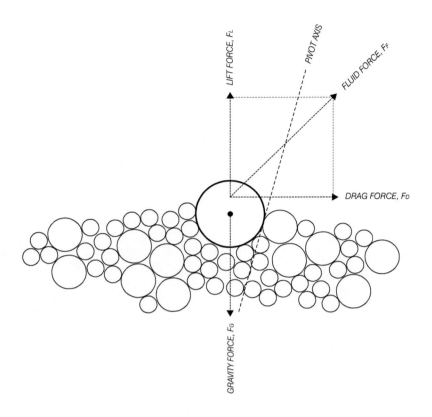

LIFT FORCE, F_L

PIVOT AXIS

FLUID FORCE, F_F

DRAG FORCE, F_D

GRAVITY FORCE, F_G

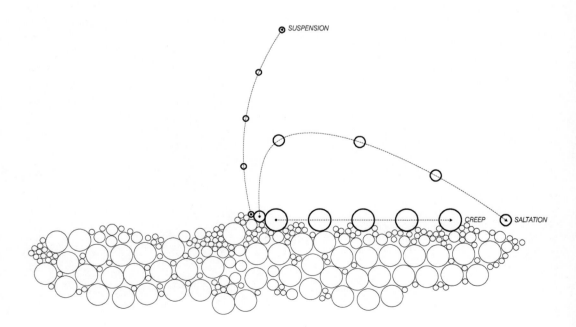

SUSPENSION

CREEP

SALTATION

Aggregates are loose agglomerations of particles or granules. These exist in great abundance in nature, such as sand for instance. In their bound form, granular materials constitute the largest amount in volume of construction material used today. Bound aggregates include, for example, cement and asphalt. However, granular materials in a loose unbound state are hardly ever deployed in architecture. Some exceptional examples include sand used in the bed of foundations of ancient Greek temples to reduce the impact of seismic movement, or as sound insulation in light timber ceilings or walls.

Granular materials belong to the so-called 'random heterogeneous materials'. Salvatore Torquato describes these as follows:

> In the most general sense, a *heterogeneous material* is one that is composed of domains of different materials (phases), such as a composite, or the same material in different states, such as a polycrystal ... [In] many instances the 'microscopic' length scale (e.g. the average domain size) is much larger than the molecular dimensions (so that the domains possess macroscopic properties) ... In such circumstances, the heterogeneous material can be viewed as a continuum on the microscopic scale, subject to classical analysis, and macroscopic or *effective* properties can be ascribed to it ... In many instances, the microstructures can be characterised only statistically, and therefore are referred to as *random heterogeneous materials*. (Torquato 2002: 1–3)

The discontinuity of granular materials and the resulting instability of aggregate formations – and, moreover, the insufficient understanding of their physics – seem to make them a rather unlikely candidate for exploration and use in architecture. As Philip Ball stated, 'only in recent years have scientists begun to appreciate that, to explain how granular media behave, they must invent new physics. Engineers have long developed rules of thumb for handling these materials, but physicists want general principles that are broadly applicable and that account for observations at a fundamental level' (Ball 1999: 199). Aggregates are therefore not located within the realm of biological inquiry but instead rooted within the domain of physics. They constitute one of the most exotic areas of inquiry described in this book, requiring a large amount of basic research before characteristics and properties may be utilised towards particular performative domains. Interestingly, aggregates display characteristics that make them an excellent area of study with regard to the Emergent Technologies and Design agenda: responsiveness to extrinsic stimuli and a resultant self-organisational behaviour, leading to a dynamic pattern formation that can be analysed through physical experiments and subsequently instrumentalised. In this way an instrumental design approach based on the performative capacity of loose aggregates constitutes a radical departure from all common architectural design strategies based on assemblies and assembly processes, as aggregates are neither organised by specifying the location of connections or joints of elements nor embedded in a binding matrix. As loose accumulations of vast amounts of separate particles, aggregates form as dynamic

12.1 (above opposite)

Forces acting on a sand grain in an aeolian environment. The lift force (FL) results from an increase in velocity and a decrease in pressure due to airflow compressing above the grain. The drag force (FD) is the resistance to the flow coming from the sand bed. The resulting force is the fluid force (FF) that pivots the grain around its neighbour. (Drawn according to Siever 1988.) MArch Dissertation of Karola Dierichs, February 2009.

12.2 (opposite)

Suspension, saltation and creep. Wind impacting on a sand grain can have three different effects: the grain can either be suspended as in a dust storm, it can saltate (Latin: salire, to jump), or it can creep, depending on the grain size and density, and also the wind speed. (Drawn according to Bagnold 1941.) MArch Dissertation of Karola Dierichs, February 2009.

 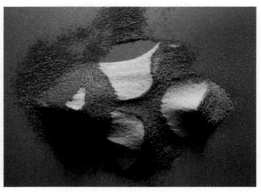

12.3

Processes and patterns of sand-dune formation
were extensively studied on the island of Sylt. MArch
Dissertation of Karola Dierichs, February 2009. Photo:
Karola Dierichs, 2009.

12.4

One frame of a time-lapse photography of a sand-dune
formation process undertaken in the laboratory. This
process can be analysed by using sands of different
colouration in order to show the deposition and mixing
process. MArch Dissertation of Karola Dierichs, February
2009.

equilibrium patterns under the influence of extrinsic influences, such as gravity and wind, dead weight and internal friction resistances. Hence, designing – a term that may need to be critically revised or extended in this context – with aggregates is opposed to a history of construction based on imposing shape on material constructs with a high degree of control. Thus the research in EmTech, as for example the project that illustrates this text and is explained in the following paragraphs, aimed at exploring aggregate formations beyond a conception of aggregates as shapeless materials to be controlled by elaborate enclosing formwork. This would have disregarded their innate capacity of pattern formation according to specific influences and constraints. The greatest potential of aggregates may lie in *not* assigning such subordinate role to granular substance, but, instead, in utilising the way in which granular substances can change their degree of stability. Thus, one of the most interesting and distinctive properties of granular materials is their capacity to shift between solid and liquid states: 'when submitted to small mean stresses, the shear strength is also very small and the granular material can flow almost like a liquid ... on the other hand, when the mean stress is high,

the granular material will be able to bear high loading ...' (Hicher 1998: 1). Of particular importance for design research based on deploying granular behaviour is their innate capacity to flow and set. This ability of aggregates to shift between solid and liquid states is what makes granular materials fascinating, as it underlies their capacity for dynamic pattern formation due to stresses, which may be induced either by natural forces, as for instance by wind and water in the case of sand dunes, or alternatively by human intervention. One of the key publications with regard to the former is Bagnold's *The Physics of Blown Sand and Desert Formation* (1941), in which he posited that:

> The geomorphologist, aware of the vast periods of time during which his processes have acted, is rightly doubtful of the ability of the physicist and the chemist to imitate them usefully in their laboratories. He is, in consequence, generally averse to the experimental method of research. It seemed to me, however, that the subject of sand movement lies far more in the realm of physics than of geomorphology.   (Bagnold 1941: xix)

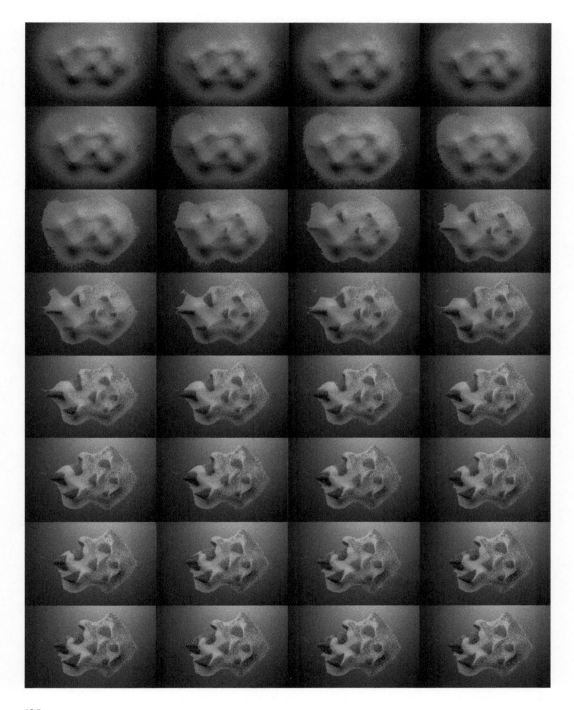

12.5

The time-lapse photography allows study of the entire development of seven sand piles being gradually eroded through a constant airstream of 21 km/h. Windward faces and leeward sides form within seconds. This process can be analysed by using a lighter coloured sand of the same grade that is taken off at the leeward sides. MArch Dissertation of Karola Dierichs, February 2009.

12.6

Aerodynamic surface roughness is related but not equal to the height, density and articulation of the surface elements. The illustration shows a notational system mapping the roughness relationship of existing dunes and new dunes occurring in aggregation cycle one on a specific test site on the island of Sylt, Northern Germany. MArch Dissertation of Karola Dierichs, February 2009.

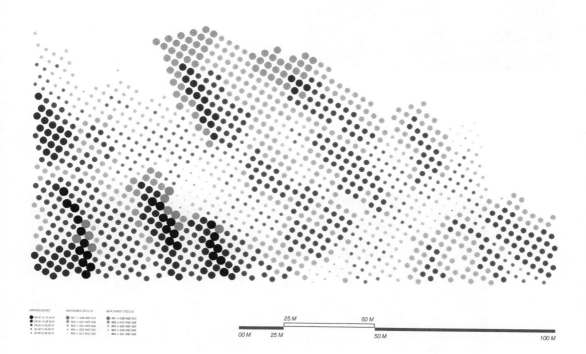

12.7

The illustration shows a smaller area of the proposed new dune field, which is modelled in terms of its possible growth in order to identify a possible pile configuration for complementary laboratory testing. MArch Dissertation of Karola Dierichs, February 2009.

12.8

The relationship between pouring or draining sand and the geometric layout of hole patterns was tested in an number of experiments. The sand-pile formations were evaluated in relation to variables including the angle of the base surface and also the amount of sand to be poured or drained, pouring speed, and funnel size and configuration. Through changes to the parametric setup, different sand formations emerge. Diploma Project of Gen Takahashi, AA Diploma Unit 4, Unit Masters: Michael Hensel and Achim Menges, 2006.

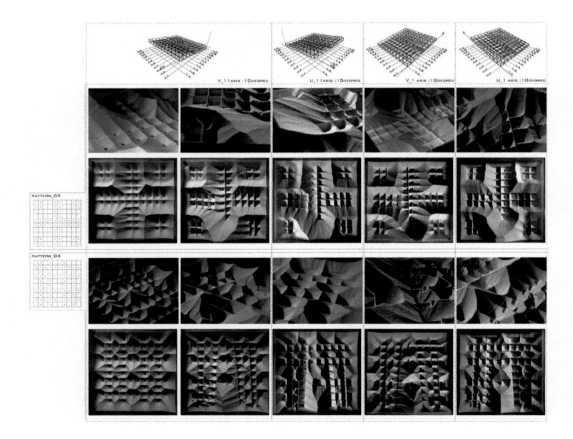

12.9

The experiment depicted explored a combination of wind-blown sand aggregation and draining the sand through multilayered, differentiated lattices, which in turn results in pile formations in lower layers and below the lattice datum. Sand thus gets captured, drained in highly specific ways and formed against a series of constraints on top, within and below the lattice datum. Diploma Project of Gen Takahashi, AA Diploma Unit 4, Unit Masters: Michael Hensel and Achim Menges, 2006.

Key determinants of the specific behaviour of granular materials are the geometry of the granules or elements and their mechanical properties, the geometry of the arrangements, and the extrinsic forces that act on the arrangements. Also, when aggregates accumulate, such as in sand piles, they can reach a critical limit leading to a sudden catastrophic change, an avalanche, only to build up afterwards in a similar way, while remaining poised at the critical limit. Philip Ball described this characteristic:

> There is something very peculiar about the sand pile that displays this behaviour: it is constantly seeking the *least* stable state ... States like this, which are susceptible to fluctuations on all scales at the slightest provocation, have been known to physicists for a long time. They are called critical states ... Instead of constantly seeking to escape the critical state, the sand pile seeks constantly to return to it. Bak (Bak *et al.* 1987) called this phenomenon self-organised criticality, reflecting the fact that the critical state seems to organise itself into this most precarious of configurations.
>
> (Ball 1999: 213–14)

Interestingly, granular materials can also be anisotropic, meaning that 'their response to a given stress depends on the orientation of that stress. This is due to the arrangement of the particles' (Hicher 1998: 12). Geometric anisotropy due to a varied orientation of tangent planes in the contact area of granules leads to mechanical anisotropy with different mechanical stress paths. This characteristic can be utilised in a number of ways, directing stresses through multiple load paths, or releasing stress strategically in certain regions of an aggregate to cause a change to the liquid state so as to remove granules or particles in specified areas. For example, while in most substances the pressure at the bottom of a column of matter is directly related to its height, the pressure that results from a tall column of sand is independent of its height. Another interesting aspect is the stress distribution below

piles of sand, where the stress is minimal below the highest point of the pile.

For the most part, working with granular substances demarcates a decisive shift from the predominant mode of designing static arrangements towards reconfigurable and self-organising structures with multiple stable states. Herein lies a considerable intellectual challenge for researchers and designers alike who are interested in exploring the potential of loose aggregates.

Karola Dierichs' MArch dissertation (2009) focused on the formation of sand dunes on the northern German island Sylt with the aim of intervening in geomorphological processes. The research commenced with extensive studies into dune types and related dune-formation processes. This was followed by extensive laboratory studies utilising wind tunnel experiments to investigate sand formations and the mixing of granules over time, with additional granules added over time. In order to investigate the movement and mixing of granules, sands of different colours were used. In order to verify the validity of these experiments, in situ experiments were carried out and compared with the results of the laboratory experiments. These experiments served to suggest ways of intervening in highly sensitive dune landscapes that are under threat of being washed or blown away. In this context, strategically placed sand deposits may serve to replenish the dune-formation processes. Other types of interventions may include a graded binding of the loose aggregate by mixing finely calibrated amounts of cement into the sand to locally and temporarily stabilise dunes for architectural purposes, as a more nuanced approach than simply importing unrelated interventions that may affect the dune formation process in one way or another without partaking in it. Earlier research undertaken by Gen Takahashi at the Architectural Association in London showed some possibilities in this direction (Hensel and Menges 2006: 286–95), using lattice type structures to collect and drain sand, so as to embed the architectural intervention within the processes of wind-blown sand accumulation and dune formation. This research into intervening in 'granular landscapes', utilising

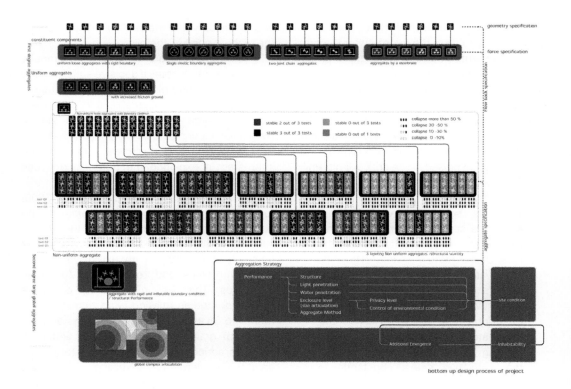

12.10

The table shows six particle types tested in relation to the probability of the resulting aggregation forming a structurally stable configuration. For each type–environment combination at least nine tests were conducted. Diploma Project of Eiichi Matsuda, AA Diploma Unit 4, Unit Masters: Michael Hensel and Achim Menges, 2004.

natural granules and forces acting upon them, constitutes only the very beginning of an integral approach towards natural landscaping and architectural design, and constitutes most definitely an exhilarating area of future research.

In addition to utilising natural granules, it can also be of interest to design the elements which an aggregate may comprise. Initial research in this direction was undertaken by Eiichi Matsuda at the Architectural Association in London (Hensel and Menges 2006: 262–71), as well as Anne Hawkins and Catie Newell at the Rice School of Architecture in Houston (Hensel and Menges 2006: 274–83). Eiichi Matsuda conducted extensive experiments with tens of thousands of three-axial cross elements to deduce their aggregation behaviour and pattern

based on varied pouring strategies of the elements. A pneumatic formwork was utilised for these experiments, so that the formwork could be easily removed by deflating it after the pouring process. Once the formwork is removed the aggregate settles into a stable state based on the number of contact points and friction between the elements. This is dependent on both the geometry and the mass and surface roughness of the element. The research continued to investigate the possibility of deriving different aggregate densities to be utilised for modulating light penetration, self-shading and airflow through each aggregate formation.

EmTech students undertook a further development of the system by changing the size of the element to human scale. Initial experiments

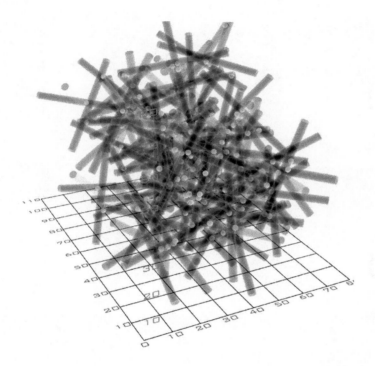

12.11

The illustration shows a computational experiment conducted in a physics simulation environment. Through the simulation of the influence of gravity acting on the aggregates, their distribution patterns can be computationally derived. This enables tracing the contact points between the individual aggregate elements as well as their formation tendencies and structural behaviour. Diploma Project of Eiichi Matsuda, AA Diploma Unit 4, Unit Masters: Michael Hensel and Achim Menges, 2004.

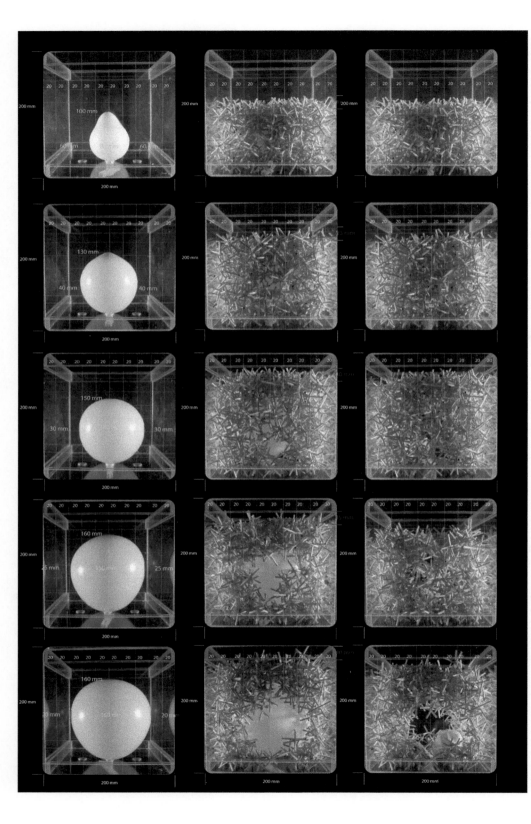

12.12 (opposite)

The illustration shows an experiment of pouring designed aggregate elements into a test container filled with a pneumatic body. This experiment demonstrates the capacity of aggregates to form a self-supporting structure over a cavity produced by an inflated formwork. After deflating the pneu, the aggregates settle into a stable configuration and a cavernous space emerges. Diploma Project of Eiichi Matsuda, AA Diploma Unit 4, Unit Masters: Michael Hensel and Achim Menges, 2004.

12.13 (below)

In order to investigate the tendency of each geometric element type to aggregate with different densities, a large number of aggregation tests were conducted. The table shows the identification of resulting zones of densities (from left to right) for different element types (from top to bottom). Diploma Project of Eiichi Matsuda, AA Diploma Unit 4, Unit Masters: Michael Hensel and Achim Menges, 2004.

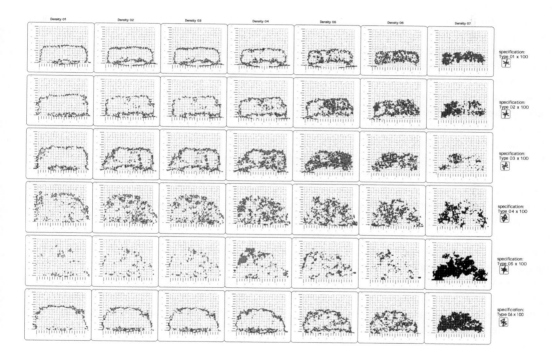

took place at the Architectural Association's workshop facilities in Hooke Park in Dorset. This involved the fabrication of several hundred elements of 900 × 900 × 900 mm, 600 × 600 × 600 mm and 300 × 300 × 300 mm that were tested in various aggregation patterns under static and dynamic loads. The elements were aggregated over a pneumatic formwork made from inexpensive off-the-shelf plastic bags. This set was then further developed as a scheme for a canopy located on the terrace of the Architectural Association. In order to prevent a catastrophic structural failure, the aggregate was planned to be first compacted to increase contact and friction between the particles, subsequently fixing them in strategic locations with ropes. While the canopy may not be constructed on the terrace of the Architectural Association at this point in time, it is nevertheless intended that it be constructed at a later stage at the Hooke Park facilities so that the long-term effect of horizontal loads onto the aggregate and the additional binding strategies can be examined and analysed.

As is evident from the above, the vast majority of experiments with aggregates have as of yet been undertaken physically. This is mainly due to the fact that computational methods only capture certain aspects of granular behaviour and that such methods need to be combined and evaluated with regard to their usefulness specific to modelling and simulation purposes. For the purpose of analysing the behaviour of granular materials 'in a dense state and submitted to static and dynamic loading', Bernard Cambou suggests a combination of:

> experimental analyses which demonstrate the main features of granular materials; micromechanical analysis using homogenisation techniques or numerical modelling (Discrete Element Method), which allow the understanding and the modelling of the behaviour of granular materials from the knowledge of local phenomena; phenomenological modelling [for] which [it] remains necessary to use numerical tools such as Finite Element Methods, allowing many kinds of boundary problems to be solved.
> (Cambou 1998)

The term 'discrete element method' (DEM) describes a number of computational methods that serve to model the motion of a large number of particles or granules, even with non-spherical geometry. DEM is limited by processor capacity, which in turn delimits the number of particles modelled and the length and complexity of the simulation. Treating granular material as a continuum, such as a fluid, allows for utilising computational fluid dynamics (CFD), which serves to analyse fluid flows through numerical methods and the use of algorithmic procedures. In any case, setting up a computational logic requires to quite some extent empirical data, which can be compared with the computational outcome in order to verify it. This entails that the particular aspect under investigation will already have been isolated. And in the latter also lies the predicament, an isolated view of an isolated scale-specific condition or behaviour. At this stage the research of Emergent Technologies and Design into aggregates has not proceeded far enough to engage such methods in a manner that corresponds with its agenda. More basic research is necessary, while keeping an eye on the development of computational methods and tools. In the words of Philip Ball 'what is particularly exciting about these systems is that not even the scientists studying them have yet acquired an intuition that allows them to predict what they might see in a given experiment' (Ball 1999: 222).

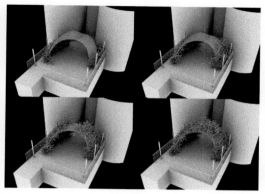

12.15

Based on the initial tests in Hooke Park, an 'Aggregate Canopy' for the roof terrace of the Architectural Association in London was developed. The rendering shows the pouring and aggregation process. Phase 1 Studio Work of Selim Bayer and Kyle Schertzing, 2009.

12.14

The image sequence shows a full-scale test of an aggregate with designed particles. The individual particles were manufactured at the Hooke Park workshop in Dorset, using local wood. The aggregate particles were then poured over a pneumatic formwork. After removal of the formwork, the aggregates settled into a structurally stable arch configuration with a considerable load-bearing capacity. Phase 1 Studio Work of Selim Bayer and Kyle Schertzing, 2009.

Bibliography

INTRODUCTION

Bertalanffy, L. von (1969) *General Systems Theory: Foundations, Development, Applications*. New York: George Braziller.

Bertalanffy, L. von (1976) *Perspectives on General System Theory*. New York: George Braziller.

Brown, J. H. (1994) 'Complex Ecological Systems', in G. A. Cowan, A. Pines. and S. Meltzer (eds), *Complexity: Metaphors, Models, and Reality*. Santa Fe Institute: Studies in the science of Complexity. Reading, MA: Addison-Wesley, 419–43.

De Wolf, T. and Holvoet, T. (2005) 'Emergence versus Self-organisation: Different Concepts but Promising when Combined', in *Engineering Self-Organising Systems: Methodologies and Applications*. Lecture Notes in Computer Science/Lecture Notes in Artificial Intelligence. New York: Springer, 1–15.

Otto F. (1971). *IL3 Biology and Building*. Stuttgart: IL University of Stuttgart. 27.

1

EVOLUTION AND COMPUTATION

Bateson, W. (1894) *Materials for the Study of Variation, Treated with Especial Regard to Discontinuity in the Origin of Species*. London: Macmillan & Company.

Berril, N.J. and Goodwin, B.C. (1996) *The Life of Form: Emergent Patterns of Morphological Transformation*. Rivista di Biologia-Biology Forum 89.

Darwin, C. R. (1859) *On the Origin of Species by Means of Natural Selection, or the Preservation of Favoured Races in the Struggle for Life*, 1st edn. London: John Murray.

Eldredge, N. (1995), *Reinventing Darwin*. London: John Wiley & Sons.

Gould, S. J. (1977) *Ontogeny and Phylogeny*. Cambridge, MA: Belknap Press.

Gould, S. J. (2002) *The Structure of Evolutionary Theory*. Cambridge, MA: Harvard University Press.

Thompson, D'Arcy Wentworth (1917), *On Growth and Form*. Cambridge: Cambridge University Press.

Weinstock, M. (2010 forthcoming) *The Architecture of Emergence: The Evolution of Form in Nature and Civilisation*. London: Wiley AD.

2

MATERIAL SYSTEMS, COMPUTATIONAL MORPHOGENESIS AND PERFORMATIVE CAPACITY

Gaß, S. (1990) *Form-Kraft- Masse Experimente*. Stuttgart: Karl Krämer Verlag.

Goethe, J. W. ([1796] 1987) *Schriften zur Morphologie*. Frankfurt: Deutscher Klassiker Verlag.

Grafton, A. (2002) *Leon Battista Alberti: Master Builder of the Italian Renaissance*. Cambridge, MA: Harvard University Press.

Hensel, M. and Menges, A. (2006) *Morpho-Ecologies*. London: AA Publications.

Mayr, E. (2002) *Die Entwicklung der biologischen Gedankenwelt*. Berlin, London, New York: Springer.

Menges, A. (2008) 'Integral Formation and Materialisation: Computational Form and Material Gestalt', in B. Kolarevic and K. Klinger (eds), *Manufacturing Material Effects: Rethinking Design and Making in Architecture*. New York: Routledge.

Sasaki, M. (2007) *Morphogenesis of Flux Structures*. London: AA Publications.

Terzidis, K. (2006) *Algorithmic Architecture*. Oxford: Architectural Press.

Winfree, T. A. (1987) *When Time Breaks Down*. New York: Princeton University Press.

3

MATERIAL SYSTEMS AND ENVIRONMENTAL DYNAMICS FEEDBACK

Bettum, J. and Hensel, M. (1999) 'Issues of Materiality'. Unpublished Paper commissioned by Sanford Kwinter for a planned journal entitled *Rumble*.

Oke, T. R. (1987) *Boundary Layer Climates*, 2nd edn. London: Routledge.

Rosenberg, N. J., Blad, B. L. and Verma, S. B. (1983) *Micro-climate: The Biological Environment*, 2nd edn. London: John Wiley & Sons.

Weinstock, M. (2010 forthcoming) *The*

Architecture of Emergence: The Evolution of Form in Nature and Civilisation. London: Wiley AD.

4
FIBRES

Jeronimidis, G. (2004) 'Biodynamics', in M. Hensel, A. Menges and M. Weinstock (eds), *Emergence: Morphogentic Design Strategies*. *Architectural Design*, vol. 74, no. 3. London: AD Wiley Academy, 90–6.

Neville, A. C. (1993) *Biology of Fibrous Composites*. Cambridge: Cambridge University Press.

Turner, S. (2007) *The Tinkerer's Accomplice: How Design Emerges From Life Itself*. Cambridge, MA: Harvard University Press.

5
TEXTILES

Engel, H. (1999) *Structure Systems*, 2nd edn. Ostfildern-Ruit: Gerd Hatje.

Seiler-Baldinger, A. (1994) *Textiles: A Classification of Techniques*. Bathurst: Crawford House Press.

Semper, G. (1860) *Style in the Technical and Tectonic Arts; or, Practical Aesthetics: A Handbook for Technicians, Artists, and Friends of the Arts*. 2 vols. Frankfurt am Main: Verlag für Kunst und Wissenschaft.

Wolff, C. (1996) *The Art of Manipulating Fabric*. Iola, Wisconsin: Krause Publications.

6
NETS

Bach K., Burkhardt B., Graefe R., Raccanello R. (1975) *IL 8 Nets in Nature and Technics*. Stuttgart: University of Stuttgart.

Engel, H. (1999) *Structure Systems*, 2nd edn. Ostfildern-Ruit: Gerd Hatje.

Otto F. (ed.) (1967) *Tensile Structures: Design, Structure and Calculation of Buildings of Cables, Nets and Membranes*. Cambridge, MA: MIT Press.

7
LATTICES

Happold, E. and Liddell, I. (1978) 'The Calculation of the Shell', in B. Burkhardt (ed.), *IL 13 Multihalle Mannheim*. Stuttgart: Karl Krämer Verlag, 60–97.

8
BRANCHES

Ball, P. (1999) *The Self-made Tapestry: Pattern Formation in Nature*. Oxford, New York, Tokyo: Oxford University Press.

Engel, H. (1999) *Structure Systems*, 2nd edn. Ostfildern-Ruit: Gerd Hatje.

Jirasek, C., Prusinkiewicz, P., *et al.* (2000) 'Integrating Biomechanics into developmental plant models expressed using L-systems', in H. C. Spatz and T. Speck (eds), *Plant Biomechanics 2000: Proceedings of the 3rd Plant Biomechanics Conference 2000*. Stuttgart: George Thieme Verlag.

Mandelbrot, B. B. (1982) *The Fractal Geometry of Nature*. San Francisco: W. H. Freeman.

Mattheck C. (1998) *Design in Nature: Learning from Trees*. New York: Springer.

Prusinkiewicz, P. and Lindenmayer, A. (1990) *The Algorithmic Beauty of Plants*. New York: Springer.

Wagenführ, A. (2008) *Die strukturelle Anisotropie von Holz als Chance für technische Innovationen: Sitzungsberichte der Sächsischen Akademie der Wissenschaften zu Leipzig*. Technikwissenschaftliche Klasse 2, Heft 6. Stuttgart: Hirzel.

9
CELLS

Gibson, L. J. and Ashby, M. F. (1999) *Cellular Solids: Structure and Properties*. Cambridge: Cambridge University Press.

10
MASS COMPONENTS

Dieste, E. (1997) 'Architecture and Construction', in A. J. Torrecillas (ed.), *Eladio Dieste: 1943–1996*. Exhibition catalogue, Junta de Andalucia.

Fathy H. (1986) *Natural Energy and Vernacular Architecture: Principles and Examples with Reference to Hot Arid Climates*. Chicago: The University of Chicago Press.

Gates, C. (2003) *Ancient Cities: The Archeology of Urban Life in the Ancient Near East*

and Egypt, Greece, and Rome. London:
Routledge.

11
CASTS

Fathy H. (1986) *Natural Energy and Vernacular Architecture: Principles and Examples with Reference to Hot Arid Climates*. Chicago: The University of Chicago Press.

Kull, U. (2005) 'Frei Otto and Biology', in W. Nerdinger (ed.), *Lightweight Construction – Natural Design: Frei Otto – Complete Works*. Basel, Boston, Berlin: Birkhäuser, 45–54.

12
AGGREGATES

Bagnold R. A. (2005 [1954, 1941]). *The Physics of Blown Sand and Desert Dunes*. Mineola NY: Dover.

Bak, P., Tang, C. and Wiesenfeld, K. (1987) 'Self-organised Criticality: An Explanation of $1/f$ noise'. *Physical Review Letters* 59.

Ball, P. (1999) *The Self-made Tapestry: Pattern Formation in Nature*. Oxford, New York, Tokyo: Oxford University Press.

Cambou, B. (1998) 'Experimental Behaviour of Granular Materials', in B. Cambou (ed.), *Behaviour of Granular Materials*. New York, Wien: Springer.

Hensel, M. and Menges, A. (2006) *Morpho-Ecologies*. London: AA Publications.

Hicher, P. Y. (1998) 'Experimental Behaviour of Granular Materials', in B. Cambou (ed.), *Behaviour of Granular Materials*. New York, Wien: Springer.

Siever, R. (1988) *Sand*. Scientific American Library. New York: W. H. Freeman.

Torquato, S. (2002) *Random Heterogeneous Materials: Microstructure and Macroscopic Properties*. Interdisciplinary Applied Mathematics, vol. 16: *Mechanics and Materials*. New York: Springer.

Project credits

AA TERRACE MEMBRANE CANOPY
Architectural Association, London
Emergent Technologies and Design
programme, 2006–7

Project coordination
Michael Hensel, Michael Weinstock, Achim
Menges
Design and construction coordination
Digital modelling coordination: Omid Kamvari
Moghaddam
Structure coordination: Daniel Caserta
Segraves
Material and fabrication coordination: Bulut
Cebeci
PR and documentation coordination: Karola
Dierichs
Design and construction
Irina Bardakhanova, Maria Bessa, Arielle
Blonder-Afek, Bulut Cebeci, Yi Wen Chen,
Karola Dierichs, Christina Doumpioti, Andres
Harris Aguirre, Omid Kamvari Moghaddam,
Sreedhar Mallemadugula, Cyril Owen Manyara,
Akanksha Mittal, Matteo Noto, Onur Suraka
Ozkaya, Elke Pedal Baertl, Gabriel Sanchiz
Garin, Daniel Caserta Segraves, Defne
Sunguroğlu, Manja Van de Worp, Christy
Widjaja
Engineering consultants
Buro Happold, London
Project coordination: Mike Cook, Wolf
Mangelsdorf, Toby Ronalds
Engineering team: Kevin Berry, Jamie Goggins,
Chris Hulmes, Jean Pierre Kim, Marissa
Kretsch, Tom Makin, Ivan Muscat, Greg
Phillips, Toby Ronalds, Ricardo Sequeira
Software collaboration
Robert Aish, Director Bentley Research,
Generative Components, Bentley Systems Inc.
Membrane technology consultants
WG Lucas and Son
Membrane cutting and labelling
Automated Cutting Services Ltd
Membrane sewing
London College of Fashion
Steel nickel plating
Fox Plating

Sponsors
AA Workshop, Bentley Systems Inc., Kamkav
Construction Ltd., MPanel Support Team,
OCEAN Research and Design Network, Online
Reprographics

SHELTER AND VIEWING PLATFORM
Hacienda Quitralco, Aísen Region, Patagonia,
Chile
Emergent Technologies and Design
programme, 2006–7

Client representative
Martin Westcott
Client coordination team
Martin Westcott, Melanie Leibbrandt, Robin
Westcott
Project coordination
Michael Hensel and Juan
Subercaseaux
Design supervision
Michael Hensel, Juan Subercaseaux, Michael
Weinstock, Achim Menges
EmTech design team
Maria Bessa, Bulut Cebeci, Christina
Doumpioti, Andres Harris Aguirre, Elke Pedal
Baertl, Defne Sunguroğlu, Manja Van de Word,
Christy Widjaja
Engineering consultancy
Buro Happold: Lawrence Friesen, Nikolaos
Stathopoulos, Defne Sunguroğlu
Seismic analysis
Arup & Partners: Nikolaos Socratus
Software: GSA Version 8.3 © Oasys 1997–
2008 Oasys Ltd.
Construction coordination
Michael Hensel and Juan Subercaseaux
Construction team
Maria Bessa, Bulut Cebeci, Michael Hensel,
Andres Harris Aguirre, Melanie Leibbrandt,
Elke Pedal Baertl, Juan Subercaseaux, Defne
Sunguroğlu, Manja Van de Word, Christy
Widjaja with Jaime, Juan, and Segundo

NET-BRIDGE

Hacienda Quitralco, Aísen Region, Patagonia, Chile

Emergent Technologies and Design Programme, 2007–8

Client representative
Martin Westcott
Client coordination team
Martin Westcott, Melanie Leibbrandt, Robin Westcott
Project coordination
Michael Hensel and Juan Subercaseaux
Design supervision
Michael Hensel, Juan Subercaseaux, Michael Weinstock, Achim Menges, Daniel Coll I Capdevila, Defne Sunguroğlu
Design phase 01
Pooja Bali, Antonio Capone, Santiago Fernandez Achury
Design phase 02
Design coordination: Santiago Fernandez Achury
Construction coordination: Tomasz Mlynarski
Construction scheduler: Evan Greenberg
Design team:
Santiago Fernandez Achury, Sean Ahlquist, Hiva Bakhtiari,Pooja Bali, Antonio Capone, Moritz Fleischmann, Renata Elizondo, Mehran Gharleghi, Evan Greenberg, Tommy Johnson, Yukio Minobe, Tomasz Mlynarski, Elina Pavela, Amin Sadeghy, Gennaro Senatore
Engineering consultants
Expedition Engineering
Tim Harris, Julia Ratcliffe, Andrew Weir
Construction supervision
Michael Hensel, Juan Subercaseaux, Daniel Coll I Capdevila, Defne Sunguroğlu
Construction team
Antonio Capone, Santiago Fernandez Achury, Sean Alquist, Gharleghi, Evan Greenberg, Tommy Johnson, Tomasz Mlynarski, Elina Pavela, Gennaro Senatore, Michael Hensel, Subercaseaux, Daniel Coll I Capdevila, Defne Sunguroğlu, Santiago Subercaseaux, Ivan Cheuquepil, Gerardo Cheuquepil, Juan Carcamo

Sponsors
Woods Bagot, Architectural Association, OCEAN Research and Design Network
Transport and travel logistics
Juan Carlos Selman, LAN Chile

Author biographies

Michael U. Hensel

Dipl Ing Grad Dipl Des AA Architekt AKNW
Professor Michael Hensel is an architect,
researcher and writer. He was co-director
of the Emergent Technologies and Design
Master Programme at the Architectural
Association in London from 2001–2009, where
he developed the curriculum and research
agenda with Michael Weinstock in 2000. He
taught at the Architectural Association from
1993–2009. Since 2008 he has been Professor
for Research by Design at the Oslo School of
Architecture and Design. Michael Hensel has
held visiting professorships and innovation
fellowships in Europe, the Americas and
Australia.

Michael Hensel is a founding member of the
OCEAN network, originally founded in 1994,
and registered as an association focusing
on research by design in 2008 in Norway.
He is also a board member of BIONIS –
the Biomimetics Network for Industrial
Sustainability – as well as an editorial board
member of *AD* Wiley and *JBE – Journal for
Bionic Engineering* (Elsevier Scientific Press)
and permanent collaborator of *Arch+ Magazine*.

His PhD thesis focuses on establishing the
theoretical framework for 'Performance-
oriented Design: A Biological Paradigm for
Architectural Design and Sustainability', which
he pursues at the Centre of Biomimetics at the
University of Reading.

Michael Hensel has published and written extensively, including:

Ertas, H., Hensel, M. and Sunguroğlu Hensel,
   D. (2010 forthcoming) *Turkey: At the
   Threshold*. London: AD Wiley.
Hensel, M., and Menges, A. (eds) (2006)
   Morpho-Ecologies. London: AA Publications.
Hensel, M., and Menges, A. (eds) (2008a)
   *Versatility and Vicissitude: Performance in
   Morpho-Ecological Design*. London: AD
   Wiley.
Hensel, M., and Menges, A. (eds) (2008b) *Form
   Follows Performance: Zur Wechselwirkung
   von Material, Struktur, Umwelt*. Arch+ Vol.
   188. Aachen: Arch+ Verlag.
Hensel, M. and Sevaldson, B. (eds) (2002) *The
   Space of Extremes*. Oslo: AHO Oslo School
   of Architecture and Design Publications.
Hensel, M. and Verebes, T. (1999)
   Urbanisations. Architecture & Urbanism 3.
   London: Serial Books.
Hensel, M., Menges, A. and Weinstock M.
   (eds) (2004) *Emergence: Morphogenetic
   Design Strategies*. London: AD Wiley.
Hensel, M., Hight, C. and Menges, A. (eds)
   (2009) *Space Reader: Heterogenous Space in
   Architecture*. London: John Wiley & Sons.
Hensel, M., Menges, A. and Weinstock M.
   (eds) (2006) *Techniques and Technologies in
   Morphogenetic Design*. London: AD Wiley.

Achim Menges

AA Dipl (Hons) RIBA II Architekt AKH

Professor Achim Menges is an architect and director of the Institute for Computational Design at Stuttgart University. Currently he also is Visiting Professor in Architecture at Harvard University's Graduate School of Design and Visiting Professor for the Emergent Technologies and Design Graduate Programme at the Architectural Association in London.

He taught at the AA School of Architecture as Studio Master of the Emergent Technologies and Design Graduate Programme from 2002 to 2009 and as Unit Master of Diploma Unit 4 from 2003 to 2006. From 2005 to 2008 he was Professor for Form Generation and Materialisation at the HfG Offenbach University for Art and Design in Germany. In addition he has held visiting professorships in Europe and the United States.

Achim Menges research focuses on the development of integral design processes at the intersection of evolutionary computation, algorithmic design, biomimetic engineering and computer aided manufacturing that enables a highly articulated, performative built environment. His research projects have been published and exhibited worldwide and received numerous international awards.

Achim Menges' institute is part of the German Competence Network for Biomimetics. He also is a member of the Smart Geometry group.

Achim Menges has lectured widely and published more than 50 papers and articles on his research over the last five years.

Recent publications include:

Hensel, M., and Menges, A. (eds) (2006) *Morpho-Ecologies*. London: AA Publications.

Hensel, M., and Menges, A. (eds) (2008a) *Versatility and Vicissitude: Performance in Morpho-Ecological Design*. London: AD Wiley.

Hensel, M., and Menges, A. (eds) (2008b) *Form Follows Performance: Zur Wechselwirkung von Material, Struktur, Umwelt*. Arch+ Vol. 188. Aachen: Arch+ Verlag.

Hensel, M., Hight, C. and Menges, A. (eds) (2009) *Space Reader: Heterogenous Space in Architecture*. London: John Wiley & Sons.

Hensel, M., Menges, A. and Weinstock M. (eds) (2004) *Emergence: Morphogenetic Design Strategies*. London: AD Wiley.

Hensel, M., Menges, A. and Weinstock M. (eds) (2001) *Techniques and Technologies in Morphogenetic Design*. London: AD Wiley.

Menges, A. (ed.) (2008) *Systemisches Denken und Integrales Entwerfen: System Thinking and Integral Design*. Offenbach: Hochschulverlag HFG Offenbach.

www.achimmenges.net

Michael Weinstock
RIBA

Michael Weinstock is an architect. Born in Germany, he lived as a child in the Far East and then in West Africa, and attended an English public school but ran away to sea at age seventeen after reading Conrad. He spent years at sea in traditional wooden sailing ships, and gained shipyard and shipbuilding experience. He studied architecture at the Architectural Association from 1982 to 1988 and has taught at the AA School of Architecture since 1989.

His personal research interests lie in exploring the convergence of emergence, natural systems, evolution, computation and material sciences, and he has taught and published on these topics in Europe and the US since 1998. He is a member of the editorial board of AD Wiley.

Academic activities at the Architectural Association School of Architecture in London:
Academic Head since 2006
Director of the Emergent Technologies and
   Design Master Programme since 2000
Master of Technical Studies since 1997
Member of the Interim Management Group
   from June 2004 to August 2005
Diploma Unit Master from 1995 to 2001
Intermediate Unit Master and Technical Studies
   Tutor from 1991 to 1994
Workshop Technical Tutor 1st Year from 1989
   to 1990

Other academic activities since 2005:
University of Reading – Research collaboration
   with Professor George Jeronimidis and the
   Centre for Biomimetics
TU Delft – International Advisor to Delft Design
   School doctoral programme
Yale School of Architecture – Integrated Design
   and Seminar course 'Evolutionary Design and
   Digital Fabrication'

ESARQ, Barcelona – Visiting Professor to
   the Genetic Architecture graduate research
   programme, and director of 'Taller Vertical'
Università degli Studi Roma Tre, Rome –
   Visiting Professor

In press:
Weinstock M. (2010) *The Architecture of Emergence: The Evolution of Form in Nature and Civilization*. London: AD Wiley.

Index